Portobello Voices

Portobello Voices

BLANCHE GIROUARD

First published 2013

The History Press, The Mill, Brimscombe, Port Stroud, Gloucestershire, GL5 2QG
www.thehistorypress.co.uk

British Library Cataloguing in Publication Data.
A catalogue record for this book is available from the British Library.
ISBN 978 0 7524 99369

Designed by Matt Hervey

Picture Credits
Page 2, Portobello Road from the Westway, c. 1980 © Charles Marsden-Smedley
Page 10 (top) © Royal Commission on the Historic Monuments of England
Pages 10 (bottom), 12, 14, 15, 17 (bottom) and page 19 (bottom) © RBKC Library Services
Pages 13 and 16 (bottom) © Spencer family
Page 16 (top) © Ronald Cohen, London
Page 17 (top) © Ken Russell / TopFoto.co.uk
Page 19 (top) © www.urbanimage.tv / Adrian Boot
Page 143 © David Helmore
All other photographs © Blanche Girouard

For my parents

Acknowledgements

My thanks, first and foremost, must go to the traders of Portobello Market who allowed me to hang around their stalls and take up their time. They were all unfailingly friendly and helpful and I cannot emphasise enough how much pleasure I derived, and how much I learned, from the time I spent with them. My thanks also go to the antique collectors, designers and local residents who made time for an interview, showed me around their homes or studios and shared their passion for Portobello with me.

I deeply regret that I was unable to use all of the interviews I recorded. I have made a selection which I hope reflects the many facets of the market. It is, however, only a sampler of Portobello. The market is awash with interesting, brilliant people worth listening to and I hope that this book will inspire readers to search others out for themselves.

A number of people have helped me along the way. Paul Thompson showed me how oral history should be done, gave me the opportunity to try my hand at it and was a constant source of advice. Georg Philipp Pezold encouraged me to follow my dream of becoming an oral historian and had unerring confidence in my ability to pull it off. The missionary community of Ouagdougou allowed me to practice on them. Caroline Dawnay had faith in my project and worked hard to help me get this book off the ground. Nicola Guy and Declan Flynn, at The History Press, fielded endless emails without complaint. Dave Walker and Timothy Reid, at Kensington Library, searched out and scanned photographs under considerable time pressure. Nic Kasic, Tom Vague, Sarah Koneczna and Geoffrey Roome were a fount of local knowledge, advice and contacts. A number of friends also went out of their way to help me. I particularly wish to thank Matt Hervey, who designed the book and Katy Barron who tolerated it. I also wish to thank Charles Marsden-Smedley, Arabella Pike, Victoria Kingston and Johnny Cornwell. And last, but not least, I want to express my deepest thanks and love to my parents who were unstinting in their support and always ready to read and discuss what I had written.

Contents

Stalls opposite the Imperial Playhouse (later the Electric Cinema) c. 1930

Stalls opposite the Electric Cinema, c. 1970

The Story of Portobello Market

In 1731, a master mariner called Robert Jenkins was sailing home from the Spanish colony of Jamaica when Spanish coastguards boarded his ship and accused him of piracy. Tying Jenkins to the mast, the Spanish Captain 'took hold of his left Ear and with his Cutlass slit it down, and then another of the Spaniards took hold of it and tore it off, but gave him the Piece of his Ear again.'[1]

Jenkins held onto his ear, keeping it pickled in a jar. 'After many hardships and perils' he got back to England where he brandished it before a committee of the House of Commons and told them, in gruesome detail, what had happened.[2] The story got around, other West Indian merchants took fright and Parliament asked the King to seek redress from Spain. When all diplomatic efforts failed, the King commanded the Navy to retaliate. And thus it was that in 1739 the War of Jenkins' Ear commenced and Vice-Admiral Edward Vernon stormed and captured the Spanish port of Porto Bello in the Gulf of Mexico.

The Victory of Portobello thrilled the British. They lit bonfires in the street and bought commemorative medallions. Babies were named 'Vernon', pubs 'The Admiral Vernon' and a certain Mr A. Adams, living in a farmhouse near Notting Hill, renamed his farm 'Portobello Farm'.

At this time the area around Notting Hill was known as 'Kensington Gravel Pits' and only a small cluster of houses straddled the 'Great Road' which we now know as the A40. On this road was a toll gate – Notting Hill 'gate' – and from the toll gate to Portobello Farm, and beyond, a country lane, shown on maps as 'Portobello Lane'.

A century later city dwellers still walked down Portobello Lane for relaxation. 'This is one of the most rural and pleasant walks in the summer in the vicinity of London,' Thomas Faulkner wrote. 'Nothing could be heard in the tranquil silence but the notes of the lark, the linnet and the nightingale.'[3]

'From West to North, from North to East,' an old inhabitant recalled, 'scarcely a house was to be seen. Corn fields and meadow land on every side.'[4]

Looking up Portobello Road from Elgin Crescent, c. 1904

By 1851 there were a few cottages on the lane, at the Notting Hill end, most likely inhabited by men involved in building grand Victorian housing estates like the Ladbroke Estate, which runs along Kensington Park Road. And then the railway arrived – first, in 1864, to 'Notting Hill' station (now Ladbroke Grove) then, in 1866, to Westbourne Park station. Three hundred Irish navvies came over to work on the line which, once completed, carried workers into London on half-hourly trains.

By 1874 Portobello Lane was lined on both sides with shops and houses. In 1851 there were 214 inhabitants, all but three of them born in England; by 1891 there were 2,000 and many of them came from abroad. In spite of its exclusive housing estates, Notting Hill was now a working-class suburb with a large immigrant population.

Portobello Market came into existence in the late 1860s or early 1870s, possibly as a result of local Romany gypsies trading horses on the lane. It soon took off. 'Columbus discovered Portobello in 1502' wrote Sir William Bull M.P. 'We discovered Portobello Road about 370 years later … on Saturday nights in the winter, when it was thronged like a fair … On the left-hand side were costers' barrows, lighted by flaming naptha lamps. In the side streets were side shows, vendors of patent medicines, conjurors and itinerant vocalists.' Local residents flocked to the market during the day, 'not

Joanne Spencer (Gary's great great-great-grandmother) who sold salad and rabbits from a basket, c. 1904

W. Edwards fruit and veg stall, c. 1920

only for the sake of the excellent quality of the food ... but also for the sheer enjoyment of the cheery cries and the surging crowds and heavily laden stalls.'⁵

'Here,' wrote Ernest Woolf, in 1909, 'one can see mechanic and artisan life in its best and truest form ... the happy and sturdy husband with pipe in mouth, looking after his children, perhaps with one on his shoulder, whilst his better half is bargaining for the Sunday joint or resolving on the most toothsome trimmings.'⁶

Things became rather less cheerful after the First World War. In the harsh economic climate that followed, street traders (many of them veterans) started setting up their stalls every day of the week, upsetting the shopkeepers. In 1920, hoping to calm the situation, the National Federation of Discharged and Demobilised Sailors and Soldiers applied to the council to get the market officially extended. The council rejected the application but had no statutory power to stop them. And so the market became a daily affair, all entirely unregulated. At six o'clock a whistle was blown and traders ran with their barrows to a pitch. Some even slept on pitches overnight, just to be sure of a good location. In 1927 the London County

Mr Brooks' vegetable stall, 1958

Council finally restored order, passing an Act which gave boroughs the power to regulate street markets and license pitches to traders.

In the 1920s the north end of Portobello Road acquired a flea market, where rag-and-bone men (known as totters) sold the old clothing, furniture and bric-a-brac they had collected. In 1948, when Caledonian Market closed, the antiques dealers arrived. The addition of bric-a-brac and antiques to food gradually changed Portobello from a local market to a national institution. Suddenly it was the place to be.

In 1956 Muriel Spark's protagonist Needle was (literally) haunting the antique stalls of Portobello[7] while, two years later, Paddington Bear became a regular visitor with 'a good eye for a bargain'[8] and Tom Courtney (in the spoof thriller *Otley*) acted the part of a light-fingered Portobello antiques dealer pretending to be a spy and exchanging a booby-trapped suitcase in Notting Hill underground station. In 1966 the market hosted The Beach Boys and Cat Stevens found himself 'walking down Portobello Road for miles' seeing 'cuckoo clocks and plastic socks/lampshades of old antique leather/nothing looks weird, not even a beard/or the boots made out of feathers'. In 1971 Portobello met Walt Disney, as the characters in

Bernard Lewis, Hilary's father, c. 1959

Ben Spencer, Gary's grandfather, c. 1950

Emma Kirk, Josie's aunt, c. 1954

Anne Spencer, Gary's grandmother, c. 1958

Bedknobs and Broomsticks, looking for an old magic book, cheerfully chirped: 'Anything and everything a chap can unload/is sold off the barrow in Portobello Road.'

The market became a regular haunt of musicians. The punk rock band London SS wrote a song called 'Portobello Reds' and wandered down the market wearing fluorescent leather coats. Some say that Joe Strummer's lyric 'hanging about down the market street/I spent a lot of time on my feet/when I met some passing yobbos and we did chance to speak' refers to the formation of The Clash – its members described by the Sex Pistols' guitarist as 'four-square Portobello boys'. Brinsley Forde, founding member of the reggae group Aswad, lived on Portobello Road and the band used to give impromptu gigs under the Westway. Richard Branson saw an opening and soon Virgin Records was established in Vernon yard, just off Portobello Road.

Portobello's popularity remains undiminished. In 1992 Blur's Damon Albarn sang 'air cushioned soles/I bought them on the Portobello Road on a Saturday'. In 1999 the market saw the arrival of the film *Notting Hill* in which Will Thacker (played by Hugh Grant) lived behind a blue door just off Portobello Road and walked, reflectively, through the market in a two minute, four season, sequence to the strains of 'Ain't no sunshine when she's gone'. Paulo Coelho's *The Witch of Portobello* came out in 2007 and Ruth Rendell's thriller *Portobello* in 2008.

Today more than a million people a year visit Portobello Market – now considered one of the top ten tourist attractions in London. By ten o'clock on a Saturday morning the market is seething and by midday you can only pigeon step along it. The advent of tourists has brought with it a demand for hot food and souvenirs. Fake Chinese handbags and cheap mass-produced clothes proliferate. It's all too easy, now, to miss what worthwhile goods the market still has to offer.

Portobello is the last street antique market left in London. Early on Saturday morning the arcades still throb with antique dealers. On Friday morning fabulous vintage clothing is still fingered, under the Westway, by bizarrely dressed fashionistas, wardrobe mistresses, fashion designers and stylists. And throughout the week, come wind, rain or shine, costermongers are still out selling fresh fruit and vegetables.

How long this will continue is debatable. Property developers are turfing dealers out of the antique arcades. Supermarkets, on-line shopping and a lack of local parking are decimating the costermongers. And designers are taking sneaky photographs, rather than buying vintage clothing.

Aswad outside the Golden Cross on Portobello Road, c. 1980

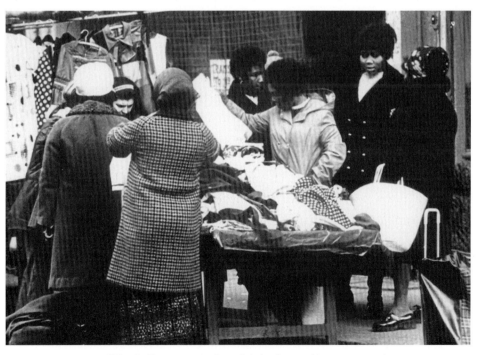

West Indian women shopping in the market, c. 1970

Preparing for market, 2013

It is easy to rail at the developers and the council for their failure to protect the market. But, as Geoff says in his interview: 'When's the last time you spent any money down there?'

If you go down to Portobello market and have a chat with the traders, you won't be disappointed. If you go down and buy something, you'll help to preserve it.

1. Robert Jenkins' deposition to the King, as quoted in *The Universal Spectator* and *Weekly Journal*, No. CXLI, 19 June 1731
2. *The Gentleman's Magazine*, June 1731, Vol. 1, p. 265
3. Thomas Faulkner, *History of the Antiquities of Kensington* (1820)
4. Kensington, Notting Hill and Paddington by 'an old Inhabitant' (Griffiths and Co., 1882)
5. Sir William Bull M.P., *Some Recollections of Bayswater 50 years ago* (Bayswater Chronicle, 1923)
6. Ernest P. Woolf, *The Interesting History of Portobello Road* (1909)
7. Muriel Spark, 'Portobello Road' from *The Ghost Stories of Muriel Spark* (New Directions Publishing Corporation, 2003)
8. Michael Bond, *A Bear Called Paddington* etc. (William Collins, 1958); Florence M. Gladstone, *Notting Hill in Bygone Days* (T. Fisher Unwin Ltd, 1924); Barbara Denny, *Notting Hill and Holland Park Past* (Historical Publications, 1993); Simon Burke and Jerome Ungoed-Thomas, *Notting Hill and Bayswater 1989/90*, (London Handbooks); Richard Tanner, *The Notting Hill and Holland Park Book* (Historical Publications, 2004); Sarah Anderson, *Inside Notting Hill* (Umbrellabooks, 2007)

Tourists in the rain, 2013

'There is a magical intellectual journey to go on with these things'

MARION, ANTIQUE DEALER

This was a DESPERATELY poor area. From the time this area was built it instantly went into decline and filled up with really poor people. Every room in the house a different family and all the rest of it. And then the depression and the war. I remember it from the late '50s – how MEAN the streets were. There was hardly a car parked around here. When I first remember it, there were LOADS of West Indians. It was very lively. My mother and I used to go up to the top end of Portobello Market and I can remember a pan of her-rings, two feet wide, piled up, filleted and scaled in front of her. Great big pile of them. A shilling. And we used to buy watermelons – which were quite exotic in those days.

I can remember the old people moaning and groaning 'Bloody antique dealers bought up all the shops round here.' Because next door there was Mr Stout, an old fashioned grocery. This side of me there was a lino shop. Panton's across the road was a chemist. Admiral Vernon's was once an undertaker. Harris's was a chandler – where they made the coffins. There was a sweet shop. There was a butcher. Poundland was Woolworths and what is now Best One – or something – was Marks & Spencer's first food shop. I can remember also a shop along there – all it sold was plantains. Bright green bananas.

We now only have one butcher the whole length of Portobello and that's the little halal place right up the end. The current developers in this immedi-ate part of the world have hyped up rents like crazy. I think it's unsustain-able. In fact I'm sure it's unsustainable. So when, for instance, the bank's leases came to an end, the landlords want a modern, very high rent. So the bank says 'No thank you' and walk away and take away their ATMs, which are the life blood of the market.

Without the street market, this street is not worth a cup of cold water. Okay? Because it is the ugliest street in England leading to two of the poorest wards in Europe. My argument with the developers is you have something here unique. You have something that all the world comes to see one time or another. All sorts of people turn up – Princess Margaret, the Duchess of Alba, Liberace, Claire Bloom, Brian Epstein, Claudia Schiffer – because it's different, it's interesting. What the developers want to do is take that which is unique and make it like everything else. You don't take that which is unique and turn it into the same as everybody else because you will kill it. And that is what is happening.

Anyway, let's go back to the beginning … My father was an East Ender born right at the beginning of the last century. His father died when he was thirteen and that day he went out to work and worked until he was taken off to hospital when he was seventy-five and never came out. He was an antique dealer and it was very, very tough. Dad said in the old days you got something beautiful and there were perhaps five people in the whole country who would buy it. And if they didn't want it you could look at it for twenty years. Because people didn't travel. There was no internet. It wasn't international. So you were dependent on your three or four people who you know who might come in.

I can remember he had seventeenth-century Chinese vases in colours – perfect, beautiful. Set after set after set of them. Nobody wanted them. He had a two and a half feet high bronze and ivory figure of a lady with borzoi dogs standing each side. Art deco. And if we didn't have it five years before we sold it, I do not know how long we had it. Today it's like gold dust! It's beyond gold dust.

Dad traded through the great crash of 1929. He said you could walk through Mayfair and the bailiffs were emptying out the contents of a seven storey mansion onto the streets. You could buy the contents for fifty pounds. But nobody had fifty pounds.

When the pound came off the gold standard in 1931 gold coins were worth more than their face value. So, for several months, he went round all the pawnbrokers buying up all the guineas. Everything went into the melt. Even as late as the '60s, in one day, he said, he put one hundred thousand ounces of the finest Japanese art silver that anyone had ever seen in their lives into the flames. And he said it broke his heart – the stuff that he alone melted.

My darling, he had to. I'm sure that farmers get very fond of their animals but they have to be sausages. My father had a wife and four children. And then he had an unmarried sister and a mentally retarded brother who was brain damaged at birth. Then he had another sister who just sort of sat there. And it was endless.

Historically it's always happened. When the nobility had jewellery made, had plate, silver and gold made, that was considered a way of storing your wealth and the minute you needed it, you melted it. Louis the fourteenth had furniture cased in silver when he was a young man. But the only existing silver furniture from the late seventeenth century now is in England. Because everything that was in France was melted.

My father used to take me to the Victoria & Albert museum every Sunday and we used to pore over everything looking at what made it old. I once was trying to describe this process: it's like when a doctor does a medical diagnosis. Start off, is it old? Then, where does the material, where does the pattern, designate or come through or pass? You can read patterns. Some patterns are French; some patterns are Turkish; some patterns are South American. And then there's all sorts of interchanges.

And you look at colour. There is a range of colours you can make from vegetable and ancient mineral dyes. Mauve was an imperial colour because it was so expensive to produce. But, in the second quarter of the nineteenth century, suddenly they discovered this chemical dye, mauveine, which gave this horrendous purple and it swept the world. Once you see that in a piece of embroidery, it's out.

And then you look at more specific things like, for instance, hands. In the nineteenth century tiny hands and feet were admired. So when you see something that's got tiny hands and feet that's purporting to be, say, sixteenth-century, it isn't. In the sixteenth century – think of Leonardo's paintings – you get beautiful large hands and feet that really worked. You can even say the same thing about images of horses. In the nineteenth century they liked to see the Arab dished face for a horse. Again little tiny, itsy-bitty feet – not what you want on a horse. A horse ought to have big proper feet. And when you see things that have got no naughty bits you know that they are nineteenth-century, almost without exception.

And so you go on. You can analyse and analyse and analyse your way through what it is and there's no way of explaining it to people. You sort of imbibe it … subliminally.

One thing that's terribly controversial – no two people agree pretty well – is the issue of cameos and intaglios. One person will say 'Oh, it's clearly Roman.' The next person will say 'It's probably nineteenth-century.' You can argue until you're blue in the face. And quite frankly it's terribly hard to tell, apart from sometimes, when people sign them. Let's say you have an intaglio of the Duke of Wellington, signed by the famous makers. They would also, on the Tuesday of every week, sit and work at something that was a copy of an ancient stone; that you could sell to the Duke of somewhere or other – even the Duke of Wellington – as a Roman one. In the eighteenth century there was no way of testing those things. They dug up antiquities all over Italy and they used to get, say, two arms and a leg and make a complete figure out of it – complete with head and a dog. You end up with these famous collections of Roman marbles in stately homes and probably, on average, seventy percent of these marble carvings are eighteenth-century.

My dad taught me EVERYTHING he knew. And he learned from people who traded in the nineteenth century so I know things that other people just can't know. You put them in the back of your mind and once or twice in a lifetime they become useful.

The other day we sold a silver crucifix, cast in the form of sticks of wood with a little figure on it. Beautiful quality. It was in a late nineteenth-century English box. Made for it. And so the person I bought it from in the market, who was in the silver business, said it was late nineteenth-century.

I could tell, just by looking at the loop at the top which had little bobbles of silver round it – in what's called the pea pod pattern – that you could date it to within ten or twenty years at the very beginning of the seventeenth century. Now that early seventeenth century marks a point at which Charles the First had an archbishop called Laud. Charles was a Protestant but he was attracted to elaborate Catholic practices. (And of course he married Henrietta Maria which was the stupidest thing he could possibly have done; he was highly educated but stupid). And so Laudian style, which is very Italianate, came in, in the short period of his reign before the Civil War. And that's when you can put this thing.

Did I tell the dealer? Look – how long did it take me to explain it to you? You think these people have any idea? No! You don't tell them at all. There's no point in upsetting them. This is not a win-lose situation. I gave the price that was wanted and there was no argument about it. They sold something that was late nineteenth-century unmarked silver and I bought something that was early seventeenth-century unmarked silver.

You see mountains of nineteenth-century because this explosion of standard mass-produced, often mechanically produced, stuff came out on the market. And when it's different it sort of jumps out at you. It sort of waves at you – 'Hello' – in the most extraordinary manner. I remember going to a little antiques fair and I could see at the end of the hall a little tiny bronze figure and I could tell by its stance at what, forty, fifty feet … this is mannerist. I made a beeline for it. But to be able to spot something that's only that big, at that sort of distance, because it just stands out to you, you have to have a trained eye.

Because I came from old school antique dealing, I like things that are as near a unique object as you are likely to get. I can't look at the ordinary stuff that's bought and sold. It has to be something that's got something extra to really touch me. It's objects that speak to you.

There's a story about everything. Did I tell you about a little mug made of leather? It was made for a child. Thick black leather, so it's quite rigid, and a silver rim round it to go at the child's lips so they didn't touch the leather. And round it engraved 'Hannah Bridges' and the date '1660'. It was a little girl's tankard: you could see the little teeth marks. You never gave a child water. You hoped they'd survive so you gave them weak beer so that they had a better chance of growing up instead of being killed by the water. It's magical. And it just brings it back. It's just a creation of that time.

There is a magical intellectual journey to go on with these things. They are SO wonderful. About a year ago, I bought in the market a gold cross as a nineteenth-century copy of the much older piece. And I thought to myself 'No, this is not a nineteenth-century copy. This is an old piece.' It was a particular form of cross: Byzantine style. And it was very, very finely engraved all over with a rather elaborate loop at the top. And across it, and vertically on it, was a Latin inscription. A very good customer saw me looking at this thing and he said 'I'm interested in that.' And I said 'Well, when I've worked out what it is, you'll be the first to know.' I said to him, when I'd studied it, 'It is Byzantine. It's either very early – like sixth-century – or it is from the Latin kingdom in 1206. The Franks, the West, on the Crusades, sacked Constantinople and set up the Latin kingdom for a short time. So it's either very early or the thing that tipped Byzantium over eventually.' So anyway he bought it and he took it off to his friends in the British Museum – who are, you know, really, really great academics. He came back a week or two later and he said to me 'They say 'It's either very early – say sixth-century – or else it's Latin kingdom!' And that gives me enormous pleasure. Because nobody

loves it but it's magical to have something that is as much as a thousand years old, just sitting there unhonoured and unsung and you rescue it from its anonymity. And there is unbelievable joy in that.

Do I always get it right? No, of course not! When my lad was two, I bought a terracotta plaque – a relief of a nude young man, his back view. It was a very beautiful thing and I thought, 'It's either nineteenth-century – very high quality students' work – or it is fifteenth-century.' And because it was as clean as a whistle and I was an exhausted working mother of a two-year-old, I thought 'It's Edwardian.' They used to do lots and lots of high quality, academic copies of things. So I put a ticket on it and I put it in the shop. I had it for four months during which time several hundred very, very high-end dealers walked into the shop. (In fact THE London sculpture dealer saw it and he said, 'I'll have it. I'll just go to my car and get my cheque book to pay for it.' Well he's still coming back!)

So, anyway, another guy came in and bought it. It took him twenty years and an adventure like in Indiana Jones to actually 'prove' that it was from the workshop of Verrocchio, who was Leonardo's master. It was a study for the executioner in 'The beheading of John the Baptist'. And the guy who got the money: first of all he had to part with a great deal of it to partners and, since which time, he's drunk the lot.

A very, very well-known and famous dealer said to me afterwards 'Did I see it?' And I said to him 'Darling you've walked past it ten times!' And the guy who said 'I'll get my cheque book', he MUST know. But other people have said to me if this had happened to them, it would have destroyed them. And I think this is madness. This is just a game and it wasn't written for me. It was written in his stars that he'd buy it, have all these adventures and then, one day, sit down and tell me about it. It's amazing. And the poor chap. I just feel sorry for him because it's done him no good at all.

Life is not a competition: it's a journey. And we all know where we're going to end up. I just take the pleasures of the business. I find it an exercise that I enjoy. And I think the ability to earn a reasonable middle class living by doing as little as I do is quite an achievement!

Okay darling?

'You can honestly say there's not much I haven't collected'

REUBEN, ANTIQUE DEALER

I was born in 1939. Of course I'm a Londoner. South Londoner as you can probably hear by my accent.

We were a musical family. We used to play proper quartets – Corelli and Bach and all the classical stuff. My father used to play the bass viol. I'd play the recorder or treble viol. My mother would play the harpsichord and my sister would play the violin or the treble viol or recorder. Eighteenth-century instruments of course. In fact Pa made the harpsichord and the bass viol 'cause he couldn't buy one; we weren't rich enough.

My father was a Crime Prevention officer at Scotland Yard. He collected everything like myself. We had a big house, a two-storey house. Four bedrooms that had. We had a big front room that was full up. Never had pictures on the walls, had goodies on the wall.

From four or five years of age I collected. Pa encouraged me to buy all types of curiosities. And you got things for nothing then. It was only pennies in those days. Who understood antiques, or cared, just after the war?

We used to go down East Street every Sunday and buy lots of weird and wonderful things. I remember buying a nice Gurkha knife for a shilling. A nice eighteenth-century flute, also a shilling. Old money, you know: 5p today. I remember we bought three eighteenth-century watches for ten shillings once. Repousse silver watches, double case watches. One was by Graham, who's now a very famous make. But of course it came and it went like everything else.

Pa was very knowledgeable. He had a wonderful collection of early books and he'd read every one and understood 'em. Of course it rubbed off on me. And if you're interested, it's surprising how you'll remember it.

And that's how it all started really, with my father and us going down East Lane. And of course, later on when the Portobello came around, I came down the Portobello.

The Portobello was hardly going when I first came here. I must have been about sixteen, fifteen. Not very old anyway. It was more a junk market than an antique market as such. You never had the really posh shops we've got today. And it was a street market: there was very few arcades.

At that time I was collecting early gramophones – from 1878, when they were invented, up to about 1910. We used to advertise in a magazine called the *Exchange and Mart*. You'd be surprised the stuff I got in those days: tin foil phonographs; alloy phonographs; Berliner gramophones – all the early stuff. All three pound, two pound, five pound. All of great value now. Penny and slot phonographs – which was the rarest you could get – ten pounds each. Dog model gramophones for five pound in their boxes. Wonderful stuff. Really wonderful stuff …

I had a wonderful collection in the end. There was a chap in the gramophone society, an older man, and he couldn't believe what I had in the years I'd collected. He'd been collecting for God knows how many years and he had about forty machines and I had a hundred and thirty. And I collected all those in two years.

Anyway an American came down and I sold the collection for one thousand five hundred pounds. Which was a lot of money for a kid of seventeen. Especially in those days when you only earned two and six a week. Today it would be worth two hundred thousand I suppose.

I left school at sixteen. Didn't have many plans, no. No one ever thought of university in those days. It just wasn't done. Whoever went to university in those days except the very, very rich? The first job I got was working in a bookshop. But I didn't like the fact that I had to travel to Moorgate every day in an underground. So I stayed there a week. It was a bloomin' good job really. I always regret that. But anyway, that's what I did. Then I got a shop working in a record store. Which was a bit downmarket really. I could have had such a good job. But there you are. Life is like that.

The next collection was musical instruments. I used to come down here every week and I used to buy an instrument, maybe two. I wanted all the early instruments. Eighteenth-century stuff. I wouldn't touch anything later than 1850. Hurdy-gurdies, flutes and clarinets were plentiful. And they were all pennies. I sold that lot off gradually. I must have had six hundred then. Never counted. I must have had.

When I was twenty-two, twenty-one I became a bus conductor. Why? Money of course. It was twelve pound a week I got for that. I was only getting three pound fifty in the record shop. That was fun that was. Especially all the girls on the buses. But anyway, let's leave that there.

If we passed a junk shop and I wanted to get off, my signal to my conductor was three rings on the bell and he'd stop. And if anyone said anything he used to say 'My conductor's gone to the toilet.' I used to put all these blessed things under the stairs, where you put the cases normally. I mean, they knew what I was up to. They must have done. 'Cause when I got back to the depot I used to give them all these weird and wonderful things – 'Can you put that over the counter for me, and look after that for me?' I bought a stuffed turtle once and put it over the top …

And then I used to take every Saturday off, change my Tuesday, to come down the Portobello. And eventually the CDI called me and he said 'Reuben,' he says, 'I notice you're changing every Saturday, or if you can't change it, you become sick.' He said 'Reuben, if you do it again, I want a doctor's certificate to say why you were sick and why you didn't come in.' 'Well I won't bother to do that,' I said. 'I resign now.' He said 'Pardon?' I said 'I resign now.' He said 'Have you got a job to go to?' I said 'Yes, I have. I've been dealing antiques. I've been going down the Portobello.' Well … he wasn't cross. But I think he was a little bit amazed how I'd got away with it. 'Cause it had been going on about a year it had.

That's when I really started coming down here and dealing. You had a look round, see what you can buy, and then sell it later on for more than you paid for it. That was the idea. At six o'clock, five o'clock in the morning there was really good trading going on, in the dark with our torches.

I'd be sold out by seven o'clock. All the dealers'd been round and picked me like a bone because I was too cheap. But it didn't matter: you made a week's wages. That was good enough for me. I just thought quick sale, you know, 'cause you could always get more in those days.

I dealt for two reasons: one to make money and one to make money to make another collection. I'm a born collector. I'm not a dealer. No question about that. And I've had some good collections, let me tell you. Because I'm very changeable, you know, or was. You name it, I've collected it. I mean big collections: Christmas tree lights and Christmas tree decorations; early radios; early electric light bulbs – from the Swan lamp, right up to about 1900 – one of the best collections of those in the world; early banjos, of course, which was the best collection in the world, no question; early gas cookers; early electric motors – but I mean early historic ones; scientific instruments; things I've even forgotten I've collected, probably … I had a vast collection of early Valentine cards, lovely collection of those, Chinese shoes. All come and gone.

It does become manic. I don't know what makes you change either really. But you do. Something else comes along. Like I bought a collection of early wireless valves, so that was my next collection. Everything else had to go and I bought the wireless valves. That's what you did really. You sold one collection to support the other. I had chemist curios, chemist jars. I had a wonderful collection of early enamel signs. I had every one in South London I think – another story! Was I lifting them? No, no no. Someone else was. I don't think they lifted them, actually, but they used to get them. Who cared where they came from? They weren't worth anything. They really weren't. Then I collected pub mirrors, early lavatories – the coloured lavvies, toilet bowls. I had a lovely collection of those an' all. I've got photos. I'll show you some other time.

Pa encouraged it. It was Pa's encouragement made me do it really I suppose. And it's in the blood. 'Cause my uncle … my uncle … The fact with me is this: my father, who I call Pa, was actually my uncle. My mother was my auntie. My real father was married but his wife died. My mother died. He got remarried again and, obviously, the second wife didn't want the children – I suppose that's what happened – and we were put in a home.

So my real father's brother, who I call Pa, said 'Oh, we'll adopt them, the two children', which he did. So I was at a home in Weir until about 1943. Pa took Rosie before me, cause she's older. Does that make sense to you? You've got the story. Anyway … Ernie, my father, was madder than me. He really was a mad collector. He collected everything under the sun.

What makes a collector? I don't know. I really don't know. It's a disease. No question about it. It's something that's in your blood and you cannot get rid of. Once you're a collector, you're a collector.

I'm not a dealer. Not in my heart. I hate selling my things. But you've got to sell one to support the next collection. You know what I mean?

I regret selling the banjos, perhaps, 'cause that was a wonderful collection. I ended up with a thousand banjos. Look at them. All these banjos are pre-1900. These ones with heads on are pretty unique. That's a Negro's head. He had glass eyes. And that's a periwigged gentleman: a Georgian gentleman's head. They're 1840, I suppose, 1830. That was made of whale bone, that banjo, by a sailor. All made of whale bone. That went to the Nantucket Museum of Whaling.

33

I wouldn't say I could play them. I could get a tune out of most of them. But I was interested in the history of them. What did I discover? Nothink, to be honest. It's very difficult. They say the banjo comes from America but I think it's an English invention. It's a thing that originally came from Africa really, isn't it? Put a skin across an instrument, put a string down it – what is it? A banjo?

I used to get people from all over the world come to visit me because it was the only collection like it in the world. I sold it to Japan, which I regret to this day. I should never have sold that collection.

I'm retired now, for health. I had empyema. I was in hospital for three months. They thought I was going to die for seven weeks. I didn't. Still here. And I've had various illnesses. I've had cancer. But I've got over them all. Because you've got an interest in life, you get over these things. When you're just so interested in other things, you don't worry about things like that 'cause you're forever learning. Even now I'm learning.

The plan now? Just enjoy life and buy what I can, when I can. That's it really. Come down 'ere to meet all me old mates. Sell a little bit if I've got something to sell. And if it goes, good, I buy another instrument with it. I've started collecting musical instruments again. I've got three hundred instruments now. I've got them round my bed at home. If they fall on your head, they fall on yer head … and what a way to go! I've had a damn good life and I've had more things than most people will ever handle in their lifetime. Certainly not now. They won't handle it now. It's not there.

Another thing I collected, early cameras. I forgot that, yeah. Collected pistols, early pistols. I had a lovely collection of them too. I collected ethnic weapons. I had three thousand of them.

You name it, I've collected it really. You can honestly say there's not much I haven't collected, I don't think.

'You can still buy wonderful things'

NICHOLAS, ANTIQUE DEALER

I'm always proud to say that in thirty-five-odd years of business I've never dealt in anything commercial. I don't deal in things that are hot now. I deal in things that are interesting.

> – *I'm Stephanie and you're Nicholas.*
> – *Hello Stephanie! You made it!*
> – *I did, I did.*
> – *(He picks a picture off wall) Ooph … There you are. Then you can have a proper look at it.*
> – *Thank you very much …*
> – *That's what's called a sand picture made from natural sands from the Isle of Wight …*
> – *My speciality. I'm just publishing a book on the whole thing. Did you know they started as table decorations in the eighteenth century? If you were a really rich client and you want to have a party for five hundred of your closest friends you just call up one of your star architects (who's probably building a house for you anyway) and they say 'Oh, we can just break through the back wall and add a supper room to it. And then we have a jolly party and then demolish it again.' So you get in all the Royal Academy painters to decorate everything. Then you do your table decorations. You get in the Mister Sandman who will make you an Old Master or Snider's hunting scene– whatever you want – in the middle of the table. You have to*

imagine the table fully decked out and the candles and the mir-
rors to reflect everything. Then the sand – particularly if it's got
marble dust and quartz in it – is going to glitter and shimmer
and everyone's going to think this is the most marvellous thing.
And it will be ruined the moment you sit down to eat your
meal. That's part of the whole thing; everything is for
one night only. It's just extravagant … beyond extravagant …

    Mr Zorbel was one of four people doing these for King
George the Third. Allegedly the king said to him 'You should
find a way to fix it.' So Mr Zorbel made a sticky surface … put
sand on … another sticky surface … more sand … and built it
up so it was fairly flat. It would take him four months to make
one because it takes so long to dry layer by layer.

    This is not by Mr Zorbel himself. This one is probably by a son
or nephew and they get progressively less good. I like it because it's
small and because it's a sand picture and I'm just obsessed with
sand. It is just VERY sad. I think this is probably my fourteenth.
– Well it's lovely to have something that one loves.
– I do … yes … I do … Now I think you said three hundred
  pounds. Can we make that a slightly more attractive price?
– Um … it won't be very much more attractive, I'm afraid,
  because I know what I have in it! How about two hundred
  and eighty?
– Good-o. That pays for the taxi that takes me home. Nicholas,
  it has been a pleasure.
– It has been a pleasure to meet you too. When you are in
  Portobello, come and say hello!
– Thank you very much. Goodbye.

I have a number of things that I collect. I suppose the thing that I've been collecting the longest is books that date before the year 1700. I loved the Tudor and Stuart periods at school and when I got into this business I discovered, to my astonishment, that you could buy a book from the time of Shakespeare and Milton. They were very, very inexpensive many years ago.

This is Sir Francis Bacon's *Sylva Sylvarum* or 'A Naturall History … published after the author's death by William Rawley, Doctor in Divinity, one of his Majesities Chaplaines.' Out comes a moth – there've been a lot of them around lately.

This is from 1635 – one of the very earliest editions. It's just literally chapter after chapter after chapter of little experiments that Sir Francis Bacon made. Bacon was a brilliant mind: he wrote notes on hundreds of different things that interested him. You know … when you're walking along the beach and you're near the water's edge and your feet go into the sand and it fills with water: Why? In fact he died as the result of a scientific experiment. It was in the middle of the winter and he was then in his '60s. And he thought 'I wonder if it's possible to freeze something for a few days?' They had some chickens and he was on a journey to somewhere. He got out of his coach in a snow drift and was packing the chickens full of snow and ice to see if he could preserve them. Of course what happened was he got a very bad cold, which became pneumonia, and he died.

You could get a modern reprint of that book but it's rather nice to actually have an original. Because you can actually, viscerally, experience it the same way that somebody did nearly four hundred years ago. That, to me, is interesting.

And there's nothing like the smell of an old book. They smell differently from century to century because of the paper that was used, the leather that was used. I always think the older books have this lovely kind of organic aroma to them; they'll smell vaguely of smoked meat. But by the time you get to the nineteenth century they stop making them with rag paper and make them with wood pulp and the leather was tanned at high speed in very acidic conditions. And in the nineteenth century they had gas lighting which put sulphuric acid into the atmosphere which reacted with the tanning agents in the bindings of books and the stuff that was used in the wood pulp paper, which is why that deteriorates so quickly. I've had occasions when I've opened the covers of a book and parts of the pages start falling out like confetti because the books have essentially rotted. Whereas I'll show you one here … This book will be celebrating its five hundreth birthday next year and look at that paper – it's as tough as nails!

Then I've got a collection of little bronzes. This is a nice little piece I bought this week. It's a little – probably seventeenth-century – figure of Neptune that was made in Venice. You can tell by the style and the colour of the metal.

Bronze is a metal of widely varying recipe. Strictly speaking, it is copper and tin. But tin had to come from places like Cornwall. You had to order it and then wait a couple of months – because it had to come by sea – and it was jolly expensive. Therefore they would use things with a high copper content and put other base metals in to strengthen it. If you actually look at this metal there's a slightly rose tint to it, which is quite often indicative of Italy because they had to use things with a high copper content.

Here's a one-armed woman. This was supposed to be Venus combing her hair with one arm stretched out, but they made it without that part of the arm. In the Renaissance period, if a bronze came out of the mould and it was imperfect they didn't melt it down again. It wouldn't have put anybody off that they were missing a bit because these emulate ancient sculptures of Rome and Greece, which of course they were familiar with. If you get a Roman bronze that's dug up and it happens to be missing a leg, well you're not going to be in the least bit worried about that. So they wouldn't have minded.

It was a harking back to the classical world that drove the Renaissance. They wanted to recreate what they thought was the ideal age: the Classical Age. They wanted to make great sculptures like the Greeks and the Romans did. I mean the first commission that Michelangelo ever had, when he was a teenager, was a fake! It's the Tondo that's in the Royal Academy. And that was commissioned specifically to be like a Roman sculpture.

Most of the Roman and Greek little bronzes were gods that you prayed to. You actually put them on your household altar. Whereas when you get to the Renaissance period, this was art for pleasure. These little figures were made for collectors; they were designed to be picked up and handled. Though they did have antique shops in ancient Rome. There were antique dealers and they sold Greek sculpture. I believe there's even some documents survive where the antique dealers in Rome are complaining 'Oh, you just can't get the good old stuff anymore.' It's amazing! So it carries on and carries on. It's quite funny.

What makes people collect? Now that's a very good question. Some people just buy an antique because it happens to be something that goes in the house. Other people collect because they have a tremendous aesthetic sensibility. I think you would call Todd and Tim aesthetic collectors with their extraordinary sculptures and paintings. And then there are other people for whom it's a much deeper thing.

In a sense your collection is a reflection of your identity. And maybe, sometimes, you need that. Maybe it's a sort of insecurity that makes you want to have those things because you feel 'Who am I? Why am I here?' You've got something there that tells you something about yourself.

People who are book collectors are often rather autistic. People who collect books in certain ways, shall we say. You can get into the finer points of books. You may have a first edition but there's the first edition first issue and the first edition second issue because there's a 't' on page sixty-seven which has been left out in that one and that one. It can all be very, very categorised and you can cross reference everything and you can list it and you can fill in all the gaps. And the collectors for that tend to be people who don't communicate very well except, funnily enough, when they're talking about their collections. Then, all of a sudden, they open up and become incredibly eloquent.

I've never looked at it that way. I happen to like books of a certain period because of what they're about and what they tell you about the people. It's rather like transporting yourself into the mind of somebody in the seventeenth century. You get a feeling about what was meaningful to them.

There are some people who collect not for the objects but for the thrill of the chase. One friend has an ENORMOUS collection. There must be over twenty thousand items in it, many of which are just put away in boxes. He'd say 'I like going out. I like the joy of discovering something. I like the to and fro of negotiating.' He once said 'If it disappeared tomorrow it would be great because I'd just start again.'

And then I sold something to a chap this morning who said 'I've got no room. Why am I buying this great big thing?' But he buys it because he relates to it and he loves it. And a lot of us buy something for that reason. Sometimes an object is just simply beautiful, in its own lovely way. One sees the beauty or the intrinsic merit in an object and it's very sad when you see it on a table on a rainy day, its condition already fragile. It's now being virtually driven to the end of its career. And in a sense you almost feel 'Well my God, I think I ought to step in and buy that for just a few pounds', just so that you can preserve it.

Could it be anything to do with personal feelings of abandonment? I suppose it could be. My dad died just after I was fifteen, my mother died just before I was fourteen and I then went to live with an aunt and uncle. But I mean one's whole life was disrupted. And I suppose after that you perhaps try to heal yourself by surrounding yourself with things of your own … so that in fact you've got more power over it. Because if you've lost somebody – if you've lost a parent particularly, or both parents, or if your parents have cast you on the waters a little bit – this way you can surround yourself with things which, I suppose, act as a kind of insulation between you and the world. So that you've actually got this kind of wall of safety which you've built yourself and made your own choices over it. And they have a sense of comfort about them. It's rather nice to come in and see them. It's like seeing a well-loved friend, isn't it? There's nothing more comforting than to spend time with people that you're close to.

Why do I deal? Antique dealing is a very independent way of life. Many of us in this business are square pegs who couldn't find round holes, or wouldn't fit into round holes in any other walk of life, but here we've all found a level to function and enjoy life and to contribute something which we might not have been able to do in anything else. Because we would have probably ended up doing jobs we hated, being some of those poor people on the Tube in the morning with those terribly long faces.

Whereas here, you might have gotten up four hours before anybody who got on the Tube and gone to some extraordinary place – some boot fair or antique fair – and actually had a really interesting morning. Maybe seen some amazing things, maybe been lucky enough to buy something great, or actually not bought anything but just met up with friends and had a cup of coffee and an interesting conversation, which could range from anything from politics to astrophysics. We've got people from every walk of life that have drifted into this. We've got actors, actresses, doctors, school teachers, business people. One guy was a nuclear physicist. Then you get a certain group of people who've done it since they were quite young; I started doing this when I was about twenty-three. It's a business for autodidacts, if you like: people who have educated themselves.

When I go out and buy, I empty everything out of my head and I just kind of float about as if I'm some kind of disembodied spirit wandering around. I always say 'The objects find me.' You can just put your hand on something and not even realise why you picked it up. I went to a fair three years ago and I'm looking at this photograph album. And I keep seeing this other thing. It keeps catching my eye. It looks like the enamel badge off the radiator of a car. So I'm thinking 'What the hell. I don't want to look at a wretched car mascot badge!' I bought the album then picked this thing up and looked at it and said 'Oh'. It was a Charles the First roundel in enamel – what they called 'Surry Enamel' – made in the suburbs of London. They had pewter alms dishes which had a little circular boss in the middle. And this was probably from one of those.

If, over many years, you've gone around umpteen museums and galleries and looked at a zillion catalogues and looked at objects and talked to friends, your memory is impregnated with a huge visual library of imagery. So the eye and the subconscious do the work. Your hand goes out to something because your subconscious mind tells you 'Pick that up, it's good' and your conscious mind is lagging far behind. It's very interesting.

One of the biggest failures for us as a profession, actually, is that we are not getting the message across to people that you can still buy wonderful things and you don't have to pay very much money to have them. You've got an awful lot of media-driven stuff on television. It's either about people going round boot fairs buying real junk in order to make a fiver or the very, very scholarly Road Show where they show people masterpieces that they've been sitting on. What is needed is some presentation to say 'Well actually, there's lots of things around which are very interesting culturally and old and beautiful and very affordable.' And, in many, many cases, you'll be able to buy an item that is really well made and beautifully designed and will cost you a lot less than something brand new.

People often used to ask me 'What should I buy?' I always said 'The most important thing is, you must buy something that you like.' So how do you find out what you like? Go to museums. Walk around and see what takes your fancy. Go and view auctions. Buy a couple of reference books. Because at least then you've got some idea before you start. It's very hard to throw yourself in at the deep end and just start picking things off tables. If somebody says to me how come I know that bit of pottery is seventeenth-century and this piece of pottery is nineteenth-century – well, it's only taken me thirty-five years!

Then start going to antique markets, antique fairs, antique shops. Pick things up, look at them – ask questions. You don't have to buy it straight away. You don't have to buy it if you don't want it. Never let somebody else influence you or tell you what to buy. Just buy what you like.

I think the chances of stumbling across a real bargain, possibly even a masterpiece, are possibly even greater now than they've ever been. Because a lot of the people who are in the antique trade today do not have the grounding in it that the people who've been in it for much longer have. So although the objects are not as plentiful today, there are a lot fewer people who will recognise them.

A friend of mine in Portobello told me of somebody he knew whose neighbour was an elderly man. A little while after he died, he could smell burning. And his family were in the house next door and they had a big bonfire in the garden and they were burning his books which were all sixteenth-century. But they had no idea that they were worth anything. They just thought 'Oh look, all the spines are off. They're all really crumbly. On the fire!' He said it was pretty much too late.

Antique dealing is a business where there's negotiation on price. But there's ways of making offers and there's ways of not making offers. You ask

somebody the price of something and they say, 'It's one hundred and twenty pounds.' I've seen people who've said, 'Would you take forty?' Well sorry, go away. Because that's an insult! So don't insult somebody.

You can say 'I really like that but I've got to watch my pennies a little bit. Is there any leeway in the price?' Then people are generally very good. But don't say it's too expensive if you don't know what you're looking at.

People come here for a chat as much as anything else. I once said to a very dear friend – a customer and a collector – 'I think this is a very self-centred business. Am I doing anything for anybody else?'

He said 'You have no idea what you do for other people. You're a refuge for many people who are working very hard in other things and they can come and spend a little time with you, and look at something nice.' He was in a very high-pressure job. He would walk into my place, we'd sit and talk and I'd show him some things. And you could see, over the next half an hour, the stress would slowly melt away and he would relax and then would start to laugh and chat and look at things. And the personality inside him would emerge. He was no longer this stressed out executive salesman who had to travel round the country, dealing with unspeakable people. He was now the guy who loved the past and history. That was his joy and it shone out of him. His great ambition in life was to retire and to become an antique dealer. Sadly he didn't make it.

You also get customers who'll say 'We're having a dinner party. Come and have dinner.' So there's all that. It's a very, very multi-layered, multi-faceted thing, this business. I know people who'll say 'Antiques and business are a contradiction in terms.' They really are. I mean most of us are not conventional business people at all, the way we work. A regular accountant would look at this and throw his hands up in horror. But there again, for a lot of people it's not a business: it's a way of life.

'Everything ends up at Portobello'

BARRY AND POPPY, ANTIQUE DEALERS

POPPY – We were talking about why people start becoming dealers and I was saying, were you a collector as a child? Because I think that's often the case: people beatling around as children end up collecting as adults or dealing. And I was laughing with Barry because I was such a precocious child. On the top floor we had a room which I turned into a museum. It was mostly natural history – shells, minerals, fossils, those sorts of things – and then I had elephants' tusks and eighteenth-century prints – things that had come in job lots and bits that my parents had – and I used to charge dealers, when they came round, to come and have a look at it. And of course they all did, because I was their friend's daughter!

I was born in Chester in 1974. My parents were both dealers. It was a very easy job in those days; it was the end of the big period of house sales when you could really buy fantastic things and there was enough to go round. They used to come home every day with two carloads full, and it would all be sold by seven o'clock in the evening.

They dealt from home. The other dealers used to come at about five and it was quite glam really: there'd be Scotch and Campari and all these women would arrive in fur coats with their husbands. Business was done in the first hour and then they'd all go out to dinner. And it would all happen again the next day. It was easy. It was a ball. Dealers were making a fortune and it was cash.

I went to art school, studied fashion and wanted to be a designer. When I left I came to London, got a job with two dealers and a job in the fashion industry. Antiques won. I just can't keep away from it – that's the problem!

BARRY – I grew up in a village in Kent. My dad was the local bobby. My mum was a housewife. There was no antiques or anything like that involved. I went to Sandwich secondary modern school because I failed my 11 plus. I left there as soon as I could and went to catering college. But I only lasted there about nine months because there was a fire. The fire started as I recall – well I should recall, because I started it – in a sort of locker room and spread.

I went to work as a cook on a pirate radio station in the Thames estuary. I did that until the government closed them down. Then I opened a coffee bar in the house I was living in. It was an old shop downstairs so I just knocked a hole in the wall, put a big door in – didn't think about a licence – went to the Cash and Carry, bought loads of Kit Kats and things, bought a coffee machine and put a counter in. That didn't last very long because I moved to London.

This was in the '60s. I became a hippie. Big time. Everything that it entails: long hair; lots of dope; I suppose acid as well. And this is also the time I became interested in antiques. Hippies liked India so I started buying rugs and embroideries. You'd hang them round your pad. You'd have them billowing from the ceiling.

Did I work? Course you didn't work! You'd buy a couple of ounces of dope and you'd sell it in quid deals to your mates and cover your own expenses. I was actually living off Kensington Church Street in a road called Camden Walk – quite a swanky place these days. Rents were cheap. I was sharing the flat and it was fifteen quid a week between us. None of us were working. You didn't want to go to the Dole because they would tell you to get a job. We had other things to do, like go to Kensington Market and hang around, or take some acid and go to Kew Gardens. That's what we did – it was a full-time job, believe it or not.

My friend, Paul, and I met an American lady in London who had a lot of psilocybin tablets – magic mushrooms basically. She was off to Copenhagen and she said 'Do you want to come and sell them all for me – I've got ten thousand of these things.' So we headed off to Copenhagen. We sold all this and then we started buying cannabis and taking it up to Sweden where you get more money. After about six months we just decided that was enough; we'd better come back to England. We were on the ferry from Gothenburg to Immingham and Paul said to me 'What we gonna do now?' I said, 'I've got no idea.'

He said 'Let's become antiques dealers.'

And I went 'Yeah, that sounds like groovy. Let's do that!' We had one thousand kroner each – which was probably about six hundred quid – and it was in one single one thousand kroner note. We came back to England and we went to Sandown on the south coast, near Folkestone. We went into an antique shop and I said 'What do we buy then Paul?'

He said 'We buy Art Nouveau, that's the latest thing.'

So we said to the woman 'Have you got any Art Nouveau?' We bought all these jardinieres and bronze candlesticks – things that I don't have any-thing to do with these days – and we spent all of our money. She must have thought it was Christmas, this lady. We brought it all to London and took a stand in Antiquarius on the Kings Road. It was the first week it opened. We put it all in there and we didn't sell a thing. We didn't sell a sausage. Course we didn't 'cause we'd obviously paid top prices in this sort of rather swanky antique shop on the south coast. And basically it just all went pear shaped: we sat there for months, not selling anything.

We didn't really care because we still had our lifestyle in London. But it was hard to pay the rent and I think we just gave it up. I took what we had to the Portobello road and rented a stand in the Red Lion Arcade. So I was by then an antiques dealer. I was selling it, but I was selling it for less. I didn't care. One afternoon a bloke came who I knew, who I used to buy quite a lot of dope from, and he said 'Do you want to go to Pakistan?' 'Yeah!' I said. 'When?'

He said 'Now.' So I closed my stand, went home, got my passport, and went to the airport. I never went back: left my stuff there. I suppose they took the stuff – good luck to them, they can have it!

I spent the next nine months round the north-west frontier, buying vast quantities of dope. I started seeing things from the Indus valley culture in the antique shops there: big stone friezes, Buddha images and things like this, which I thought were really fantastic. But we didn't have any money: the guy who sent us out there didn't pay us anything.

I flew home and took a stand in Camden Lock. I started going to junk shops all over London, of which there were thousands, buying eastern things and African things. And I went to Christie's in South Ken – South East Asian and Indian art they called the sale and it was every week! You'd basically spend a couple of hundred pounds and have a car full.

Then I started buying and collecting rugs. I had Caucasian rugs and I think I was probably a bit of a show-off. I was a bit proud of them, very full of myself about it all. So anyway I got robbed and I lost everything. It just put me off the antiques thing entirely. I never wanted to buy another thing.

So I started this cafe in Acton Park. Did that for a couple of years and then I went bankrupt. Coke was my undoing. It took all my money and really made me like a paranoid wreck. Not good. Not good at all. Something I'm not very proud of. So anyway, I lost my business. A friend of mine gave me a job as a labourer for his building company. I'd never picked up a hammer in my life but I quite enjoyed it.

Then one day I went to Bermondsey market. It was the first time I'd been to an antiques market since I'd been robbed: I couldn't look at an antiques market for years. I saw a basket, a big African basket. And I thought 'That's a fantastic textile – because textiles are my thing – and no one will ever pinch that!'

I bought it and I then bought every single basket. I'd go to the Portobello road every Saturday and I bought thousands of them, from the late nineteenth, early twentieth century, up to the Second World War. I became the leading authority on African baskets and they became worth more and more money. Because of the baskets, I got back into African things and I started buying calabash. So I was doing that and being a builder. Occasionally, latterly, I took a stall at Portobello, mainly selling baskets. Because I was new, it was all fresh stuff and I would sell so much it was fantastic. I got a bit of a taste for it so I took a stand in Lipka's arcade which was where Poppy was.

I tried to find an excuse, really, for talking to her because I did really feel it was impossible, it was ridiculous: I was twenty-five years older than her. So I didn't do anything about it for yonks. And then one day – this is so embarrassing – I saw in the paper they had this Indian classical concert. I quite like that and I thought 'I'll buy two tickets and ask Poppy.' So I did. I bought them about three months in advance and I couldn't ask her. Every week I go down there and I think 'Right, I'm going to do it this week.' I'd go round there and I'd go 'No I can't! It's stupid! I might freak her out. She'll probably go "Ughhh! Creepy old guy!"' The day before the concert I just went there and blurted it out. I said 'Do you want to come out to a concert tonight … Oh God what have I said?' And she went 'Oh that would be nice!' So we went out and that was it.

Poppy and I moved in together. I was still building and I found that then I really started getting very, very jealous of the idea that Poppy was out buying stuff and I was just going getting filthy. So we decided I'd have to give up my job.

POPPY – For the first year and a half, two years, we couldn't do wrong. It was just fantastic. And then suddenly the banks collapsed. The business started going off a few months before and it just completely buggered us up. Suddenly, like all antiques dealers, we didn't have any money.

BARRY – There's a myth that in times of credit crunch, because they are not getting any interest, people will actually invest their money in an object or an antique. Of course they don't. To buy an antique you have to have a record of buying antiques. People don't suddenly think 'I'm going to buy an antique' because they're terrified. They wouldn't know where to start. If you buy antiques, you buy antiques and if you don't, you don't.

POPPY – The other big problem with the business itself is that antiques are fantastically unfashionable. I'll watch my peer group, who are now young people making very good incomes living in nice London flats or houses, and there isn't an antique, there isn't a painting, there isn't a dining table. It's all from Heals. They want new. I suppose it's what came with Kelly Hoppen and Anouska Hempel – minimalism really. These very, very low-key, pattern-less textiles, milky colours, don't suit antiques. Regency textiles are bright green and gold. They're not taupe.

BARRY – And what the style magazines tell us are antiques are absolute rubbish! They're sort of painted furniture with chicken wire. Distressed. It's the 'I saw you coming' look. It's junk. Absolute junk.

POPPY – Even though Portobello is a London landmark, as far as antiques are concerned I think that people think that it's just tat. I don't think people realise that a lot of people are actually dealing very good things and it's actually feeding the whole of the London antiques trade and people from the Continent, America, Japan and all sorts of places. In fact it's a pool: everything ends up at Portobello.

BARRY – It's the only place in the country …

POPPY – because Bermondsey's gone, Camden Market's gone.

BARRY – I think the council also think it's just a little bit of bric-a-brac down there. They want to make it pedestrian like Covent Garden. They want it to have sort of old English humbug shop, cheeky chappy Cockneys selling scarves and ties and a preferred route – the yellow brick road – for walking right from Notting Hill Gate. With signposts and buskers.

Why aren't we fighting harder to protect it? Antiques people don't like being led. We are individuals. And that's one of the problems: we can't organise. We are sole traders: we're not good at unions.

POPPY – I think most antique dealers you meet were often not very good at school. Often rebellious teenagers, stubborn, not very good at sharing, not very good at being told. What will happen? I think it will go. I think the whole thing will go.

BARRY – And it will end up with those magnifying glasses. Not even reproduction. Bogus antiques. Ersatz antiques. And then we will all be working on the Internet, just dealing from home.

POPPY – We're quite snooty about antiques really. Good antiques are fantastically well made – great examples of whatever period or nationality they are. And it also requires application; you have to learn about them.

BARRY – You learn through the cheque-book, making mistakes. Buying something and not selling it or paying too much. Very early on, I bought a model of Queen Victoria that was Nigerian. It said on the back 'Queen Victoria, Lagos 1898'. It was a really rough and ugly representation of Queen Victoria, probably two feet high. I paid ten pounds for it. I took it to the Portobello road and I sold it to a friend of mine. He gave me forty quid and sold it for seven thousand. That is a fantastic lesson for me because I now know what to pay for such things. And don't be frightened of putting a good price on it. Go for it.

You mustn't get hurt if you sell something and somebody sells it for more. It happens with all dealers. Oddly enough, there can be two dealers and you can both make money out of each other. You might have similar tastes but one person might see something the other person doesn't or know somebody who might prefer that sort of object. That is how it works – at no point does anyone say 'Hey that's not fair' otherwise we'd all spend our lives just hating.

POPPY – The most fun – and this only happens with really good friends – is if something really fantastic turns up and you know that that person's spotted it as well and you can go halves on it. Then, if it's really successful and you make a lot of money out of it, you can celebrate. You all go out to dinner; you all have champagne. That's the most fun.

BARRY – What we don't like doing are these things they call rings. People will come to us and say 'I hope you're not after what I'm after!' and you'll say

'Possibly I am.' 'Well, why don't you talk to me?' We get asked that a lot. In other words: 'I'm going to buy this. I'm in charge of the ring. And if you want to join the ring, you'll talk to me.' It's bullying. And my reaction to that is 'No'. But if you don't go in, they'll say 'Right. We'll make you pay.'

POPPY – A friend of ours, when he was a very young man in the '70s, went up against the big furniture knock. There were a pair of Anglo-Indian cupboards and they were mega, mega. He'd just sold his house for ten thousand pounds, his wife was about to drop her first child and he thought 'I want to buy these.' The knock approached him and said 'You're going to come with us and be in with us.' He said 'No, I'm not' and they said 'Right, you're going to be taught a lesson.' So they did. I think their bidding cost him twenty-five thousand. He said he loaded them into his van, having got no house, a pregnant wife and no money, got about a mile down the road, got out and threw up.

BARRY – He was determined. He was bloody minded about it.

POPPY – The only way to get them off your back is let them teach you a lesson and they will leave you alone.

BARRY – How do the rings work? I'll show you. We've got one object and we decide we all want that, so let's not bid against each other. It goes for a hundred but it was worth five thousand. Then the three of us go outside and we write on a piece of paper how much we'd pay for it. I might put two hundred, you might put three hundred, Poppy might put one hundred and twenty. That means you will end up with it, because you offered the most. But you've now agreed to pay three hundred … so out of the balance between the one hundred we've paid and the three hundred, there's a difference of two hundred pounds. So you'd give me a third of it and Poppy a third of it.

POPPY – The idea is that every dealer makes a cut. Also the dealer that ends up with it has paid out less. But it's a complicated gamble.

BARRY – It's real poker! If it's a big ring, they say what they'll pay out loud. They go round in increments until someone says 'That's enough for me.' And then they will get paid out. If there's eight of us, you will get paid out an eighth of the balance between what it costs and where you dropped out.

POPPY – I hate doing it, actually, because I find the maths almost impossible.

BARRY – And it's illegal because you're stealing from the vendor. We don't go to auctions to go home with a hundred quid. If we see something we like, we want the thing!

POPPY – We want to get it home and clean it, and get all the books out and look it up and talk about it.

BARRY – There's nothing better then, after a long day, putting it on the table, opening a bottle of wine and getting the books out – of which we've got thousands. What fun to go through – 'There's one!' 'No that's not the same!' – and pin it down!

POPPY – We buy things on a weekly basis that we've never had before. Every time it's a learning curve. And also, when you're looking at something, you start learning about something else. It takes you off on a tangent. If you're learning about, say, a French lacquer box, that might take you on to Japanese Nambam. So you're constantly seeing the connections between different cultures and different materials and styles. And that's very nice. If we buy something and we're not quite sure, we say 'Let's go and see if they've got any in the British Museum or the V & A.' If they haven't, go to the Study Room, ask the expert, see what they think.

Dealing on your own can be quite a lonely business. You can be stuck in some auction house at the back end of nowhere on a rainy day, competing against other people in the room. It's all very clandestine and you've got all day there and six hours between lots.

BARRY – Whereas, with two of us, you just say 'Let's go to the pub!'

POPPY – We're a good balance. Barry's more impetuous and I'm a bit cautious. Barry will say 'Now come on, you really ought to just stick your neck out and buy that!' and I will say to him 'Just leave it. Put it down!'

BARRY – We get up at four to go to Portobello. We get there early for parking and also because we want to buy something. We leave the arcade at three, three-thirty.

POPPY – Luckily the bit that we're in is very jolly. We'll generally have a bottle of fizz and gossip.

BARRY – Saturday morning is really when we sell. Some days we don't sell a thing. Other days you have a bumper day. For us, a good day would be half a dozen sales.

Poppy – It can be very frightening. Because the problem with antiques dealers is, it doesn't matter if you've got a million pounds or a hundred pounds: you will spend to the last shilling you own. So if you don't sell something, and you haven't got any money because you've spent it all, you're really stuck.

Barry – We sometimes need to sell on a Saturday because we have no money. I mean no money. We've spent it. And if we don't sell on that Saturday, the following week is really … fraught.

Poppy – It stops your buying power because you become nervous. Bills start coming in. It can be very nerve wracking. We've reached times where we're absolutely hanging off the cliff edge and I'm tearing my hair out with anxiety and worry and you'll say 'No, no, no. It's fine. We'll sort it out.' And, actually, we always do.

Barry – We have got a lot of stuff. So we just pick something and say 'Look. That is worth five hundred pounds. Didn't really want to sell it, but come on. It's only stuff.' Everything we have is for sale under certain circumstances. There are just a couple of things – sentimental sort of things – that are not really for sale.

Any regrets? No! You can't beat being self-employed! When I was building I was self-employed, but it's not the same. Then I was working for you and if I didn't show up at your house to do the work you could phone me up and say 'Hey, where are you? You said you'd be here at eight!' At least now we can actually – well, we can't afford it but we COULD – stay in bed all day.

'It's a healthy obsession'

Tim and Todd, collectors

Tim – We were both brought up abroad

Todd – I grew up on the seaside in South America and the West indies and lived on little islands, so it was very easy to collect shells. I had a little museum in a cupboard in my room where I used to charge my brothers and sisters to come and see the shell of the week, rotating display. I had all my shells labelled and I catalogued them: used to mark where I found them, how deep the water was, what day it was.

Tim – My parents lived in Nigeria when I was little and then we moved to Fiji. So my first collections – rather like Todd – were shells and insects and natural history. But I was always interested in old things.

I was pretty obsessed with antiques. It's just you couldn't get anything in Fiji – though I remember finding some Georgian silver in a sort of fete sale. We used to come to England regularly. I was pretty obsessed with historic houses, churches, monuments and I had this weird sort of yearning to know more about them. We had a couple of books about historic houses in Britain and I used to devour those. And then my school was designed by Pugin so I was in some quite interesting buildings. But, again, you don't get out very often if you're in boarding school. So it was rather vicarious …

Todd – When you grow up abroad, churches are the one place that have old things. For instance in Peru there were big baroque churches from the seventeenth and eighteenth century filled with gold and amazing ornaments and fantastic paintings and sculpture. I just loved going to churches.

TIM – In Fiji you didn't have wonderful gilded things but you did have French mission churches built in the 1860s and '70s, filled with plaster statues and stained glass – bondieuserie. My mother wrote a big book on the history of the missions so we spent a lot of time with the clergy and got into the back of sacristies and looked at the mildewed vestments all falling to bits. I've always been interested in religious architecture and art. Always rather loved what someone once described as the 'millinery aspects' of the church. And, in fact, when I first came to London, because you could buy them quite cheaply, I started collecting religious statues. By the time I met Todd my flat had become quite famous really, because it had been decked out with all this stuff.

TODD – I'm sure some people thought that Tim's taste was very bizarre but I'm not frightened of Catholic objects. I quite like them. And also I just liked the idea of mad collecting habits.

TIM – When we first met, in a rather sort of seedy night club, we talked about marble busts. I'd just acquired my first marble bust and that was very, very exciting. We instantly started going to all the markets together.

TODD – We both started collecting much more eagerly and also we encouraged one another to buy more things.

TIM – We've been coming to markets for twenty-five-odd years now. And viewing auctions and reading books.

Sadly, nearly every street market in London is in decline. The familiar refrain is 'Oh, the stuff isn't as good as it used to be.' But we can still go to the market and for a couple of quid buy a wonderful nineteenth-century plate or something, take it home and eat off it.

TODD – We've just bought two very beautiful eighteenth-century Chinese export plates for thirty quid. People say 'Oh, you're so lucky finding good things' – and we have found remarkable things at markets – but we are persistent. I mean we go … When we're in town we go every weekend and we comb the market.

TIM – About twenty stalls we do and we do them quite briskly. I'm afraid some arcades we don't even bother going in.

TODD – We're sort of, in this way, like a dog. You know how a dog will find a nice bone somewhere in a park and he'll always come back to the same place.

It's the same thing. You become obsessive. And because we were both, as children, collecting, we have a good eye. I remember I used to go out diving virtually every day when we lived on the seaside. I could scan across the reef and find a seashell a mile away. So we're like scanners. We quickly rip through the market and we'll find something we recognise from a mile away.

We know exactly what we like straight away. We're very decisive. If we have to hesitate, then it may be not the right thing for us. It's very much an instinctive or intuitive emotion. You just like something and that's it. You buy it.

TIM – There are things we can't afford.

TODD – Of course. We don't have all the money in the world. We're not really interested in buying things that are already very, very expensive because they're sort of discovered. We prefer things that are unloved. But we spent six hundred pounds in the market this morning, which is probably more than most people spend.

TIM – Sometimes we've found amazing things. You've just got to get them.

TODD – We have bought some incredible things: renaissance bronzes; wonderful terracottas …

TIM – A very important piece of sculpture for a hundred and fifty pounds. It's now in the National Gallery of Scotland. That was a great thing. Everyone still mentions that.

TODD – So much circulates just unknown.

TIM – Most dealers haven't the time or the resources or, quite frankly, the knowledge to research things properly. They just want to make a quick profit.

TODD – They reach a dead end and they don't know how to go any further. But both Tim and I have spent our lives in archives. We know country house collections very well. We know most of the museum collections. So we have a very broad knowledge. We seldom buy a fake.

TIM – There's this little old lady and man who always have works by Paul Klee, Kisling, Botero, Foujita – sort of second or third rank people – on their stall. Always just a few hundred pounds. Quite often signed as well. They sit there and if anyone says 'What's this?' They say 'Ooh, I don't know dear; I just got it out of a house clearance.'

Todd – We've had friends of ours, who are curators in museums, saying, 'I've just found a really wonderful sketch '

Tim – 'I think it's by Foujita, Botero or someone.'

Todd – And they're not bad copies.

Todd – Do the vendors know? Of course they know!

Tim – They make them!

Todd – You can really tell with most of the stuff: if you know your onions, it's not that difficult. Instantly we buy something we research it. And we have acquisition books: we write down where we bought it, what we think it is, how much we paid. Just for pleasure.

Tim – At the end of the year we have a little reminiscence about what we've bought and we go through and categorise the objects.

Todd – We have a natural affinity for lots of different kinds of objects.

Tim – But there are very distinctive themes. There's sculpture, portraiture …

Todd – Ceramics, glass …

Tim – A lot of things people would not want to show – like religious pictures, or things with a death theme, or cheap nineteenth-century oleographs or broken sculpture.

Neither of us are the sort of people who put things into store. I've always displayed my collection, and that's been really important to me. There are photographs of me aged two with my little collection all laid out. And then I've got photographs of my room at school and my bedroom at home with all my natural history and everything and then when I first came to London I had an incredibly over-decorated room in a little shared house. So it's almost like a little kind of carapace. Like some animals which create these kind of bowers or whatever.

Todd – A lot of people are nervous about sending the wrong signals to people so they don't want to put things in their house. That's why so many people put up posters and boring old Ikea furniture. It's perfectly all right if you want something bland that doesn't really say anything about you at all, apart from you're just like three hundred thousand other million people. A lot of people just don't have any confidence to try and express themselves in a way. Whereas we feel comfortable amalgamating huge quantities of very diverse objects in small spaces. It doesn't daunt us at all.

Also I think you have to have this sort of obsessive gene. It's really something that you're born with. I mean you're either a collector or you're not. And it's not just about owning it. It's about having an object to look at at your leisure …

TIM – And it's the chase as well.

TODD – It's the pleasure of finding something, discovering something. It's the same thing as going to the beach. You might go to the beach and there's not a single shell. You might one day walk by and find there's some incredible triton … just sitting there on the shore. I've always said 'This is my first eighteenth-century crucifixion' or 'my first bird's egg' – implying that there's going to be a lot of them. Because I like the idea of comparison. And I think all collectors do. It's about novelty too. It's so brilliant to always find new kinds of objects you've never looked at before. Life's so much more rich and enjoyable when you feel that anywhere you go there's scope to find something entirely new and just change your life – even for a short while. It just gives you a new view of the world. What's under the table? Oh, a goat … I got it years ago …

It's a big goat. A mouflon, I think. I bought it at an auction in Islington. I had to take it home on the bus because I didn't have enough money after I'd bought it to take it in a taxi. I had to change buses at Camden Town so I put him on a wall. I remember these young girls coming up to me and saying 'Oh, is that your goat?' I said 'Yes'. And they said 'It's cruel keeping a goat in town. What do you feed it?' And I said 'Not very much'. It looked like it was just sitting there quietly.

We've had it for years and years. It went to Hampton Court and sat in the director's office for about eight years. It was supposed to go in the freezer to have a treatment for insects. Then I brought it home and on the way back I stopped all across London taking pictures, like Queen Eleanor's bier coming back. Quite benign isn't it?

TIM – Shall we walk around?

TODD – This is like the Kunst und Wunderkammer. Strange ethnographica.

TIM – Antiquities or Victorian fake antiquities. English nineteenth-century little cabinet busts

TODD – Lots of shells and dried birds' heads and insects …

TIM – A deer's embryo from the famous Cedric Crossfield of Portobello Road. He gave it to me for my birthday …

TODD – It's drying up.

TIM – I keep talking to Sam Alberti about putting more formalin in it. These are kangaroo paws. Mounted in silver. Sort of colonial souvenir … The cast of a Moah egg. A huge ostrich, I think. Lives in New Zealand.

TIM – Here in the loo, after Guido Rene, a repentant Mary Magdalene and a repentant St Francis.

TODD – It's nice to have big oil paintings in the loo.

TIM – This used to have more popes. We had a bit of a problem with damp in the corner so a whole load were taken down. Are we making a statement? No. Occasionally Catholic friends say 'I can take everything, but not the crucifixes in the lavatory.' But it's just another room to fill up.

TODD – There's only so much space.

TIM – Here we have the livery of the Earl of Ashburnham. This head was made in Japan; it's a portrait of an English man. He's quite recently been moved here.

TIM – It's very arranged, this house.

TODD – The pleasure has to be display too. Creating a sense of atmosphere is, I think, really important. Because it's not strictly about individual objects: it's about putting things together. It's about creating a setting.

I think we've been most influenced by going to country houses. English country houses are so wonderful because – unlike boring old museums nowadays, all done by graphic designers and lumped in this terrible confusion – they very often display, in very beautiful ways, paintings and fantastic tables full of sculpture, mixed up with natural history and all sorts of little family heirlooms.

And I think what most people say when they come to our collection is that it's playful. It's not pompous. Children come here and they just love looking at a stuffed seal, a strange piece of sculpture or something. So it has nothing to do with brilliant objects. It's all about wonder: great surprise and wonder and seeing things you never see.

TIM – Occasionally you come across people who find it incredibly creepy because every other room has a skeleton or a nun or a rat or something – but those people often have rather fevered imaginations and have seen too many horror films.

TODD – I think it would be very difficult for anyone to say what they found in the collection that dominates the whole thing … but it sort of hangs together, just as an expression of us. It's home.

TIM – If I'm travelling and lecturing or staying with people for a long period I really get quite sort of heart sick about wanting to be with my objects. There's a wonderful quote from Newton, teasing the third Earl of Pembroke who was the great collector of ancient marbles. He talked about how he likes playing with his stone dolls … ! I rather love that phrase. I find what can really make me feel very happy is pottering around rearranging. This whole house constantly gets kind of … titivated. We do a lot of moving furniture.

TODD – All the time. Tim takes the lead.

TIM – Quite often you need to soften Todd up.

TODD – It's not that I mind them moving. It's just that sometimes I don't physically want to do it all. I get tired. Come upstairs. … This is our trophy wall …

TIM – A lot of our taxidermy and animal heads have gone and a few more will probably go as well because they take a lot of room. And also I think we prefer being surrounded by pictures than moose and things. … So this is where we sleep. Big seventeenth-century crucifixion.

TODD – There's nowhere else in the house that it will fit.

TIM – A few soldiers. I have to be controlled sometimes, portraits of soldiers.

TODD – This one's completely dotty. He looks like he's a Hollywood subject because he's got this sort of diaphanous background. And that one's got a cheeky look about him which I really like. A funny little smirk.

TIM – He's nice to wake up to. He's Lord Robertson of Oakridge as a young man. Rather a handsome beast. It's by a society painter who's famous for doing a portrait of Edward the Eighth in 'tennis outfit' which caused, apparently, a bit of a frisson. She's the Countess of Rosse by Oliver Messel, her brother. This one's obviously an Englishman dressed up as an Indian soldier with an Indian helmet on. So, I'm afraid, another soldier … This is a nineteenth-century kitchen with an old pump.

TODD – Seventeenth-century panelling.

TIM – We've been trying not to hang things on it … But not very successfully.

TODD – And guests that stay here wake up and see Saturn eating his children. Delightful souvenir!

TIM – This is our bathroom … Embossed memorial pictures. Done in the 1870s or '80s … That's an oleograph. They're meant to look like oil paintings and they're usually printed on quite cheap paper, so they're rather fragile. You get a lot of virgins and children and saints and things. That's another one. With a dead father figure …

TIM – The dining room. There used to be a big collection of taxidermy – big stuffed birds in boxes – in this room. It had a strange atmosphere so in the end we sold most of the birds and hung these pictures.

TODD – Some people have this feeling about buying pictures of other people's relations. We don't buy because we're trying to show any pedigree. We just buy because we like the faces.

TIM – I would have hated to have inherited a whole load of boring Knoxes of Londonderry. This leaves us free to collect as many abbots and nuns – and Van Dykes – as we can.

What we like about religious portraits is that very often they were done by good artists for rich families of interesting sitters in an elaborate setting with memento mori and really interesting iconography. They're incredibly rich in lots of different ways.

Take this picture. Someone might just say 'That's a nun.' But this is a founding portrait for a convent that was established by Elena de Toledo in Florence by her son Ferdinand de Medici in the late sixteenth century. It shows the Pope surrounded by nuns who were all handmaidens, as it were, to Elena de Toledo. They all came from these very aristocratic families. They were the Knights and Knightesses of Malta. And he's holding a papal bull establishing the convent. It's by a really good painter called Filippo Tarchiani who did lots of paintings in Florence in the late sixteenth century and it's also got its period frame. So you can just buy a painting and, all of a sudden, everything unfolds. This was confiscated when Napoleon arrived in Florence and there's a number on the back for the confiscation. So you can see the whole history of the convent unfolding as well.

TODD – I love pictures but I have a real feel for sculpture. I was saying to somebody the other day that I think I'm good at sculpture because I'm slightly colour blind. I think it's an appreciation of form and shape and light and shadow … It's something I really respond to. In the front hall we have all this shadow relief and it just picks up the light. It's like going into a Pharaonic tomb. We don't know who they all are. This was the Duke of Albany, Victoria's son. This is certainly Prince Albert here, by a German sculptor called Grass – mid-nineteenth-century.

TIM – This is a bit of a marshalling yard because this is stuff we're getting rid of. Our collection does have a back door. We regularly sluice it out and clean it out. When we fall out of love with something we just sell it or pass it on. I think that's quite healthy really.

TODD – We had a dinner party last night. We were going to get rid of these bones and one of our guests – who's a great friend of ours – came over and she said 'What are those? I'll take them all.' They're whale vertebrae. Traditionally used by sailors. They'd cut the fins off them and use them as stools because they have these abrasive bottoms so on deck they wouldn't move. She's going to sit on them.

TIM – She's got a huge flat in Notting Hill. So this is our kitchen …

TODD – Everything's Harlequin. Nothing has to match …

TIM – I quite like the fact that it's not just that we have a living room with historic things and then the kitchen is all mod cons. It's right the way through. In a funny sort of way it is a kind of retreat from the world. Because once you've closed the front gate this is a totally different world from Poundland, Halfords and all those fried chicken establishments outside. That's something we're not very interested in. We are interested in architecture and art and stuff like that. We're not interested in celebrities and media particularly. Nothing depresses us more than a night spent watching television. When we go and spend time with our family and they're all glued to the television we almost lose the will to live.

TODD – The house is certainly a retreat, that's for sure. It's not so much to get away from the big nasty world. It's just that this is OUR world.

It is an obsession but it's a healthy obsession. We never have any money because we spend all of our money buying things. But every time I do this I think, well, it's just like putting money into the bank because although we don't buy for investment, we're not chucking the money out on fast cars …

TIM – … gambling or drinking it away.

TODD – My father's a businessman and he puts his money in things he can't see with people he doesn't know. The nice thing about us is that we get things that we know about, that we have an instinctive feeling for and we get the pleasure of looking at them all the time. And if you know what you're buying, what does it really matter?'

We don't give a damn about what people expect the place to look like. We don't care about things being fashionable. We don't care about what people think. It's just really what we want to do.

'It's a hunting ground'

John, collector

Give your feet a good wipe …

I give talks on my collection. Groups pay three hundred and fifty pounds to come round, maximum of twenty people. I get them all in here and I spout for three hours. I'm a mad collector and I like to show it off, like girls show off their dolls. I say 'Ask questions! The ruder the question, the better!' I like it: stimulating, you know. And they always say 'How did you start? Who did you start with?' And I say 'Of course, the great secret of collecting is not to have children. Because they're very expensive, children. And I haven't got any children so I spent it on antiques. You start with nothing – it's very important to start with nothing – and then you get a bit more and you refine your taste.'

This is one of the loves of my life. And it is a good collection. I sometimes say 'I've got the best collection of Victorian – 1830 to 1930 – tiles in the world.' The Tiles and Decorative Architectural Ceramics Society come round and I say that to them. And I say 'Look, I can see the hair rising on the back of your neck and you thinking 'This big headed bugger Scott'. And I say 'I quite like that.'

I say 'I *say* this. Tell me!' And I'm hoping that someone will say 'Good Mr Scott, with the greatest of possible respect to you, old Fred has got a much … ' because I'm desperate to meet Old Fred, aren't I? And that's the thing, to find someone who's similarly mad is my dream. Because we can have a real chat!

I don't really like the word Victoriana because it has a slightly disparaging ambience to it, doesn't it? And this is a Valhalla – that's the way I feel – for worshippers of the great Victorian architect designers. They're all the

Victorian experts, aren't they? With Dresser at the top. Pusey, Voysey, Street, Thomas Jekyll. All the famous people. Eric Gill. I don't want anyone to forget that Christopher Dresser was the greatest and Morris was ranking tenth or twentieth … He's nice but he's nowhere near like Dresser. Dresser is the king and I extol his work …

I was born in Wallasey, near Birkenhead, and I was raised in Birkenhead. My parents were divorced when I was about one, I think, and my father lived all his life in Barbados. My mother married again and we lived in a 1910 house – arts and craftsy – full of furniture and clocks and things which were owned by my stepfather's father and grandfather.

So I was raised there. And I'm very fond of Birkenhead. I lent about twenty things to the V & A exhibition on the Cult of Beauty. And I don't put 'J. Scott Collection'. 'The Birkenhead collection' – that's what I put. Kind of feeling of poor old Birkenhead. Because I always like to tell people 'Liverpool was the second port of the Empire. And after the war, in 1947, we were the largest empire the world has EVER known.' Seven times bigger than the Roman Empire, which is something to get your mind round. So the second port of the empire was something. And posh people came over, worked in Liverpool – dirty Liverpool – and lived in Chesh-i-yah, in the Wirral. Very posh, you see. I always think of H.G. Wells and George Orwell. As authors, I love them. Do you remember Tono – Bungay? Counter Jumping? Do you know what a counter jumper is? I really should try and conceal from you my snobbish accent. I can drop back inter Burkenhed. As ah say, ah was brart op in Burkenhed, and ah can slip raht bluddy back inter it, just a the drop of a bluddy hat, ah can!

My mother was brought up in Wallasey and she was sent to a finishing school in Switzerland by her father, who was an architect. When she heard me saying 'O Mother, look over ther' – just that word 'ther' – I went to a smarter school, not a Birkenhead school, and I started speaking better. And then I went to Radley, which was even more posh, and THEN to Oxford – my dear!

I was good at games and head boy. I was the chap who led everything, the charges: 'Come on chaps! Together!' There were far more intelligent people in the school. They should have been honoured. But no one was honoured in the 1940s and '50s: it was, were you good at games? That was everything.

Oxford was lovely of course. My only claim to fame in life is that I got into Oxford without examination or interview. I had a marvellous time in National Service. I served the Crown in Malaya, fighting in the jungles in a war we won. The Americans lost in Vietnam. We won in Malaya. I went to see my father afterwards and I didn't know what to do. (I've never known what to do. Didn't want to be a train driver even.) I said 'Would you pay for me to go to Oxford?' And he said 'Yes'. So I wrote to a master at school called Ivor Gilliat (a wonderful man whom I adored). A week after he got the letter, he went to Henley – because Radley's a rowing school – and he met the Admissions Tutor of Corpus Christi College. 'Hello Ivor,' said … (I can't remember his name. It's terrible old age, terrible. And also M.E. UGH. I'm not dead – that's all I can say … I'll remember it probably in about two hours' time). 'We haven't had anyone from Radley recently Ivor!' 'Well, we've got a chap.' (I can imagine it!) 'He'll never set the Thames on fire, academically, but he's a good chap. Plays rugger quite well!'

Enough! Absolutely forbidden today! And I do feel a burden in many ways. I really do feel a burden on my life. And one of the burdens is I was so lucky to get into Oxford, I've got to acquit myself well before the Lord. Because I really believe that when you die, you – and everyone – we're all going to go up and we're going to knock on the Pearly Gates like that (knock, knock, knock) and hope that we'll be admitted. I don't believe in Hell but I do feel it might be difficult. … Are they going to be opened?

I do believe in the Lord and I believe everyone should just work very hard to do good deeds. Which is what we used to do. And you get brownie points as you go along, you see. There are three things I do in my life: look after my properties; the Notting Hill Gate improvements group and my collection. One of my favourite things is picking up litter because I don't have to open a file and write someone a letter or an email or something to tell them they should do it. Just do it.

Everyone should do that. They must live their life on the basis that that is going to happen. Everyone wants to get into the Elysian fields, don't they? I've decided that what I'm hoping for is a look of slight reproach -'Not bad but could do better' – and maybe sent away to spend a little bit more time. But not shutting the door completely.

When I went up to Oxford I didn't know what to read. I said 'That P.P.E. sounds a nice, general thing.' They said 'You're reading Law.' Because it had become a School where if you were a bit … Why, I don't know. I mean it's fairly black and white.

I wasn't very well educated. I've spent too much time playing cricket and rugby. I got a third. Everyone says 'Oh, John, you were playing rugby so hard. You didn't have … ' But it wasn't like that at all. I did spend a lot of time playing rugby but I worked VERY hard to get my third.

I started collecting when I was at Oxford. Piranesi drawings of ruined Rome. I've got a kind of macabre sense. There are three types of people: static; dynamic and melancholic. Have you heard that? I'm melancholic. Better to be dynamic. Anyway, the first things were Piranesi engravings; there are lots of them round the house. Love them. Particularly the macabre ones, the Carceri … It's something to do with the sad person, the melancholic. I don't beat people. I don't lash up girlfriends and beat them with whips. Nor do I give them whips to beat me. I'm not at all like that. It's more melancholia, the darker side. I mean my favourite author is Edgar Allan Poe. I think he's the most wonderful writer.

When I left Oxford I became a solicitor, but didn't like it. I should not have become a solicitor. My dear uncle – he's a solicitor and bachelor – wanted me to come in and take over his business eventually and pay him a pension. I should have been a chartered surveyor. That's what I should have done. But I've never wanted to be anything particularly. And I've always lacked confidence, believe it or not. Great lack of confidence in myself. Now, when I'm too old to do anything, and my body is suffering and my mind is suffering, I've got tremendous confidence. It's very freeing. I can talk to a king or a queen!

Why didn't I become a dealer? Good question. Although I could see how you could make a bob or two, it wasn't quite *de rigeur*. It wasn't the kind of thing that you did at that age. They'd got a plan for me: I was going to get qualified as a solicitor. So that was a regular thing to do. But buying and selling! It was still something in the '50s. No, I didn't feel like that.

I wasn't very good at law. And actually my uncle, who was my favourite man in the world, wrote me a Dear John letter. I hadn't pinched the petty cash but I'd made a bit of a balls-up. And he said 'I think you'd be happier … .' God that was a terrible time. I didn't know what I was going to do at all. I didn't know what I could do. Of course I should have got a job in another firm of solicitors. But I didn't like it at all.

So I thought 'What do you like doing?' My uncle had lent me £2,650 in 1961 and I bought a little house in Hammersmith and did it up, laid the floors, wallpaper. And I thought, 'I like doing that. So I'll go into property.' It wasn't quite interior decorating. That wasn't posh enough. I had to do something … Wasn't going to go into TRADE.

I worked for two public property companies and I left them to make more money myself. I set up in 1971. By '72 I was a millionaire and I made my backers a million. But in '73 everything collapsed, and I was a minus millionaire then. And it was very, very, very, very, very, very difficult [he pours the tea].

And that was another very difficult stage in my life. Very depressed indeed. Pills galore. Ludium L21. Can't remember anything that happened this morning or this afternoon … but Ludium L21 I remember. That was the drug. And I got over it. I got going again. In fact my collection is built on the money which I've made from property.

People say 'Why did you collect?' And I've thought and thought and thought. I like to give an answer. Loneliness. Definitely loneliness. I'm an only child. Quite hard to admit really. People don't like to admit things. The English are terribly reserved, aren't they? I'm not reserved now, in my 77th year, I let it all hang out now! Let me pour you some more tea … .

Much more importantly, bringing things back. It's like a hunter going out of the cave in the morning: primeval. You've got to get something to bring back to feed your wife and children don't you? So I bring it back, put it on the mantelpiece. When I've brought it back it's there. Yes, I have got a book. And I've got a problem. Because I always stick a sticker on it with the date. And I look it up in the book and I can see the date and recognise it from the date. Can you guess what's happened? The stickers have come off! Because they don't make them like they used to. If you see old fashioned ones they've been there since 1890.

I love the market. An awful lot of my things – I would say probably 15-20 per cent of my collection – has come from there. It's just what you might FIND … I can tell you about the clock. I went round and I saw a clock. I got it in my hand. And I was looking at it. It was a Voysey clock. It was wood and it was hand-painted: 'Time and Tide wait for no man'. It was in poor condition and it was twenty-six pounds. This was in the late '60s. And I thought 'No, twenty-six pounds … ' Anyway, didn't buy it. And John Jess bought it for thirty-two pounds. He sold it about four years ago to the V & A. And I think he sold it for one or two hundred thousand.

Glass was one of the first things I started collecting. Because I had this little house, I had to furnish it, didn't I? That was one of the main things, the drivers. Didn't get anything from home. And I found you could buy a pair of Cadbury old legged Victorian chairs for two pounds each, but Times Furnishings they were three pounds fifty each. It was cheaper to buy old ones. And a bit of charm and attraction about it. And the same thing with drinking glasses. Nearly all these are Powell glasses which are England's greatest glass makers.

I've moved from area to area. I was very keen on Art Nouveau because it's got a kind of whiplash. It's into the field of the macabre and the sinister, and the uncertain. And I do love Art Nouveau. I always call myself the last of the Empire Loyalists so I collect English things. I'm very Anglophile. But – the contrariness of life – my favourite artist is a Frenchman called Hector Guimard who designed the Paris Metro.

That's a marvellous piece of Guimard metalwork out of his house, Castel Beranger, in Paris. And this is De Morgan here. I don't know who these are by – the metalwork is so beautiful, isn't it? People hated Victorian stuff: 'It's catastrophic!' My mother hated it. I said 'What's bad taste Mother?' She hardly hesitated: 'Albert Memorial'. This is when I can remember asking her, sixty years ago. She never really saw this because she died thirty years ago. But you see how bright and beautiful it is.

There's quite a lot of stuff here … see if I can recognise anything that came from Portobello.

I bought that painting in Portobello Road for about twenty quid a good forty years ago. I liked it because it's evocative of the '50s and it's a White Star liner, or Cunard or something, coming into Dar es Salaam. I bought that in Portobello road, it's Cloisonné. It's a very kind of Art Nouveau Japanese thing. Very much 1910. That's by Alfred Gilbert: it's *Perseus Arming*. These are Christopher Dresser teapots here, Dresser stuff.

Portobello Road is a place to pick up tiles. I started collecting tiles because they were cheap, when I was going through one of my bankrupt periods in the '70s. They've got a bit more expensive now. I've been a big collector of Christopher Dresser and I do promote him. For instance, I was the person who bullied the V & A – I'm always bullying people, I call it friendly bullying – to do an exhibition on Dresser which was very successful.

Dresser was the greatest designer of the period. And we were the greatest empire in the world. And we were very rich. And when there is great wealth, there are normally good people to use that wealth and good architects to design beautiful buildings. Why does it appeal to me so much? It's a love of the past. It's a love of things as they were. And my mind is kind of addled with the love of familiarity. Nostalgia is a kind of river running through me all the time. Nostalgia for the age of Empire and the way we lived. We were the best in the world! I know you've got to move with the times. But I mean I'm very, very disturbed that the Post Office has shut. It's right across the road. It was very convenient and there was a post box. Now I have to walk ten minutes. And to post something that I need to get a stamp on, have to go to Notting Hill Gate! This is an ENORMOUS upheaval. And I'm not going to be able to use cheques very soon. I don't know what I'm going to do.

That's one of the *pièces de resistance* that I found in Portobello Road: the centrepiece of the great pavement laid in Cliveden. One of the most famous pavements ever laid. And – what's her name, terrible woman? – Lady Astor said 'No I don't like it. Take it up!' She had it removed and piled in a basement. It's Minton: the head of the Medusa, that had all these serpents flying round it. Fantastic.

These kind of things do turn up. Amazing things. So it's a treasure trove. And it's a hunting ground. I say to people 'It's like fishing'. I've been fond of fishing. I like coarse fishing. I don't like trout fishing (that's nice but posher and, funnily enough, I rather like the unposh). You throw your float out. These funny old men do it. Have you seen them, on the river, watching the float? Because when it goes like that … you don't know, it might be the largest carp EVER! And then it turns up. And the float lies flat. That means that the fish has lifted it off the bottom. And then it starts moving away as it pulls. Very exciting. TERRIBLY exciting.

This is an imitation mosaic tile. The chap I bought this from pulled me over a year after I bought it and said 'I've just found a cutting in an old Times and it said "This was a Roman mosaic found in the city of London, unearthed in 18–"' And there was a photograph of it. It's Shrigley and Hunt and they obviously thought 'That's a bloody good thing. We can sell tiles on the basis of that. Let's make it into a teapot stand and make the whole thing ceramic.' And it's a series that a number of people did which I collect. I think it's very lovely that. And it was quite modestly priced. But when, of course, the great John Scott collection of TILES is sold, I mean …

I don't mind how it goes, honestly, the J. Scott collection. People say 'Oh John, you should have a museum of your own here.' Not a chance. Anyone doing that would want about twenty million, wouldn't they? People with peaked caps to show people round, insurance, cleaning. Sell the lot. Go back and let someone else have some fun.

I like to get something every Saturday. I like to be there at seven but it's eight-thirty in the end, I'm afraid, because I'm getting old and I can't do all these things that I hoped I was going to be able to do. And I don't succeed because age is getting me down. So I always bully people 'Get on with it now, whatever you do. Get on with it now! Tomorrow will be too late!' You're a long time dead. You say it could be quite restful? Yes. I'm actually dreaming of that. Very nice indeed.

'It's our turn now to get
our arse kicked'

Geoff, financial services

I started life as a scrap metal dealer. Then I sold my business and I met Bo. She had a little antique business in Nottingham. She was in the middle of a divorce and I'd just been divorced and we started doing the antique fairs down in London on a Sunday.

It was quite hard to get in those. One Sunday I had an ear operation and I didn't go down. And when Bo came home she was all upset: the fair organiser had said 'Out of fifty-two fairs I can only let you have fifteen.' So she was distraught because, for us, that was our main living then. So I said 'Right. The following week, when I get better, we'll drive down to London: we'll go to Bermondsey; we'll go to Portobello; we'll go to Camden. We'll go and we'll find somewhere.'

We got to Portobello Road, Westbourne Grove, got out of the cab and I said to Bo 'This is where we're gonna be.' It just had a whole vibrancy about it; it was almost intoxicating. People running round: 'You got any Rolexes? Any Rolexes? Any jewellery? Any jewellery?' Everybody wanted stuff. Anything really that they could make a profit on.

I don't know how I drifted into wrist watches and pocket watches. I've got no idea. But I was driving Bo down and I was buying a few watches. All of a sudden I found I could make four to five hundred pound by just buying a watch and I'd got no idea what it was.

But the good thing about Portobello at that time, you could buy a watch – not really knowing what you're doing except you knew it was a Rolex – and then you'd show it to somebody. You gave one hundred for it and you ask him one hundred and fifty and he'd say 'Well I would've given one-fifty but the case isn't marked. The dial's cracked.' So you learned what they were looking for and how fussy. And then you avoided the more fussy dealers and went for the guys who'd buy the crap at a good price. That was just the market game.

Basically, when you're a dealer it doesn't really matter whether you're selling diamond rings or horse shit: it's just a price. It's just to know how much it is. And that is what makes a market interesting. Dealers will trade and trade amongst themselves and, in a kind of way, they're oblivious to the outside world. They're looking for this commodity. It's worth forty quid – they can buy it for twenty; they can make a great profit. If they can only buy it for thirty-five they'll buy it and take a short profit – might take thirty-nine. It's that sort of wheeling and dealing that made Portobello particularly great.

It really was a heady time in the '70s and '80s. You could sell ANYTHING. And the more bizarre it was, the greater the demand. It was weird. In Nottingham there was a guy had a military shop and he was a personal friend of mine. He said 'Geoff, are you going to Portobello tomorrow?' I said 'Yeah.' He said 'You can't take these for me, can you?' I said 'What's that?' He had two ivory tusks, about six foot high. They were HUGE these tusks. I took them home. I put them on the roof rack of the car and I drove down to Portobello Road.

All the way down Bo kept saying 'You're bloody mad. I don't know what you're doing with these. You'll never sell them.' Within three seconds of me getting on Portobello Road I had guys fighting to buy 'em. It was like a ping pong session: it was incredible.

To show how busy it was: we'd work Monday to Thursday, looking at auctions; work Friday morning at Bermondsey; come to Portobello on Saturday and do the Sunday fairs. People were taking great money – great wads of money. It was just a miracle. I tell you, you had to see it to believe it. I'll give you a little story …

I finished up getting a little stall in one of the arcades and I was selling watches and little bits of jewellery and I was doing all right. One day a guy I knew from Leicester stood talking to me. And an Italian came – who's a real big watch dealer now – and they started talking. He said 'Did you bring that watch?' He said 'Yeah, I brought it.' He pulled it out, this watch, and he looked at it. 'Right, okay. What did we say? Forty-eight grand?' The guy said 'Yeah.' And they stood in front of my stall counting this forty-eight grand out for this watch. It was incredible. He just put the money in his pocket and they both walked away.

When we started, all those shops were all full of antiques arcades – from Chepstow Villas down to Elgin Crescent. Every building. There was no people selling cupcakes. And one of the things I remember about that period was that just along Westbourne Grove there was a guy had a TV radio repair shop and he was the only one there on that side. He said to me 'Years ago, when I was a boy, all these shops that you guys are in now were shops serving the local community and you guys have pushed everybody out.' And now it's happening to us. It's our turn now to get our arse kicked. We're being pushed out by high property prices. Landlords have no interest in renting out arcades to people selling interesting goods. They're only interested in renting shops to whoever will pay eighty to a hundred thousand a year.

You get a potential estate agent brings somebody down who wants to open a shop selling pyjamas, say, and 'Wow, look at all these people!' But the footfall doesn't necessarily mean they take any money. So they go in there, high rents, stay a couple of years and they go. So you've got this spiral; the whole cycle will go back down again and you'll have empty shops.

It wouldn't be so much of a problem if there was a demand there for people to buy brown furniture, silver or whatever … it would be just the same. But there's just not the demand now. People don't want it. It's like my step-son. He's a captain of British Airways: he earns God knows how much. The most expensive thing he's got in his house is a DVD Blu-ray TV. About two grand. The rest is Ikea.

I don't get upset about it like a lot of people do. The market is a living thing. Most people in that market will adapt, and do adapt. I was taught as a youngster: don't fall in love with your stock. For me it's just a commodity. So now I sell money. I cash cheques, lend money, change Euros. 'Cause I move with the times.

Do I get pleasure from it? Well … like all dealing, when it's good it's better than sex. When it's not, it's crap! What I like is on Sunday morning when people come in to borrow money and they tell you all these far-fetched schemes. I get a lot of satisfaction out of seeing them come to fruition.

I think the best one we had – the one that took my breath away – was a guy came in here to borrow a substantial amount of money for a medieval iron floor. It was all kind of early welding and drilled and pot riveted with all sorts of birds and animals. And ballroom size. The workmanship was incredible. So we lent him a bit of money. He bought it, sold it, paid me off.

Another interesting one … it's a funny story this. There was a couple down the market and they sold walking sticks. She'd been around for years.

Beautifully spoken. Her husband was a huge bear of a man and they drove around in a hearse. She came one day and she borrowed a little bit of money but she couldn't service the loan.

I knew they lived in Lincolnshire. So one day I drove up to Lincolnshire. I drove around and I found where they lived. Lovely drive up, lovely gates. I went through the gates. The front was Victorian – with those typical horrible Victorian bay windows – but in the back it was beautiful early Georgian. I went round – past a pile of rubbish, couple of rusty cars – and they came out. They were kind of shocked to see me. To say it was abject poverty ... there was no bannisters there; they'd sold all the fireplaces and stuff was missing. I stood there. I had a brand new Mercedes at the time, with a sun roof. She says 'I know what you've come for. You've come to sort the money out.' So I said 'Yeah.' So she said 'Well we can't pay you and that's all there is to it. But you can have a cup of tea and shoot the shit.' So we did that. I said 'It's amazing this place, isn't it?' She said 'Yeah. We owe (let's say) twenty thousand on it.' I said 'Is that all?' She said 'Yeah. We're behind with the mortgage.' I looked at it. I thought, 'Christ, it's an amazing place.' I got talking to her. 'What's the story with this then?' She said, 'Well, we bought two medieval screens.' They sold one for a lot of money and they bought this place and a school in the same village. The story goes (she didn't tell me this but the story goes) that they were looking round the house and they found the cellar. And it was full of champagne. And they didn't come out for about a year. They drank the lot apparently. Then they started selling bits from the house just to keep going.

I went back to my car to get my phone. The car was FULL of cats and dogs. They'd got in through the roof – all these wild cats and dogs. There was about ten of them in me car, sitting all over my car, brand new car. She said 'Ah, don't mind them.'

I rang Bo up and I said 'It's a good buy this place, for twenty-five grand. It's a bit dilapidated but it's amazing.' I went back. I said to her, I said, 'Listen. Tell you what I'll do. I'll pay your mortgage off and give you some money on top and I'll take this off you.' And she said 'Oh, that'll be all right yeah!' Just like that. She said 'But I've got one ace in my pack.' We walked down the garden and there was this beautiful walled garden. It took your breath away. You went through this little door – just like these like fairytale type things and you open the door and you go into a magical garden – and there was all these wonderful shrubs. It was overgrown but it was absolutely divine. I thought 'Bloody hell.' She said 'One of the neighbours wants to buy it but we don't want to sell it.'

Over the next couple of weeks we were negotiating with the mortgage company. The next thing I know, she phoned me up and she said 'Oh Geoff, we're not going to do that anymore because we've sold the walled garden and we've paid the mortgage company off.' Then she said 'But we've got something else we can offer you.' So I said 'What's that?' She said 'You'll have to go down to Devon.'

I went back to London. Picked Bo up. We drove down to Devon. And again ... completely bloody eccentric. You wouldn't believe it unless you'd seen it. You drove into this little place. It was a Bakelite museum – full of Bakelite radios – and there was this lovely little cottage. There was a little tea room and her daughter and her husband lived there. She was an elegant sort of woman. He was as nutty as a fruitcake. And the thing that struck Bo and I: all their kids were wild. Feral. Runny noses and no shoes on. Just running around like wild. Unkempt. And one of the little kids – couldn't have been no bigger than that – was just sort of floating in the river. So I went to the house and I said to the woman 'I think one of your kids is in the river.' 'Oh don't worry,' she said. 'Whistler, go fetch her.' And the dog goes bounding down – this great Labrador – dives in the river, swims across, gets the kid – she's got her knickers on – and pulls her to the bank. It was just so feral. It was weird.

Anyway, she took me into this building and there was a slab of marble and on it was all these figures like skulls and cherubs and things. Didn't do anything for me. But Bo said 'All the hairs on the back of my neck are pushing up. Oh, it's wonderful this is.' I said 'Is it?' She said 'Look at it. Look at the work.' I said 'Jesus Christ, it must weigh about three ton.' Anyway she sold it to me. Didn't know what the hell to do with it. Then a guy came in here to cash a cheque and he dealt in antiquities. I said 'You don't have a bit of time?' I says 'It's a great big piece of marble. Bo reckons it's great. It just looks like a load of shit to me.' He went down to look at it and he said 'Yeah, it's good that.' He did a lot of research. It turned out to be made by a guy who did a lot of work for Sir Christopher Wren. It was 1666 or something and it came from Annesley Hall in Nottingham. The upshot of it was he sold it for me to the Victoria & Albert.

So we got it all sorted in the end. That's the whole thing: you never know where it's all going to lead.

I don't have a system. It's a gut feeling about their ability as a dealer – if I rate them. Some people, they'll never make any money while they've got an 'ole in their arse. Some of them, you'll lend them a hundred quid 'cause you like 'em. You might get it back, you might not. But other people are gifted, talented. Good dealers are able to find things in all sorts of weird places and make good money but they're skint in two months and then they borrow more and they go again.

I don't do it out of charity. I do it to make money. But I like what the market is and I like dealers. If you look at them like I do, when they're struggling to make a living, you sort of stand back and you think, 'I don't know how the hell you do it.' I mean there's an old lady called Joan Dunk. She's been around for years. She had a little stall outside Lipkas arcade and she used to sell old glasses, second hand dinky toys, bits and bobs. We were taking twenty, thirty grand at the time selling silver and watches. And I said 'Have you 'ad a good day today?' She went 'Oh yeah, I've taken two hundred and eighty pounds.' And I said 'Christ, that's not a lot.' She said 'What you talking about? I probably made two hundred profit. What sort of a job would I 'ave to earn two hundred pound a day?' And I thought 'Yeah, you're right actually.' It all came in perspective: 'ere was me selling silver and watches for twenty grand and we'd had a bad day. And there she was, quite content with two hundred pound. You 'ad to admire her.

A member of the council once said to me, 'Is it hard to be a dealer?' I said, 'Well you have to look at it like this.' I said, 'If I gave you two thousand pounds and you went out and got a market stall and at the end of one year you could show me the two thousand and you've lived for a year, then you can call yourself our equal. Until you can do that you can't even CONCEIVE what it's like to be a dealer.'

And that's what I find abhorrent with the council and with the landlords: they don't see this spirit that people have down here. It's quickly swept under the carpet. I get passionate about it. They have a right to make a living. The thing is about Portobello Road – you've got a chance there. It's not a shopping centre. It's not there for big shops or named shops or Costa Coffee. It's one of the few places left in London where people can still come and deal and where those who're at the bottom can make a start and get going.

See nobody really minds how much money the landlord makes. Not really. When it gets passionate is when you say to a dealer 'You can't trade here anymore 'cause I'm going to let it to Tesco.' All of a sudden you've taken their living away from them. Then they get all emotional. And they resent it because that property's only valuable because they're down in the basement. People go there because of those characters. You talk to someone,

they can bedazzle you for hours! If you get Reuben talking about his banjo collection he gets off, don't he? A lot of people get intoxicated when they talk to dealers like that. They don't really want a banjo … but they buy it.

And Barry and Popsy – I love listening to what they've bought in the week. They buy the most nuttiest stuff in the world. They came in one day. 'Oi, look at this Geoff.' It was a piece of wood with teeth on it. I would have chucked it out. They said 'It's a Tibetan comb. We're going to get one thousand five hundred for this.' You're joking! And then you've got John Scott. You can't get more eccentric than him can you, hey? But he's a lovely, lovely character.

If you haven't got a kaleidoscope of eccentrics, like Barry and Poppy and John Scott and thousands of others, there's no attraction really. It's this eclectic mix that members of the public find attractive. And the thing that always irritates me is that Portobello Road made the landlords rich in the first place and now they're actually destroying what made them rich.

But you can't fight capitalism. I often say to people who argue this case about Portobello Road, 'When's the last time you spent any money down there?' If you don't spend money down there the antique dealers are not going to survive. People who want to support Portobello Road have got to go down, buy something from Barry and Poppy, buy something from Marion, buy something from Reuben. That's what the real problem is. It's that people are not buying the stuff. Cause if they were making a grand a week, say, we wouldn't be 'aving this conversation would we? Huh?

'Nobody's gonna stop me'

HILARY, VINTAGE FUR

My father came from Germany then moved to Belgium, as a displaced person, then to England. He was a pattern cutter which was very, very difficult because you were involved in making huge cuts of fabric and if you made one mistake literally the whole batch was ruined. But because he was so precise he also had a real good knack of fixing watches.

He had absolutely no money so the first thing he did in Portobello was set up this sort of tray – a bit like when you go to the theatre and you see the ice cream tray. He had leather straps around his neck and he walked up and down Portobello Road with watches and sold them to the dealers. And he would also fix their watches.

The market inspector saw my father walking up and down regularly and he said 'Look. We're going to turn all this area into stalls. You're here every week; why don't you have a stall?' And so he got a stall in Portobello.

By this time he was married to my mother. They met in the Hammersmith Palais. She was utterly beautiful: bright green eyes and jet black hair. Was she Jewish? Of course. He fell in love instantly and they got married six weeks later.

Firstly he was doing bits of jewellery and watches. Then he started doing silver and china and clocks. He was mad about clocks. Our house was full of them and they all used to cuckoo and ring and ding and dong at all times of day and night and my mum used to say 'I don't know how we bear it.' We lived in this little council flat in Islington all cooped up but it was absolutely crammed full of antiques.

And one of my jobs – now you'd call it child labour – I LOVED polishing the black silver. Because I was a Daddy's girl. As long as it was to do with helping my father I was happy. So there I was, cleaning away, absolutely in my element.

He had a navy blue van and he painted in white 'Antiques' and 'If you have anything to sell, ring this number.' He was very creative and he was always designing new contraptions for the stall. He had proper shelving and a paraffin light. Sometimes he'd have his Primus stove and he'd put a little kettle on and it was like a little picnic. He always wore a suit, shirt and tie and a flat cap in the winter. That was the sort of uniform that men wore in those days. If we went on the beach he would just be exactly the same way. He was known as Bernard Lewis. He wasn't Lewis originally; he was Lewi. As he came through English passport control they just gave you a name that sounded more anglicised. He was happy with that: because Jewish people wanted to blend; they didn't want to stand out.

Most of the people in my dad's section of the market were Jewish. My dad had this corner position and the brown shirts used to stand on that corner on a soap box, with a microphone, talking negative about Jews and how they all had to be got rid of. He'd say 'Just ignore them' so I used to keep my head down and not look. But it was free speech. It was only when a crowd of them gathered that the police would move them on.

When he first came to England he would read the dictionary every day. He was very precise about the exact meaning of words so you had to be very careful what you said. I can still remember some of the phrases he taught me to remember like 'Never let your left hand know what your right hand is doing' and 'The truth, nothing but the truth. But never the whole truth!'

He'd led such a secretive life – coming away from Germany and Belgium, then getting his parents smuggled into a house in Holland and keeping them secret in an attic for two years – I think he just felt secrets were always the best way. Even when he was ill and I could see holes in his throat, where he'd obviously had surgery, if ever I'd say 'What's that dad?' he'd say 'That's my war wound.' I was completely in the dark about how ill he was. I had NO idea.

He was diagnosed with cancer two years prior to him dying. He chose not to have any treatment because he knew it would make him less robust and unable to work to the end. And he actually worked right to the end. On the Saturday we were all at Portobello and on the Sunday we went out to Ham House because he always liked to show us stately homes and teach us about antiques and architecture. He was so much fun: we laughed and laughed all day. And then that night he was taken into hospital and we never saw him again … [she starts to cry]. I was twelve.

Once my father had died all the fun went out of life. I tried to stay positive because my mum was a depressive so I had to always try and cheer her up. My brother had to take care of us financially. And he was brilliant. But his anger at having the responsibility. He couldn't be angry with my mum so he took his anger out on me. He used to beat me up. So I went from having this magical childhood to suddenly having this horrific, tortuous childhood.

I met someone at a party and I ended up getting pregnant. It was just the worst mistake. For a Jewish girl to get pregnant at the age of sixteen to somebody who wasn't Jewish and to bring shame on my family, who were very religious … I still live with that shame. In those days you would have had to have your baby adopted and I wasn't going to do that. So I married him. You marry out, people wear black. I was literally excommunicated.

It was an absolute disaster. He was violent and controlling and, before I left him, he managed to find a way to make me pregnant, much against my will. I was just three days pregnant when I left. I went to the doctor's with Lee in the pushchair. I said 'What can I do?' He said 'You're a married woman, you can't do anything.' So I went to a friend who said 'Don't go back. Be brave and take a chance.' After you've lost a parent you are extremely brave. So I said 'Okay'. There I was, just in the clothes I stood up in. My little boy Lee's in the pushchair in the clothes that he's got. I had three pounds in my pocket. I phoned a cousin who said 'Come over now.' So just in the clothes I was wearing, over there I went.

I was working in Putney as a hairdresser. Then I had to have my tonsils out and I couldn't work in the hairdresser's for two weeks because I couldn't be around hairspray. I thought 'I haven't seen my brother for ages. I'll just walk through the market and see how he is.' Because the stall was my brother's, after my father had died. I saw the stall had all Persian bits on it and I thought 'Hang on a minute. What's going on?'

I plucked up my courage, phoned him and asked if I could use it. He went 'All right, it's yours from Saturday.' I was like 'Oh my God!' Because I only got paid when I worked – there was no sick pay or anything like that – so I had absolutely nothing. I had no idea what I was going to do.

He thought I was going to crumble by Friday. But no. I phoned up my auntie and said 'Have you got any clothes you don't wear anymore?' I phoned my cousin who had friends in high places and said 'Have you or any friends got old clothes they don't want?' So, that first Saturday, I had their shoes and their clothes. I took thirteen pounds. What was I getting for work? Five pounds! I thought 'I'm going to be a millionaire. YAAAAAAAAAAY!'

Vintage clothing was popular so I bought antique dresses at the other end of Portobello Road and I used to launder them and spend hours ironing and repairing them. And then John Lennon was wearing 1940s fur coats. I used to see them when I was buying antique clothing in the spring so I used to save them up. September the first came and I had a running rail full of vintage fur coats from the 1940s. And that was my first day of realising that I could really be successful. Because I took two hundred pounds.

1940s furs were rabbit coats: warm and practical and padded inside. They sometimes had CC – which was the clothing coupon sign – inside them: with your clothing coupons you actually could afford to buy a rabbit coat. You've got to remember how bitterly cold the winters were in those days so you aspired to it. You'd have a rabbit coat that would last you for years and you'd look rich. In the '70s these coats were THE trend. And that's how I started selling furs.

I love fur. I love the texture of it. I love the feel of it. I love the luxury of it. I love the warmth of it. You only need a mink coat and you're as warm as toast. You never, ever feel cold again, ever … if you've got fur.

There's something very romantic about 1930s fur. Picture Hollywood: ethereal show girls wearing these glamorous furs. I think mink's a good fur. It's very strong. If you get a mink coat from the '30s, it still looks new. The only thing that will wear it out is if you sit on nylon car seats with it. Then the static rubs the fur away.

The most valuable fur is sable. A sable coat can cost the same as a house. They've huge thick fur because they come from the extreme cold of Siberia but they're as light as a feather. They weigh nothing and you can roll them up and fold them into a bag that's twelve inches by twelve inches. That's the mark of a good fur.

I suppose I would dream of having chinchilla or sable. Chinchilla's this pale grey: light as a feather, ever so soft. You run your fingers through and it just makes you shudder. I've had them but I've always been too skint to keep them.

I've sold to lots of famous people: Joan Collins; Lauren Bacall; Brit Eckland; Naomi Campbell; Kate Moss; Barbara Streisand. Courtney Love came to Portobello recently and bought a whole load of stuff. She said 'I want to look like an English countess' and I said 'Ooh … Let's try on this.'

I don't know why but women who wore furs in those days were a different shape to us. Nowadays, women have got quite muscular arms so the arm holes are too small. If someone tries on a fur that's too small for them and they stretch their arms, they split it. Because furs are already worked out. If you see a fur being made you see it watered down, stretched out, wetted down, stretched out, pinned and nailed, stretched out. A skin that would be, say, fifteen inches long suddenly becomes forty inches long. So they've got absolutely no more give.

People sometimes put furs in their attics. NO. WRONG. Or in a plastic bag. NO … DON'T. NEVER. The leather can't breathe and the fur can't breathe and it basically goes crispy. Then it tears because it's stiff. So get a fabric bag – even a pillow case – and take your fur out regularly: it needs air to breathe around it. Don't just leave it there for twenty years and then wonder why it's all falling apart when you get it out.

I take my card wherever I go in the world. People get in touch with me: like the phone call I had earlier on – I gave him a lift once in Spain. Sometimes I meet people in car parks. I don't go too far away because petrol's so expensive but if someone's got a whole collection I'll travel. I used to buy at the auctions but then there was all this anti-fur brigade thing so they stopped doing fur sales. We did have a few people who came to Portobello who were anti but I used to say 'Nothing dies when you buy from me. I sell old stuff. It's true recycling.' Because, remember, on my side of the road you've got to sell things that are fifty years old or over.

I'm in agreement with that. There's a man who sells brand new stuff and yet he's signed a thing to say everything's antique! I mentioned it to the council after he complained about me. One day my stall sort of bent over a bit, towards his side, and he moaned.

It's a bit of dog eat dog. I know people have complained about me. Especially people who've gone into competition with me. It is very stressful but once you've had a parent who's died, nothing's worse than that. So everything's … dealable. The only thing you can't deal with is ill health, but I overcame that as well. I ruptured my Achilles and I was down the Portobello in a wheelchair and on crutches. It didn't stop me. I was still there. My philosophy is this: Nobody's gonna stop me: you can't keep a good man down. My dad's words!

I love Portobello. It's the individuality of the people. Remember that each person, through their own adversity, has had to come through a lot to actually, finally, get that stall there. I think you've got to be a very challenged person to work Saturdays in all weathers. Think snow, think hail, think the most bitterly winds that come through there. I've had very, very wealthy boyfriends who've said 'I want to marry you.' I'm walking round with an engagement ring, living with someone in Spain who's saying to me 'Give up everything. Come and live with me here.' Tempting as it was I never, ever, stopped Portobello. Because of the tradition. The fact that Dad was there since 1949. I can't give that up.

This is my book. I self-published. It's a collection of poems for women about life, love and other things.

Where is Portobello Road? There you are. Number 19. I'm still shaking. Sorry about this. It's just talking about my childhood always makes me shake ...

Hunting for bargains
In the Portobello Road
Is best in the summer
It's murder in the cold.

There's nothing in the world
That could ever compare
With the rush of excitement
That's abounding everywhere.

Trash or treasure
Antique or muck
You can buy from a dealer
From the back of a truck.

Early oil paintings
Handsome Victorian pots
Valuable jewellery
Of these there are lots.

Hundreds of people
Milling about
Searching for the crock of gold
But they'll never shout it out.

Portobello Road is full
of secrets and lies
How much they paid
Is the dealer's plaintive cry.

The air is pungent
With the sweet smell of success
But you wouldn't know to look at them
You'd really never guess.

Come down quickly and
Have a fascinating time
You'll be in heaven
It's a place that's just divine.

Bring big bags
You're sure to buy a load
When you come bargain hunting in
The Portobello Road.

It's a bit naive: my work has got so much better since then. I've written a second book which hasn't been published yet. It's got one hundred and fifty poems in it. They just pop out of you. But to get the best poetry for me, I've got to be in love or I've got to be in absolute pain. And when I'm in pain, I write the best things ever. My real love is poetry. When I die, I want to be known as Hilary Proctor the poet and not Hilary Proctor stall holder.

'I would like to come back as a man'

CHERYL, COSTERMONGER

I'm a Collins. Very small family. On my father's side, there was just him and his brother Charlie. There was my grandfather before him; he was original, in the '20s. I really don't know much about him, 'cause he died of cancer before I was born. And Charlie died very young – fifty – of cancer. So that just left my dad here.

> – *Hello whad'ya like my darling? That's all right. Trying to talk about the market …*
> – *Couple of pounds of those please.*
> – *Yep. Right my darling. Have you got your little bag today?*
> – *There you are. That will be one fifty when you're ready.*

I think my dad started when he was about eleven. They was just brought up to go to work because they was so poor. They wasn't educated like nowadays. They was quite ignorant people. But they were very respectable: they all wore suits, ties. You'll see it in the pictures I give you. So respectable. So proud of their job.

My dad was a very quiet man. My mum was the boss, definitely. But she married into this game. She was a hairdresser, make-up artist and seamstress in the West End. They just met up on a blind date in Bayswater and hit it off. My mum was a businesswoman. She was a clever one. She said 'I don't wanna work in the market. Riff-Raff and all that sort of thing.' That's the bad impression you used to get in them days. But now, aah, it's lovely. I couldn't do anything else!

My mum rented a shop round the corner, in Blenheim Crescent, and she sold coal. Before central heating come in, in the '50s. We never had heat. We had one fire in the kitchen and what was in front of that? The bananas! We had to sit behind the bananas! In the '70s, central heating come in so of course she couldn't sell coal, firelighters and wood for fire in your front room. Then she got her own stall next to Dad. So that's how we got two stalls together now.

– *Hello darling, what'd you like today?*
– *Some peppers please. A red and a yellow.*
– *One and one.*
– *You can still keep asking me questions in between, honey …*

I used to stand out here when I was about six or seven. I used to freeze on the corner of the stall. My job was five lemons for a shilling. You couldn't do it now, 'cause you got special lines now: you got to stand in these lines.

That's all I did at that age. And then I went to school and I trained to be a florist and that was my trade. But when I was about eighteen I had two weeks off and the guy that was helping my father had a massive heart attack and died. So I said 'Dad, I'll help you until you find someone.' He never found no one!

Never get a break, no. Four kids and a business … I can't. My holidays are when my children go on holiday and I've got an empty house. When I'm not working I like to sleep. Rest. Peace and quiet, away from people, be left alone. It's like on stage here really, a little bit, with the lights. Win the customer over, to come back again. Yeah, it's nice to be left alone. Me and the dogs. And it's better for me 'cause a lot of traders will go on holiday so I get their trade. I couldn't adjust my body clock, neither, to getting up at all hours, sitting down relaxing. 'Cause when you come back you'd think 'Oh my God, what was that all about? Is that normality?' Ha ha! We're not normal!

How do I recharge? Chocolate. And I'm very positive mentally. Very. I don't have much negative thoughts. I just feel I'm just so lucky to be alive each day and have my health and strength. I'm just blessed with such a good nature. I couldn't do this job otherwise. I do get low days. Of course: I'm human. But boy do I fight it. Yeah I'm a fighter. Taurus the boar: that's my birth sign. I'm a stubborn bitch, definitely.

– Yes darling.
– An aubergine and some parsley. A pound of beans.
– Jus' help yourself my love.
– What are these?
– Baby cu's.
– Baby cucumbers? I'll take some.
– All right darling.

We never used to sell things like courgettes and aubergines. It was just plain boring potato, carrot and onion. It was just English Food. Real basic English food.

Why did it change? Because this area become very cosmopolitan didn't it? With black people coming in, Indians coming in the '50s and '60s –whenever it was. So we have to cater for everybody. Now we sell coriander, peppers, hot chillies …

Sprouts now: I buy a bag of sprouts it lasts me three, four days. In the old days we sold like three a day! And at Christmas we used to sell twenty bags. Now I'm lucky to sell four! And all this microwave shit. It's all convenient food. It's really taken over.

– There you go darling. Eighty pence.
– Okay, bye bye … cheers …

She used to come regular. She's about ninety. That's what I mean: that generation's gone. Cooked regular meals every night. They wouldn't have wasted their money on microwave food.

My mum cooked every day. She used to prepare the pastry for steak and kidney puddings. And afters. We used to have afters as well. Unbelievable. Best cook ever! Made jam, made all her jams. She just was an amazing woman.

I wouldn't do it now. I wouldn't cook from scratch. Sunday's a big roast dinner day. Curry Saturday night, takeaway. Absolutely shattered. Just sausages and mash in the weekdays. Something light.

– Hello. Help yourself dear.
– You're quiet today … you gonna say hello?

And years ago every fruit item was wrapped in tissue: every orange, every pear. I remember it as a child. Painstakingly. Make the show look so pretty. To bring in the custom – 'cause so much competition in them days. You wasn't allowed to touch: it was up to the stall holder to take it off and show 'em. But now, we're so desperate for customers, do what yer like – within reason!

> [A Japanese woman lays down an item with a stern look]
> – Fifty pence please.
> – No manners, look! No expression. Dead!
> [Woman looks confused, gives a vague smile]
> – That's better. Don't cost nothing, do it?

You get all different types of customers: the good; the bad; the ugly. What I hate is rudeness, plain rudeness. Just picks things up and slams it down. You tolerate a lot because you'd be fighting all day out here. It's just manners. Just have some respect for how hard we work and what we do to produce this for you. People say to me 'When was that delivered?' I say 'We get up and buy it!' A lot of people don't realise what you actually do to get a box of stuff here.

I was listening to Nick Ferrari, and sometimes he don't like to be called 'mate'. I thought 'I wonder if people get offensive if I call them luvvie or darling? But it's just a part of me. It's how I am. If you don't like it, you don't come here. If you're a nasty customer, I show NO loving towards you at all. You'll get a very cold shoulder. Yeah, you'll see me change! I'd say 'Hi there, can I help you? Good morning. Good afternoon.' Very rare I get upset. You can't in this job. It's your livelihood, it's your living. People won't come back.

> – Yes darling?
> – Can I have a half kilo of mushroom please?
> – Si … si … Trying to learn the lingo?! You're speaking very good!
>   Very good!
> – If you say so! Cheers! Goodbye …

Kilograms or Ounces? It's both isn't it? The guy that tried to keep it pounds, he died of cancer. He never see it brought back again. Someone up North somewhere. Now it's optional: you can do pounds or kilos. Stay original. This is tradition. Why must WE change? Let them change to our ways! We say 'No to the Ki-lo!'

Did we get in trouble? We took no notice! But they kept coming down on us. 'You must put kilos'. Yeah, yeah. I never did it. Never! We just kept getting warned: 'Next time, put it in!' We didn't do it. If someone said 'They're here!' we just took the tickets out. You gotta laugh. I love it. I love it.

– *Do you have any fresh parsley?*
– *Parsley? I've only got continental darling. Eighty pence*
– *You don't have Italian parsley? I just looked at the recipe and it says 'Italian'.*
– *This is it. Continental. Yeah. English is curley. Eighty pence please.*
– *Thank you*
– *Bye bye now*

The council? All they're doing is catering for tourists. I don't feel they're catering for locals at all. They've allowed the cooked foods to come here which destroyed the market. Look at this stall. Beautiful. This is for the locals. And the market: it's fantastic; calm; lovely. But tomorrow, bring the cooked foods in: it's just like a mad house. It stinks. What it does to my stomach … It makes me feel sick. If I was pregnant I'd be vomiting twenty four seven out here. And, as a customer, it's disgusting.

They don't cook it here. It's prepared at home so you don't know … They bring it here, empty it out, add water and boom – there's your dinner. You do not know how it's prepared. And then the fumes start coming over. And there's smoke going everywhere. It's not on, next to fresh produce like this. I'm so anti, it's unbelievable.

It's destroyed my business, yeah. Saturday's my worst trading day. And it's a nightmare getting through 'cause all the tourists are just walking past, looking and taking pictures of fruit and veg, like they've never seen such beautiful fruit and veg before. Nobody who buys hot food buys fruit. Years ago they would buy more fruit to eat healthily. But now they see a big load of stodgy grease. It's only nat'ral – they think it smells good. I think it smells revolting.

– *Yes dear.*
– *How you keeping, all right?*
– *Yes dear, I'm fine. I've let off steam now.*
– *I went to the pound shop. When I asked for a bottle of water they gave me six.*
– *I'll buy the other for a pound.*
– *No, you can have them. It's my pleasure.*

– Please take 50p

– No, no. Have a drink on me. Unless you've got a banana …

– Yeah, go right round. Follow the yellow brick road. Round the front. Thank you.

– This is why I'm here for locals: 'cause you get lovely people like that.

This end's the better end. Where the pound a bowls are, it's not the nicest end. Pound a bowl's killed the market: it's too cheap and it's not good quality. Makes the market look bad. You'll be very lucky to get a good pound a bowl – there's something wrong with it if it's that cheap. Just old stock at market. Or if they've got a big abundance come in and it's too hot they have to get rid of it quick. But, like I say, I just think it lowers the tone a bit.

Of course mine's better. First class. But a lot of people haven't got money and they just go for pound a bowl. It's scales. Roundabouts.

No, no, no – there's no rivalry. No way. We all grew up together. We all know each other well. It can give you tension. You just have to keep it to yourself – under your breath really. You've got to live and work together.

Now, anything else you want to ask me? How do I cope with the cold? I don't have no central heating in my front room. All of us that work here, we'll all go home and within about five or ten minutes we're like a light bulb. Bright red. Pillar box red. Because it's just too much for your skin. That's why I don't have central heating. Breaks all the capillaries in your face. I used to have electrolysis. I don't do it now. I won't bother. Past all that vanity bit.

I have to just gradually get myself warm. It can take up to two or three hours. Once I've done my cooking I put a quilt cover round me – all round my feet and everywhere – and I wait 'til it comes back. Honestly. I have to wait a few hours to have a bath: at my age I get chilblains.

Here I stand on wood. It's a bit of decking and it just takes your feet. My dad, bless him, never had this, did he? Snowing, raining, he might put a bit of cardboard box down and stood on it. He was old school. Oh, he was the best. Yes he was the best. He'd get up at half twelve, one o'clock the latest, go to market, get back here for four, get the stalls out and stood here until seven every day. No wonder he got leukaemia. Too much for his body. I do miss him daily. Every day he's with me.

Horse and cart we have for funerals 'cause that's what royalty has. To me my family's royalty: the best of the best. It comes past the stall. All the

flowers are on the barrows. And when my dad come by, everyone come out the shop and clapped him 'cause he was so missed. That I'll never forget. I was in the corsage … whatever it's called … the hearse … and he was in front of me. We had two horses. I asked for four horses but one horse was lame so they couldn't give me three! And I'll never forget … I went to the church and they had big, massive posters of my father. And loads of red roses. All in the church. When people went in they saw pictures of my dad when he was young, my mum and dad's wedding picture, big picture of my dad at the altar.

You play the music they like. I played 'Unforgettable' for my dad. Nat King Cole sung that. That's when he come out of the church. And when he went in the church: 'September in the Rain' by Dinah Washington. That was their favourite song together. 'The leaves are brown, come tumbling down, remember?' Lovely song, if you hear that …

And my mum had 'Smile though your heart is breaking' when she went in. And when she come out 'Somewhere over the rainbow'. What a song!

It's beautiful. Lovely caskets. Family plot land. I had mine on a Monday. We get the weekend out the way and then we have a whole week of grieving.

I did have my kids working here when my parents first died. We just clash. Different generations. They want to do it their way. Not polite enough to customers. I lost a few customers. Didn't want to come and work every day because they want to go out at nights. I let them have too much freedom. Wasn't strict enough with them. Too many friends' parties to go to when they should be here, Saturdays, helping.

I was never spoilt. I was never given nothing: I appreciate every single thing I got. Because that's old school. It's just how it should be. Just such respect for how hard my parents worked.

I've always said if I ever come back in this world, I'm coming back as a man. They just go and work and they're finished. If that. If they go work. Us women … Well-being a one hundred per cent person, I give all. I'm a one hundred per cent out here, one hundred per cent at home. It's very tough. I would like to come back as a man …

'Is funny, life on the market'

MAREK, GERMAN FOOD

Yes Madam, no business. People is not having money or something. Losing job. And competition's here. Everybody's selling food because thinking after few months, millionaires. Everyone. Special weekend. Saturday is only food here. That's big problem now. Very bad situation for me. Really. I'm losing about 40 per cent business like before.

How long have I been here? How long, Gulosh? 1986. September. So how many? Twenty-six years and still not rich. You see. Not fantastic. Not very good idea business like that, probably.

Food is very good: boneless leg of chicken with herbs; sausages; chicken burger very tasty. Is lots of regular customers coming for my food. Schnitzels I'm do. You know schnitzels? Pork fillets. Like Wiener Schnitzel but the German is pork schnitzel. Pork loin. And new lines am try on Saturday now. Pork fillet with mushrooms and cheese. Very, very nice. But it's not very popular at moment … I dunno, maybe alter. Chicken breast with pesto and mozzarella cheese on the top. Hot of course.

I was born in Poland. Am selling German food because I'm working with German guys twenty-five years ago. From Poland is very good food. Sausage is very similar. German, Polish – doesn't matter. But is not popular, Polish name. Twenty-six years ago when you say is Polish sausages, nobody come. German food is popular here. German sausage is very popular because the British Army is staying in Germany. Sometime I'm using Polish mustard. Very nice. Really very nice. Mustard with mayonnaise mixed. Very, very good. Very tasty. And then the writing here is 'New Polish mustard. Very, very good'. Nobody touch. I'm said, what I'm do? Because there's a couple of them like this, full of this mustard. Next week I'm write, 'Nicest, beautiful new mustard from Munich. Bavarian style.' It's two days, three days, all gone!

This Portobello Market is very popular. Famous market. Number one in the UK. I'm make application form. I'm waiting. How long I'm waiting Gulosh? Few years! Few years! But now is collapse slowly, slowly. Dunno. Dunno for future. Is funny, funny life on the market. Sometimes is very bad time, very bad time really. Later again, gone up. In market you never know.

'I wanted to be champion
of the world'

PETER, COSTERMONGER

I was born in that mews in 1951. It was a working class area then. Y'know, all proper people that done shopping and 'ad time for yer and 'ad manners. Today people are running around like 'eadless chickens, rude – not all, but a lot – no manners, no please, no thank you. I grew up with black people and Irish people. That's what you 'ad in the area. That's what it really was. They kept to themself but there was never any real tensions as such. Attitudes there wasn't. You had the riots in the '50s. I was seven or eight years of age so I don't remember it that much. But I remember lots of things being smashed up and broken. You had the right wing party 'cause Oswald Mosely had an office here. He was supposed to be a Fascist so that doesn't help does it?

I'm not contradicting meself. What multiculturals done to this country's been good and been bad. It's been good and it's been bad. There you go. Maybe I wouldn't take any money at all if there wasn't any foreign people 'ere cause that's all I serve. Everyone's here. Everyone from countries I haven't even heard of. Because more foreign people will buy in the market. Maybe they ain't got credit cards. English people shop in supermarkets. If you have a car, you go to the supermarket.

The word middle class now: if you own a house, you've got your own business, you're middle class. But you're not really. I'm a working class boy. I've been a working class boy all m' life. I left school at fifteen: I weren't too bright at school. But I got a daughter now who's thirty-four years of age. She's the director of advertising in a big company and she's middle class isn't she? So they say. But I think she's a working class girl. The apple don't fall far from the tree does it? That's how I look on it. You are what you are. I'm not one of them people with a big plum in their mouth y'know! What you see with me is what you get.

I think my family were originally fruit pickers from Gloucester. My great-grandfather came from Marylebone to Portobello in the twenties. He and Dolly Cain had about twelve, thirteen kids. My grandfather had six brothers. They all had kids and they all worked on the market. There were great characters on the market then. You always had someone out for a laugh. Having a joke. Now you've got people who don't even say 'Good Morning'. Terrible.

When I was a little baby my mother put me in the scales and weighed me! I weighed three pound at birth: I was a premature twin. I started working when I was about seven, eight. Used to stand on that corner of the mews there – this used to be an Express Dairy – and my dad used to come home from market with a box of mint and a box of parsley. I used to rip newspaper up and my sister Janet used to make little bunches and we used to sell it a penny a bunch.

Did I keep the money? Nah! The old man 'ad that. He might 'ave give us a shilling or something at the end of the day. Ha ha ha! No, no, he had the money. Think he's still got it, you know what I mean! No, but they was hard times, really hard times. I was told one day my father walked to Covent Garden market, bought something on a pram, pushed it back. We were living up there in a rotten little old 'ouse. Freezing cold. Mum come down, said 'John, 'ave you got any money? I want to get the twins some milk.' And he says 'Can you 'ang on a minute Margaret? I 'aven't took the money yet.' They were tough times.

What was he like me dad? Tough. Hardworker. He was in the Army Cadets when he was about fourteen, fifteen and at the age of sixteen he got called up for the Second War. He had his seventeenth birthday in the trenches in Europe. He see all his mates getting slaughtered. And I shouldn't really say this but that done his brain in. He had five years of real hard fighting and all he come out the army in was his demob suit. Didn't 'ave any counselling or any talking or seeing what's wrong with him or anything. He was one of many that went through that. And he come out 'ere and I think he managed to borrow ten or twenty quid off his father and went and bought a few cauliflowers and stood outside the bank and tried to sell 'em. Had nothing.

No one 'ad nothing when you think of them days. I remember if I had 'oles in me shoes I daren't tell my dad I needed a new pair. Put a bit of cardboard in 'em or sum'thing. But we ate all right. We always had food on the table. One thing I will say about my father: I've never really seen eye to eye with him but he provided the best way he could. And I take me hat off to him for that. He was a straight man. He wasn't a crook. Wasn't a thief. Awkward man, but I take me hat off to him for what he could do with limited things.

> – *'Allo, where's Daryl?*
> – *I 'aven't seen him yet Linda!*
> – *Them oranges were nice.*
> – *Were they all right my darling?*
> – *Lovely.*
> – *Where you off to?*
> – *I'm just going to have a look in here. Didn't come out at all yesterday … my feet are absolutely …*
> – *Never mind! Keep fighting!*
> – *Keep fighting!*

Did I want to go on the market? Nah, I wanted to be champion of the world! When I left school I went to this weightlifting gym. Didn't like weightlifting. Then I see some guys doing this boxing so I thought I'd have a go at it.

I didn't know at the time but my grandfather, Jack Cain, was in the Guinness Book of Records for the fastest knockout in the world. So I done the boxing. That went on for about fifteen years. I mean, I never earned a lot of money out of the business but I built myself up from a one hundred pound fighter to a one thousand pound fighter. And what it done, it kept me.

Fighting is a thing that's in yer. I loved it. Why? I can't really say. But if you're getting your 'ands taped up and you're at the Albert Hall and you're doing twelve threes, you're fighting a real tough guy, it's a one on one – just you and him – you can't pass the ball to someone if you're tired … It is the sport of gladiators, boxing. There's not a sport that comes near it for fitness. I used to get up every morning and run ten mile. EVERY morning. And I used to go to the gym in the evening and do two hours hard boxing training.

I got involved in the film world by luck. I was an amateur boxer at the time. I was only a young kid of about eighteen, nineteen, and I'd just come back from my 'olidays in Spain and I 'ad a little bit of a suntan. I was stopped on Regent Street by an Italian film director named Pier Pasolini.

I used to train with a boxing club called the Polytechnic which was the lower end of Regent Street, near where the BBC is. And I come out the gym, walking down Lower Regent Street, and I see all these people walking towards me. About ten, fifteen people. 'E couldn't speak great English, Pasolini, so he 'ad an interpreter. So he stopped and 'e said to me 'We would like to know if you'd be interested in being in a film.' I thought 'What's 'e going on about?' You know, I was a fighter, not an actor. I went 'What, a blue film?' Anyway he introduced me to Pasolini. I never knew Pasolini. He asked me did I know anything about the Canterbury Tales and I went 'Oh yeah'. I knew nothing!

So … one thing led to another and I 'ad to go to the Piccadilly 'otel, in the West End. He had the whole of the top floor of the hotel. The whole lot. Him and his crew. The lot. I told him, I said 'I can't act'. He said … it sounds strange, doesn't it … he said 'No, it's your face I like'. 'E was gay but 'e knew I wasn't gay. He knew I was straight. So we went to Cornwall, we went to Canterbury, and I played Absalon, the lover, in the Miller's Tale. I 'ad to learn scripts and my memory is … well I can't remember telephone numbers. I'm just BAD. Brain idle! Eh I punched through that. We got through that. "Eh ye they, my sweet turtle dove, this is your Absalon.' It was all old English and I can't speak any English. Anyway, I had to serenade a song. I 'ad to sing to Alison who's at the winder. How was it? Well it was no Top Tenors. Anyway, I got through that and I got through that and it actually won an award at a German film festival. The Golden Bear award or something like that.

I remember going to the cinema with some friends to see it. And … not me … but the movie was fucking amazing. He was like a Ken Russell but before Ken Russell. It was just an amazing film about this pilgrimage. Very raunchy. Very, very near the mark. I remember one part I was dressed up like a court jester and I 'ad to wear a pair of tights. And one part he said 'Peter would you mind doing this part in the nude?' So I said 'Nah', I said. 'I can't do that.'

I met all these actors, all their darlings. They're all up their own arse. They's all for theirselves. I mean there was one guy there – Michael Belfont his name was – and 'e said 'Oh they've just flown me in from Madrid where I'm doing a James Bond movie but I just managed to come down 'ere for a day as they need me.' Like, too much bull shit.

And I done lots of other things. I mean, I've never got any money but I've 'ad a colourful life. I've 'ad photos taken with Miss World. That was just a modelling stunt. Me being a fighter and her throwing a punch at me. I've done advertising. A guy just stopped me again on the street. Said I should be in advertising. This is true: I don't lie. This is all luck. I remember doing an advert in Rome. The product was a packet of biscuits and the biscuits were called 'Upper Cut' – as in punch! I 'ad a lovely four days there. I stayed in a lovely hotel, all expenses paid. I had a chauffeur drive a car for me anywhere I wanted to go in Rome. Got about six, seven hundred quid for the job and all I 'ad to do, basically, was run down the streets of Rome with a tracksuit on, me 'ands bandaged up, throwing punches. It was great.

Then I got a telegram from Pasolini. 'E was going to make another film and 'e wanted me to go out there. But no, I was doing my training. I was fighting. It was just what I loved. I wouldn't say I was good at it but I felt comfortable at it. I didn't feel comfortable trying to learn lines and be an actor. I wanted to be the champion of the world. I won the Southern Area Middleweight title. That was sweet. That was great. That was lovely. I looked at the names on it: Bunnie Stirling, Kevin Finnegan. Middle-class, world-class fighters. And my name was on there. That made me feel good. But I wasn't good enough to be the champion of the world.

I got hurt one night in a fight and I said to meself 'That's it: no more'. I was twenty-six years of age but I was still ranked number three in the country. I retired. In that game, when it starts to hurt you get out. Because getting in the ring, getting smashed in the head, is not healthy. You can't stay in that game too long. I've known fighters who've stayed in the game a little bit long and they couldn't have a conversation with you now. They're walking down the road like they're drunk.

You're a bit lost when you stop, yeah. I was a bit lost for a while. 'Cause I loved the limelight. I loved all what went with it. I mean … only skill I ever 'ad was with me 'ands, fighting. I couldn't fall back on a profession. I didn't really follow too much up after that. Me dad always had the stall and I basically just went back to work with 'im. And then I took it off 'im and I just went from there.

I do a little bit of boxing training for some people in my spare time. They want a little bit of personal one to one. I do a bit of that and I take it from there. Everyone wants to fight today but they can't fight. You fight when you're hungry. When you WANT something you fight. I was hungry to be champion. But now it's all a fashion. All these middle class (posh voice), 'Oh, going boxing tonight?' It's all these bankers and wankers … or whatever you want to call them. There are a couple of them I train they're actually not too bad at all. But you still gotta have that va va voom in you. You gotta 'ave that. You gotta 'ave that.

That's enough about me ... Maybe we should talk about the market! Not just me. You know it's really ... to talk about yourself ... Bragging. Anyway, I've nothing else to say now. I'm talked out. We can catch up again, can't we? Lovely lady! Is that al'right with you? Is that all right? We should do this over a beer really. We could 'ave a sit in a pub. Have about ten pints and then I'll make a lot more sense! Ha ha ha ha!

[Six months later ...]

You don't mind if I smoke, do yer?

Just a tea ... normal tea ... two sugars ...

It's just not viable now. Supermarkets have totally crucified the small man. They've killed the butcher, the baker, the candlestick maker. I mean you can't compete with them. We can buy bananas to go 50p a pound with, which won't get you a lot of money. You go to the supermarket and they'll be twenty-five pence a pound.

And all you're getting in the market now is tourists. Thousands and thousands. No disrespect for the tourist. They're not here to buy fruit. They don't take a bag of vegetables or a bag of fruit back to the hotel. Years ago this used to be a real working class area. Where I say you had proper people. You had a woman who 'ad three kids. Didn't 'ave a lot of money. Didn't 'ave anythink. But they bought a bit of veg in the market. You look at this market now, it's all fast food. You can get paella, sausages, 'ot dogs, pastas, spaghettis, wraps ... that's all they're selling. Because the tourist will buy that as 'e's walking along the street.

And all the properties are so expensive. The poor people that lived here they've been moved out to, say, Milton Keynes or out of London so the property developers can charge high rents for the new money that's coming in. If you 'ad more working class people in the area I'm sure you'd still be a bit better trade, which you don't. No one deals with cash now. Everyone deals with plastic. And everythink's done on line now. It's crazy. That mews at the bottom of Portobello Road: they've got an amazing fruit stall outside but they 'ave their fruit delivered. They 'ave everything delivered. They can sit indoors on their computer now and pay for it on a computer and not come out the 'ouse. And people don't know what it does. What it does, it breaks down the community. There's no community spirit. Same as public 'ouses in the area. If you ever wanted a plumber or a builder or someone to do an odd job, you go in the pub, someone would know. You go in a pub now, you've got to wait for someone to make a cappuccino before you can get a pint. And if you ain't dressed too good they look at you as if you're a bit funny, you shouldn't be there.

I just said 'I've 'ad enough.' I was digging a hole for meself. Keep trying to pay the rent up that office each week, pay your share out of the warehouse rents, keep your motors taxed, insured, petrol, paper bags you need to put the produce in. You can't go work with yer bus fare. You've gotta go work with some money to be able to buy stuff.

Relieved? Yeah. I've sort of kicked the monkey off me shoulder a bit. But I just think it's sad the way it's going. You've only got to look round London to see 'ow many shops are shutting. And empty shops. This is not a recession. This is a depression. This is like the 1930s in the States. I don't know how it's going to get better. I've no idea. I'd love to go the 'ouse of Commons with a bottle of gin, stand up and tell all 'em learned people what I think. I'd sack the lot! I wouldn't need to write anything down. It would just come out and they'd 'ave to listen to me for about two hours. I don't know what I'd say … I'd know on my third glass of gin. And I wouldn't swear either. If you swear, you've got nothing to say. You know the old saying: empty drums sound loud. So there you go.

Don't get me wrong, I miss not being in the market every day. It was no easy choice for me to give that stall up. We've 'ad that stall about seventy years in my family's name. It's a long time. It's a little bit of 'istory gone. Now I just help a couple of days a week down there if I want to. I don't do a lot. I don't wanna do a lot. I'm not twenty one. I'm sixty-one. What do I want now? Me? Grandchildren! That's what I want now. I want my daughter to 'ave a couple of nice middleweights …

'It's not like it used to be'

DIMBO AND JACK, COSTERMONGERS

DIMBO – It's terrible out here. I've been here seventy years, love. You know what I mean? And I've seen the difference of it. All day long, love, I stand here …

JACK – Taking a pound here, two pound there. It's quite frightening actually. I don't know what's going to happen. This is NOT a living. I mean we're only here because my mum's eighty-seven, I'm sixty-five, my husband's sixty-six. What else do we do? The thing is, with us, we all live together. So we've got one pot – one electricity bill, one gas bill … If we had to pay all, we couldn't do it.

We live ten minutes away. My mum was born and bred in Notting Hill. All our family were. My great grandmother had thirteen children in that first white house over there. Thirteen children and they all had stalls in the market.

When my mum used to finish work on a Saturday, I used to sit up there with my great granny Cain. When I was four, five. My mum and dad would go and 'ave a drink in Finches. She used to open up top winder and sit me up there – I remember it like it was yesterday. She used to get a little plate and we'd 'ave a lump of cheese, crusty bread and a couple of slices of Spanish onion. And she used to pour me out a little drop of Guinness. So I used to sit up the winder, drink the Guinness, eat the cheese and wait for my mum and dad to come back. How did they meet? I don't know. In a pub probably!

DIMBO – Yeah.

JACK – See!

DIMBO – Used to go to the pub and used to play darts, didn't 'e?

JACK – Yeah.

DIMBO – 'E 'ad to go to another pub to play the other team and 'e said, 'If you're 'ere when I come back, I'll buy you a brown ale.' So I sat there and waited for the brown ale. How many children? Only the one, love. I made a good job out of 'er!

JACK – She wasn't allowed to 'ave any more. My grandfather said 'Don't 'ave anymore because there's nobody to work on the stall.'

DIMBO – Yeah, you're right love. Told my 'usband that. He never used to take no notice: if it 'appened, it 'appened, di'n' it! 'E was a good man, 'e was. Local, yeah. Up Harrow road way. 'E died overnight. 'E was 'ere on the Friday and dead Friday night. 'Ow old was he Jack?

JACK – Sixty-two.

DIMBO – Sixty-two. Massive heart attack. Had his lunch and everything. When I went into the living room 'e was …

JACK – Dead in the chair.

DIMBO – Women live older. 'Alf of this market is run by the women. Women work harder than men, yeah. It's always been that way, ennit?

JACK – Oh, absolutely. My auntie Clarrie used to live in Elgin Crescent. She had a veg stall right where my granny Cain had her house. And before she came a work of a morning, she'd make a meat pudding and put it on. And then, when my aunt May used to come down to help, she'd run round, check on the pudding, make sure that the water hadn't boiled out of it, top it up, come back to the stall. She'd have the veg prepared. She'd just put it on when she went home and the meat pudding would all be done!

And my Granny Cain was far stronger than my grandfather. Far stronger. My grandfather used to do the buying for most of the family but 'e wouldn't serve a customer. Wasn't interested. He used to go to every race meeting there was. Monday was drinking day. They used to have parties over there in the pub. What did the women do? Stand here. Waited for 'em to come back!

DIMBO – If they didn't come back they 'ad to go and find 'em. Did they mind? They just accepted it. They knew what they were gonna do, so what's the point? They still went anyway. Sometimes the wives would go with 'em. Sometimes they wouldn't pull the stall out.

Jack – They used to do all theirself out with their fox …

Dimbo – My aunties and all that. Fox furs. Very smart. I always done meself up when I gone out. But not to come to work. No point out here, darling. Yeah, sensible shoes. My girls bought me these. They're lovely. Marks & Spencers. They are very comfortable. And we always wrap ourselves up when it's winter. When it breaks through we like to take all this off. But I never complained about the weather.

Jack – Nobody grumbles.

Dimbo – Yeah.

Jack – My mum stood at the stall with pleurisy and pneumonia. Any of these family, when they're sick: 'I'll work it off'. If they get pneumonia: 'Have a bowl of chicken soup and work it off.' My great granny always had a pot of stew going. Every day. They used to leave the stall when it was really cold. Just disappear. 'Where you going?' 'I'm going up Gran's; I'm gonna have a cup a soup.' You used to just help yerself. Pop up Granny's, have a cup of hot soup, back down. Pot of boiled chicken is the answer to everything in this family.

Dimbo – Well I don't think it hurts. I mean, I'm eighty-seven now, so it ain't 'urt me, 'as it?

Jack – Mother will be eighty-eight on the 1 July.

Dimbo – How will I celebrate? Out here, I suppose, love. Going to work! We don't celebrate birthdays. We're just old fashioned family. Carry on regardless.

Jack – We're here every day apart from Thursday. And we're not allowed to work Sundays. What do I do? Washing. Ironing. Cleaning. Get ready for Monday. Thursday is the same. Washing and ironing. Maybe go and get a bit of shopping. I sit down when I can. But I just don't get the time.

Dimbo – Am I always working? Oh yeah! I'm not lazy, love. I like to keep doing something indoors. When I get home of a night, I do anything wants doing. I've never watched television. I love the evening papers. And I like a Guinness of a night when I go in. I'm telling the truth – I'm not telling lies. Keeps me going.

JACK – What about your *Daily Mail*? You go mad if you 'aven't got yer *Daily Mail*!

DIMBO – Oh yeah. Me *Daily Mail*. Course. Do I vote? Not a lot love. Well, I mean, I am Conservative. I've been Conservative all me life, love. Me mum and dad was it, so I'm it. I'm with them love.

Why did they call me Dimbo? My name is Doris Margaret really. But when I was born, they tell me I was very small. They said, 'Look at Dolly Dimbo.' And it stuck to me. I'm used to it now. School? Sirdar Road. Yeah, it was all right while I was there. I didn't complain.

JACK – But then again, they was only there 'til they was fourteen. Missing every Friday.

DIMBO – That's right. But we helped along one another, love.

JACK – Some of them couldn't read or write but they knew 'ow to add up!

DIMBO – Yeah. And that's the main thing. When I left, my first job was at McVitties in Harlesden. I used to pick biscuits off of the conveyers and all that. And they sent these two great big men up to watch me. They thought I was cheating because I was so quick on the conveyer!

JACK – There was nothing for the girl next door to pack because Dolly packed it! Dolly put MacVitties on their feet!

DIMBO – Then I had a job at Vandervilles, North Acton. Making bits for aeroplanes. Feeding the machine. That's how I got me finger …

JACK – You know where they do the holes in nuts and bolts? It came down and it went through her finger.

DIMBO – That's the proof …

JACK – It's dead.

DIMBO – It's dead, love. Look. It is absolutely useless.

JACK – They wanted to take that top off and she said 'No'.

DIMBO – 'No, leave it where it is.' It does get in the way, yes. When it gets cold it throbs a bit, dun'it? I tell yer, dun I?

JACK – Sometimes she has to keep cups of hot water …

DIMBO – Dip it in …

JACK – And hold it in hot water.

DIMBO – Does it go white? Ooh it goes all colours!

When did I come to the market?

JACK – When my granddad said 'That's it. You've got to pack up now.'

DIMBO – He wanted me to work for him, love.

JACK – He must 'ave 'ad a few other people but …

DIMBO – They wanted us because they didn't want to give us a lot of money. We was cheap labour, love! In them days you couldn't pick and choose. You had to go where your parents told yer. Today, these young 'uns, they don't wanna know. They just wanna do what they wanna do …

JACK – Who's singing?

DIMBO – It's a little nursery over there.

JACK – No, that's Wednesday morning Mum.

DIMBO – Who's that then?

JACK – I bet I know who that is. It's that nutty one on the bike. The characters we used to have in this market – ah, there was loads. There was an old man called Lordie: they used to have a real good laugh with him. Used to sell plants. Because he couldn't read or write, he used to get somebody to write the tickets for him. So what they used to do, they used to put the wrong name on the plant. Of course somebody would come and ask for antirrhinums and he went straight to antirrhinums. 'But you haven't got antirrhinums in there, you've got … '! Everybody used to be laughing! Oh, there used to be murders. It was all done in a joke; they was always playing practical jokes on one another down here.

And there was a man used to walk about with a parrot on his shoulder. There's an old man down here now with a dog on his shoulder. D'you know, funnily enough, we were talking about that. I haven't seen that man for a few weeks. He was always up and down. Sometimes it makes you wonder. All of a sudden you miss these people. We used to get some lovely, lovely people in this area.

DIMBO – You're talking about class.

JACK – Yeah. Those people are not around anymore: they've moved out of the area. Once they've moved out, they don't come back … which I don't blame them. Or they might appear one day and they go 'Oh, God, look at it! 'Asn't it altered? What's gone on?'

DIMBO – 'Oh my God this market: it's not like it used to be!'

Jack – I don't know too much about that end of the market I never really venture down that end. Do they still do all the second hand stuff? 'Cause that used to go right the way up.

DIMBO – We're working 'ere. And we're 'ere to work, like. You know what I mean?
   No more, love. I'm not good at answering questions.

JACK – Tell the lady when the sirens used to go …

DIMBO – Oh yeah. When the sirens used to go, we used to just leave the stall as it was like that. Around the corner they 'ad a little shelter. We used to go in there, wait for the all clear, and come back and go to work. No, nothing stolen. Them days, they didn't steal nothing. Now, you can't leave anything here.

JACK – Oh my God. There wouldn't be a thing left!

DIMBO – You can't even walk about.

JACK – Oh I'm glad I'm not young down 'ere 'cause I wouldn't be here. I would not be here. Really wouldn't. But we couldn't do anything else.

DIMBO – Don't know nothing else.

JACK – 'Oo's gonna employ us?

DIMBO – When will we stop? Well I suppose we'll be in the box, love!

JACK – Right, I'd better go and get something done. I've gotta go over the warehouse and sweep it out. Hose it down. Keep it clean.
   All right darling. You're welcome. Bye bye.

'We're all 'alf related'

JOSIE, COSTERMONGER

See that picture?* It's by Ken Russell. That's my stall. That's my great aunt, Emma Kirk. And that's the bakers. She's reading the paper and I know for a fact she couldn't read. Yeah. 'Cause even 'er children couldn't read so there's no way she could read. Plus that was 'er son, 'Arry boy's, stall. 'Er stall was actually next door and she sold flowers. So she's definitely posing for that picture.

This was the farmer's lane. We called this The Lane: we don't know it as Portobeller. The farmer 'ad 'is farm 'ouse at the top and 'e give to the people of the area to work on. But the council took it over 'cause they were fighting for the pitches so it 'ad to be better organised.

- *Morning Jim ... strawberries are two twenty today.*
- *Blimey. They are big though.*
- *I'm usually one fifty with strawberries but I can't be that with those..Open one up, babe. Take one out and pop one in if you like. It's only one ... You've been aw'right?*
- *Yeah.*
- *'Oo you've upset today?*
- *Corrie today.*
- *Corrie? I've gone off that. I don't watch it no more*
- *Yeah. Exactly. What are these ones?*
- *Papaya.Try one.*
- *No thank you. I don't really like papaya to be honest. I'll just have some ginger.*
- *I tell you what. A fresh papaya is very good for yer tummy.*

---

* Illustrated on page 17 (top)

It's like putting antiseptic in yer belly. Honestly. A lady I knew,
she used to come and she was very ill. She 'ad food allergies. She
got onto papaya and she looked ten years younger.
'Ere, I started eating them meself!
– Seven pound please dear …

He's Jim Shelley that bloke – the *Mirror* TV critic. I bought 'is paper today. 'E's done Corrie 'e said. Ah 'e's a lovely guy. I've got a lot of good customers. And they're regulars. So that is very good for me. 'Cause no matter what, I'll always take summin', because I've got them …

– Morning dallin!
– A couple of plums and a banana please. Where's 'e, in doors?
– Nah, 'e's up dialysing …
– Oh is 'e?
– Yes, Monday innit?
– Oh, okay.
– What, did you want 'im?
– Ah nah. I just wondered where 'e was, that's all. 'E's happy ain't
*   'e? Little Johnny?*
– Oh yeah, 'e's all right. 'E's all right. 'E's satisfied. 'E's happy
*   with … what 'e got*
– Yeah …
– 'E'll do about eighteen months.
– Yeah …
– Another eighteen months, maybe two tops. But 'e'll be glad
*   when 'e gets out The Scrubs.*
– Might crash into 'Arry, eh!
– Yeah, 'e probably will, wun' he!

That guy, 'e's married to my niece and that's 'is uncle. We're all 'alf related, the old fashioned Nottin' Hill families are. 'Cause it was just us years ago.

Both of my parents were from around 'ere. My mum was born in 155 Portland Road. I don't know what her parents did. I don't think my granny worked – women didn't work then – but I know that my granddad did. But then 'e went in the First World War and 'e become ill with his chest.

My dad's dad was a totter. Rag-and-bone man. He was lovely, my granddad Joe. 'E also suffered from 'is chest: got gassed in the First World War.

When I was young 'e was bedridden and 'e 'ad the oxygen by 'is bed. But 'e did 'ave one of them big copper medal things what you get from the Army. With 'is name on.

My dad's mum was a winder cleaner and she used to go in the pub and do acrobats and pass the 'at round. She must 'ave been a right ol' character but I didn't know 'er unfortunately; she went off with another man when my dad was about six.

I 'ad two grannies and a great granny out of Bangor Street. That was the roughest street in Nottin' Hill. My aunt said to me that they would be going to their gran with 'er Sunday dinner and my mum'd 'ave the Yorkshire and she'd say to 'er sister "Ere, 'old that a minute.' To be able to walk down the street you'd 'ave to fight this fat bird who was sat at the end of the street. So she'd punch into this girl. Once you give 'er a couple of clumps, you'd be all right and they'd go on.

You 'ad to go out and fight. If I come in to my mum's and said, 'So and so's 'it me', she'd go 'Get out there and hit them else I'm gonna hit you.' You 'ad to stand up for yourself.

In them days women would sit on the steps and natter to each other and watch what was everybody up to. Everybody knew everybody. You'd know if a stranger come in that road. And all kids'd play in the street then. You'd play football, cricket, one to ten London to Paris – what they call 'opscotch.

I lived just down 'ere in Talbot Grove, which is gone now. They'd fetch their babies out in the prams and leave them outside all day. You'd go 'Oh Mrs So-and-so your baby's crying' and they'd go 'Oh yeah.' They'd get their baby, feed them or change 'em, put them back in the pram. Back out they go. They'd say fresh air was good for 'em.

Did anyone steal them? NO. D'you know what, you couldn't afford to keep the one's you 'ad let alone nick someone else's! 'Ere, you'd be doing them a turn if you took their baby. They'd think 'That's 'andy. 'Nother one I ain't got to worry about!' They would in them days. It's true!

But people got moved out. 'Alf the family got moved out to Greenford and 'alf stayed 'ere. It just got all split up.

– *How much are your lemons?*
– *They're 25p*
– *All right darling. I want to get a whole lot tomorrow. You aren't here tomorrow are you?*
– *Yeah, yeah, yeah.*

– I'll be back … [goes into shop]

– He won't be. 'E'll never be back again. 'E just keeps coming, doing things like that! All the monkeys ain't up the zoo, right. Just bear that in mind …

It's funny. See this Nottin 'Ill now – it's different. But we still all know each other. And we all know each other's business. We 'ear things and go ''Ere, d'you know that Maldy Court, 'er daughter's got pregnant.' Or ''Er daughter's just left 'er old man' or ''E's been nicked … 'D'you know what I mean?

We only gossip about each other. We wouldn't never get nobody in trouble. We'd never go nowhere about nobody. So we're all 'alf related. But see, what happened, a lot of them changed their names to avoid conscription. Or if they got in trouble …

My dad was in prison a lot. He was one of the first men to escape from Dartmoor. But they caught 'im. Took 'im back and that. 'E was only a thief; 'e never hurt anybody. I know it sounds a bit stupid but I wouldn't like to rob a person … a woman … of their purse … or a man … That ain't nice. Or to go out … like burglary … ain't nice. BUT, if you go into a firm, where there's a lot of stuff and you just go in and take it overnight when nobody knows … they'll only fiddle off the insurance anyway probably …

My dad was a good man really. 'E educated isself in prison – that's where 'e learned to read and write – and 'e'd finish any crossword puzzle. He wasn't 'alf a clever man. If he'd had a different life, 'e would 'ave been quite brainy. But 'e never 'ad nothing; 'e didn't even 'ave a pair of shoes. I think 'e did go to school at St John's but 'e only went now and again. Sometimes 'e never ate for two or three days. It was like that.

He was a totter at first, like his dad. There was quite a few totters round 'ere. Steptoe and Son got his horse and cart from down by the Barn, down by St Anne's Road. That was Chrissy Arnold's 'orse. 'Ercules.

Why totters? Well that's all they could do, innit? Really. 'Cause won't get job in the bank! Ha ha ha …

My dad's family were gypsies. Irish? NAH Romany! Don't ever say that – they'll go mad! Probably my mum's too, if the truth be known. She 'ad dark air and olive skin. Say if it was sunny, if my mum walked from 'ere to Ladbroke Grove she'd be brown.

All the old families round 'ere were gypsies. That's 'ow they come 'ere. They used to do a bit of the talk. I know a bit: 'parny' is rain. You'd go 'Oh, we've 'ad enough parny, ain't we!'. And 'yocks' are yer eyes. And if I go

'All right chavvy mushy' that's 'baby face'. 'Chavvy' is a baby and 'mushy' is your face.

Nowadays they're ashamed to say it. 'Cause they 'ad a bad name as thiefs and that didn't they? And nowadays we ain't. We're so far from it. Although my dad was a thief, I've never nicked nothing in my life. I've never touched nothing that didn't belong to me. That's how my mum fetched me up. 'Cause she said she'd chop me fingers off! Ha ha ha!

My mum was pregnant when my dad got five years. I was three when my Dad come home. I remember as a small child my mum drumming it in my 'ead not to tell anyone me dad was away. And you know, don't tell no one yer business. But see, my mum 'ad epileptic fits. Years ago, the welfare would come round their 'ouses – the poor – and take their children like that. No letter, nothing. My mum was frit of them. She'd say 'The welfare'll be round 'ere..' and you'd be 'Aagh … the welfare lady'.

Mum always worked. Dinner lady at the school. She only worked there 'cause of me. She didn't wanna leave me. Was it hard with my dad away? To be honest, I didn't take much notice. My mum loved me so much that it didn't matter. I didn't even wan' 'im 'ome!

– *Ello Dallin! 'Ow long you've got to go?*
– *Seven weeks!*
– *Seems like the longest, tha's the only trouble. Do you know what yer 'aving?*
– *No. No. 'Aving a surprise.*
– *Little boy.*
– *Yeah?*
– *Yeah, I reckon.*
– *All right then. We'll see.*
– *Yeah! See you later …*

I like people. You can tell I like people innit? I'm a social person. And I 'ave a lot of old people who come up and 'ave a little chat. D'you know what I mean? They're lonely and that.

I started working on the market with my aunt. I done that for a few years. And then this stall come vacant. So I got a bank loan down Barclays and I bought the stall and bought a van … and I paid something to 'im … . Hey, I'm whispering! Oh, you know about 'im. Was 'is name? Wally! My dad writ about 'im over there outside that betting shop. 'E writ on the pavement in chalk. Drew a picture of 'im and said … 'Wally is bent'. 'E got nicked for that my dad.

And another one … 'e got caught at the airport with quarter of a million wot 'e nicked. That's why we're not allowed to give them cash no more up that council office. I 'ave to pay it up the town 'all and take my books up there to get them verified that I paid. Or you pay by card or cheque or direct debit.

Did you know the story of our old swimming baths? They knocked that down illegally. They went the whole length of Silchester Road. Oh it was beautiful. Porchester was a shit 'ole – honestly – compared to our baths. We 'ad all the beautiful Victorian tiles and they was all lead and copper.

There was three swimmin' pools. Different sizes. One was called the tuppenny all-offs; you'd go in there with no clothes on. I never experienced it. I just was told about it.

And there was the washing baths at the end. Where there was baths. We'd 'ave our bath there once a week. Mum would put us in the tin one in the week, a couple of times, but we'd go down there for a bath. 'Cause we only 'ad two rooms.

It was all private: you was in the room with a bath and a wooden bench for yer clothes. They provided soap and you'd ring and they'd give you another lot of 'ot water. You didn't 'ave a tap. You 'ad a big copper spout inside and they'd use a spanner from outside. And she would go 'Mind out, 'ot water coming in' if you rang for it. And you'd move away. There was two classes: first and second class. I don't know the difference; I never went in first class. Maybe you could 'ave unlimited water. In second class, you could only ring once but she was my dad's cousin so we could ring three times.

It's like when I used to go swimming. They'd walk around and go 'You, out! You, out!' That's 'ow they got you out when you'd 'ad yer time. Cos otherwise you'd be in there all day and night. There was nothing else to do – we only 'ad the pool! But me, I could stay in there all the time. And if it weren't 'er on, you could 'ide. When you saw the woman comin' round you'd run in the toilet. Or there was a thing where you walk along and you could jump off so you'd go under there and 'ide from 'er.

Did people shower first? They never done all that! That's why everybody was running alive with verrucas and that, weren't it? 'Cause they must 'ave been rotten. We'd go down there with the school once a week. Some of the kids'd take their socks off. They was rotten! They'd 'ave all tide marks 'ere round their necks. There was some right soapy families round 'ere years ago, weren't they? If someone's soapy, they're rotten. They're bobby cotton. Yeah. But there was loads of them round 'ere.

My Mum also done the washing over there once a week. Scrubbed all the washing. Children weren't allowed in there: the ironers and the big clothes 'orses were all burning 'ot. It was just dangerous. And they 'ad the canteen. The lady'd make 'er own plum jam. You'd go up there for a bit of bread and jam after swimming. Or a cup of Bovril.

That was the hub of my life. They was a big hub of our community. But they was corrupt: the councillor with the metal man. 'Ad a thing going on with back 'anders. They knocked it down quick, overnight. 'E got nicked, the councilor. 'E got two years. But we still lost our baths.

– *'Ello Superman!*
– *That was the major selling point. Let's go to Josie the fruit lady and show her the Superman outfit.*
– *Yeah, let's 'ave a look. Dah Dah Dah … de de da da! He's faster than a bolt of lightning! In 'e cute! She's doing a book … It's for the good of the market …*
– *Oh excellent*
– *Shop at your local SPAR … Don't be a Stepford Wife. Come into the market!*
– *You get rubbish at the supermarket. I bought some plums yesterday. I even cooked them with sugar and it was still horrible.*
– *A farmer told me they show you a picture and they want that apple. They don't care what you put in it to make it look like that. He said 'I could grow a square apple. But when people eat it, they gonna get a pair of titties – men – 'cause it's gonna be 'ormones in it.' Three pound my darling. He's a cute little thing. 'E's like 'is mum.*
– *Bye bye.*

I love kids. Yeah, some kids do hang around the market. Generally they 'ave 'ad a 'ard life. No love, nothin'. And 'ere they get their lunch bought, they got food what they never 'ad before. Plus we're all together. We're like a family. And it's a life where they've not 'ad that life. Maybe they've been left in … like where their mums go out, 'ave parties … just care about theirself. And we're not like that, see. We're different. I don't know why but we love our children. We would never leave our children. We fetch our children up right.

And years ago, you know what you get a lot of? The dimalos. D'you know what a dimalo is? Someone who's a bit mentally retarded. They all used to come 'ere. They'd work for us and we'd pay 'em. You don't need the brains of Lloyd George to work 'ere, do ya! They'd pull the stalls out. They'd do a lot of 'eavy work. It's good 'cause they 'ave a life. You gotta 'ave a lot of patience, though, with them. They could do your brain in … in more than one ways. Like I used to 'ave Fred work for me and they used to call 'im 'Planet of the Apes' because 'e 'ad a big fat 'ead, a big fat face, 'is nose up there and is eyes down like that. Some guy in the market called 'im 101 'cause 'e looked like the little villain from 101 Dalmatians! But that's what I've always known. I was used to them all.

It's like Brian who's 'elping nearby. 'E's a poor thing. And you know what? Two weeks ago this woman come with a man and she said that 'e was a nonce because 'e looks a bit … So the man smacked 'im round the head. But what 'ad 'appened was 'e told 'er husband that she was carrying on with someone and she never forgive 'im. She come down 'ere with a big man and 'e 'it 'im. And now 'e's frit 'cause she said she'd come back. But when she comes back we're 'aving 'er. If she goes near 'im, I'll root her hair out. I'll scurf 'er … And 'e's glad, like, because we'll protect 'im. 'E knows we'll protect 'im.

'Ave you got children?' this woman was shouting out. ''E's a paedophile.' I said, ''Ere love, d'you think we've only known 'im five minutes? We know all his family, love. Now fuck off.' D'you know what I mean?

[sniff] Sorry, the smell … It's not nothing. It's that drain! I don't want you to think … It's stagnant and when the water comes it makes it smell. See, there's a drain right under there. I've got stuff what I should put down. Air freshener, yeah. If people's coming to buy food it isn't nice to smell that, is it? If you want to buy a bit of fruit. So I've got the fruit smell: orange and lemon. Ha ha ha ha ha!

> – *What did you want babe?*
> – *Five pound of cherries.*
> – *Yeah, aw'right. I won't be one minute, Blanche. Can you serve 'im? Would you do two and a half pound in weight?*
> – *Let's 'ear' you 'oller! Let's 'ear you 'oller. C'mon, 'Two pound tomaters!'*
> – *Nobody's going to do it like that*
> – *Nah. Nobody 'as. Nobody 'as.*

'Every day there is a bargain'

VEE, LOCAL RESIDENT

I was born in '33 in the West Indies. I grew up in Trinidad. I actually country person but I went to a school in PortoSpain called St. Rose's. It was the type of school that you have to pay a school fee and up to this day I keep wondering, 'Where did me mum get that money from to pay that school fee?' Because we were real – what you call back home – 'catching your arse'. Things bad. You know – you're scraping. My two brothers went to school local: up St. Joseph's. But it was like she want to give the girl the best. I guess, in her book, it's like what she didn't have she want to give it to me.

From school I worked at a bookshop. Then I work in a big furniture shop and then I came up here. Why? It was the usual thing. You see a little guy and you fancy him badly but he not doing anything. Typical West Indian man. And me mum, she suspected. She wanted better for me.

They had sent people in Trinidad to recruit young girls for nursing. And my girlfriend, Jocelyn, went in for it and got through. She kept encouraging me to come up, come up, come up. In those days you just get a passport and get on a boat. I'd never been nowhere before. I don't know what the hell I was coming to. But I wasn't scared or nothing. I just thought I coming to the Mother Country! That's what they say down there – you going to your mother country. Because in those days, Trinidad – I think the full West Indies – was run by the British.

Because I came here in the winter my friend had sent me a coat. A winter coat! When friends come to visit me, I would go and dress in it and just walk: 'Here comes Miss England!' And we would have a good laugh and say,

'My God, it's so heavy!' Because it felt real heavy. We didn't have no bit o' garment that you would put on down there that that heavy.

I came off the boat and I came straight to Paddington. Jocelyn was there waiting for me and we came straight to Ladbroke Grove. 31 Powys Square. I paid a pound a week for rent. It was about three of us renting one room so we could split it. That was a Rachman house. They say now it was exorbitant rent. I don't know; I couldn't really say the man was nasty because he give me a roof over me head. Nobody else wanted us! When I came here you could see on the windows "Room to Let. No blacks'. Back home I never knew of my colour. I always knew about the Have and the Have-Nots. But you could be black as me arse but you're rich – so you have! Nobody back home had prepared you for this. So it was something new for you to get your head around.

I didn't have much money and I knew I had to get on on me own. Someone had told me about Osrams in Hammersmith taking in staff. I went there, they give me a test and I pass it. There was some valve. Some cathode and anode. You're looking down a microscope at this little ting and you have to make sure that it's straight and it's spinning. And if it's not straight you have a little tweezer to straighten it. It was a fiddly little thing but the pay was five pounds a week. That was enough to pay me rent, buy some food, buy a little top and send a pound for me mum.

I think I was the first black in that section. I remember I had this Mrs Redwood, supervisor lady. Very nice lady. I was in a little hut on me own. A little dark room. And ever so often she'll come and pat me in the shoulder: 'You all right?' Because I heard them talking out there. I couldn't understand what they were saying – to me they was speaking so fast – but I knew they're cussing me. I didn't care. I was too thick skinned to bother. But this supervisor lady always used to come and say, 'Don't worry with them. They're not used to you. When they get used to you …' And she was so right. When they get used to me, the same girl who used to be all the time ponging me whole arse, the same English girl, she become me best friend and she sort of want to stick up for me for anything. I say, look at life eh! And that little bitch hated me so much!

When I arrived, it was so black! The night, it was black. Get up in the morning and still black. Oh my God, how everything so black? It just like the clouds on you. And we used to have this thing they call the smog and the fog. The whole place dark. You just hear footsteps coming. So you're walking but you're keeping your hands out there because you bump into people.

And the people – you see them all on the street in black, black. They didn't have no bright colour to bright up. I dunno why. That was England.

And it was so cold! There was no central heating, no. It's paraffin we had in those days. Paraffin heaters. It was like a lamp that will keep the room warm. Oh my God, that was awful. Everything used to smell of paraffin. It used to be worse when you're going in the morning to go to work: you'll get the train at Ladbroke Grove and when you get in the train, EVERYBODY smell of paraffin.

We used to go to the Electric cinema to keep warm. We called it 'The Bug House'. Oh it had lots of bugs! You would go in there and you would start to itch. It was a dirty little place. But it was cheap! Cheap! And in the winter you trying to pinch on the paraffin.

There used to be problems in no. 31 with a woman who had one room on the side there. In those days you had to put money in the meter for gas for the cooking. And every time you put a shilling in the meter, you boil a little water and by the time you take your tea and you come back out, your shilling finish because she would just use it. You could hear her door open and she bring out a big pot with pig foot – or some hard arsed food – to cook and let it cook until the money finish. Did we get cross? How could you? We were sharing. You had to share the bathroom, share toilet, share kitchen, share everything.

I didn't realise the house belonged to Rachman. Nooo! But I did meet him later. You heard of Michael de Freitas? They say he was one of Rachman bodyguards. I dunno; I knew him from home. It was me lunch break from Osram. Go down to Hammersmith. To Kings Street. And there he was. 'What you doing here girl?' And I like, 'Oh my God!' Because, you see, in those days, whenever you see a blacker's face it was such a big greeting and you're so happy to see somebody your shade around! I'm telling him where I live and I'm looking for somewhere bigger and he tell me to go to Rachman.

I remember going in through the door and there was this big tiger head on the floor. It was a rug. But I'd just come from home so I didn't know. I never saw nothing like that! So I 'Oh…oh…oh!': I think it would come and bite me! This man was sitting behind a big desk. I told him I looking for a place and he ask me, 'You want it for business?' And I, like a fool – I was so green! Just off the banana boat! – said, 'Oh no mister, me I ha' no money to open business!' Ha ha ha! Anyway, he said he couldn't help me. Weeks after I met Michael. The first thing he said: 'What's wrong with you all?

When you gonna realise you're sitting on gold? You can make big money.' I then realised the whole thing was Michael meant for me to open me leg. THAT was the business: he wanted to be my pimp! After that Michael incident I sort of thought, 'Well, who can you trust? This is a guy from home and this is what he wants me to do?'

So I always used to keep me wits about me. There were lots of parties to go to then. Yeah man! All about around this area was buzzing. I was always going down to the clubs about one, two o'clock in the morning and I would boogie all night to every tune. They were shaveens. Something illegal. I remember a few times they raided the place looking for drugs. But I never took none of that. Or Spirits. I thought, 'I don't want to drink or do things that me head go funny and then the next morning I'm looking at you and wondering, 'What did we do? How did we do it?' NO WAY!' So when I'm tired, I just put me coat on. And nobody could say they cover me. Because I know.

I came just before the Notting Hill riots. I remember a day we were coming from work and there was loads of black men out by Ladbroke Grove station. They kept shouting to us, 'Don't come out. Go home. Go home and pray for your brothers.' And I was thinking, 'Why are they saying that?' Not knowing this rioting was going on.

We used to look out the window and see the Teddy Boys, the police, the Blackers, running down the street. And then there was a girl who used to live across the road. An English girl. Nice. Blonde. They marked her house 'Nigger Lover' because she used to go with black guys. My friend Jocelyn used to be so nervous and scared. We had this big old wardrobe. Big heavy time wardrobe. Every night we had to be pulling it by the door!

I don't know what cause it. Some people said that it was because the white girls were going to the black men and the white boys didn't like it. But it stopped when they had that death. Remember Cochrane? He was from the West Indies. He got beaten.

I went back to Trinidad after five years. It was like something in your head telling you, this guy is waiting down there. He'll be ready for you. And he did write. He came up to visit too. But I always say, he never promised me anything. When I got home, well he was so busy. So many women! Like I had to be in the queue. So I came back and I got married to this other guy from Trinidad. I dunno if it was on the rebound. He himself asked me that once and I say, 'Oh I missed the bus. So I take the train'. Which wasn't nice. But all the same. We had the first boy. And then I was pregnant again so I had the second boy. And a tird boy.

From the time I came, I knew the market and I get on with everybody in the market. I remember there was a lady up at the top there. She used to have all little West Indian ting: salt fish; bits of yam; dark shade stockings. I remember Cheryl' parents. I remember Gary's dad. He was so polite and kind. You know when you meet a person like that and he's ready to do anything for you? Like you buy a chicken off him, you want it cut that way, cut this way and he'll do it for you? So where else you going but him?

After the years, me marriage broke down. And when that broke down I was skint. I have three boys to mind. It wasn't easy. The market people were the people who helped me. Up to this morning I was talking to Sheila about it. Sheila make me know what is a slate. When I pass there, I want something to cook for the children, 'Oh Vee, don't worry. I put it on your slate.' I couldn't go to no supermarket and aks for that. And my three boys all worked in the market. Kurt start working with Cheryl' parents. In the evening he'd come with a little bit of fruits, or potato. And Kevin used to work with Dimbo. He also used to bring fruits.

I don't think I have to be grateful forever but as long as I'm around I want to be grateful for that. I'll always want to support the market people. I wouldn't go into Tescos and buy a hand o' banana. NO. Or two oranges or fruits – I WOULDN'T go in there to buy that.

All me weekly food I buy from the market. There's a guy down there. Keith? He there on a Friday and a Saturday. The basmati rice I buy that there. Last week I got lentils. A chunk of cheese. Biscuit, cakes, drinks for me grandchildren – whatever I know they fancy. They're so good to me: they deliver to my door. Fruit and vegetables I usually buy from Cheryl, or I go up to the Golborne Road and they deliver it too.

In the week I come out and I get little tings. Today I went by Alan, because he was telling someone about me. He say, 'Watch her. She's a film star'. Because I'm in that programme 'Off your rockers'. That's a television show on a Sunday. It's old people doing funny things. I'm dressed as a nun on a scooter with this very loud horn and I'm supposed to hit on whoever they tell me. So I'll press me horn and shout, 'Move out the way, you silly twat. God bless you my child!' Then I make the sign of the cross, smile at them and just keep driving on. Yeah, I don't mind doing it! I getting a little money in my hand. How are you go feel silly?

I've been in a few films as well. I was a black witch in Harry Potter. They put the costume on you and they blacken you up. Yeah. All between your fingernails they blacken. I was in the corner; Harry Potter came up that way and we just had to be there like witches making a brew.

How did it all start? I don't know if I give you this story… I used to swim down Kensington every day. And it used to be a group of us. Early birds. People going out to work. And one girl there, she used to run Models One. That's the model agency with Naomi Campbell. A day I saw her and she said to me that Vogue had given her this assignment to look for an old black woman with good skin. She said she'd been in all the churches but everybody, they don't like that. They don't want to be into this thing. So I said, 'I don't mind.'

Me know nothing about that photo shoot. But I went and I did it. They put a lot of makeup on me. All me nails were polished. Beautiful Japanese designer clothes. Issy Miyake. Handmade shoes by so and so. Black pearl necklace by Tiffanys. Earrings that were so many tousands. Diamond this and de de de. Did I like it? Yeah man! It looked good!

But the point is, when I was leaving, me son keep asking me, 'Mum, where you going? Why you dressed that way?' I didn't want him to know. Because I know his mouth is like diarrhoea mouth. He can talk. And I don't want to talk about it. To me this thing could fall through. As I going down the stairs, he shouting, 'Mum where you going?' So I just shout back, 'I going whor – ing!' And I going out! The man is waiting for me downstairs and I just leave him with that!

The magazine came out and he was, 'Mum!!!!' This friend from the swimming was on her way to Ireland and she bought this magazine. She said, 'You are dark horse!' Alan Yentob (I didn't tell you, but I did babysitting for him), he was flying back. So he say on the flight he sat down and when he open the book and he saw my face he couldn't believe it! Vanessa – Richard Branson's sister (I used to babysit for her children too) – called me and she said, 'Vee, my God! I was at the hairdressers and I saw … I couldn't believe it!'

So I went to an agent and then the jobs just start coming. I did a bit with Billy Connolly in an advert for the Lotto. I'm his mum and he's sitting in front of me strumming his guitar. Me husband is at the back. A black man. And he looked at me and said, 'Woman, are you sure that boy is mine?' And I just give him the dirty look. That was 'The Lotto! You take a chance!' And then you remember this girl? What was her name? Keira Knightley. In Love Actually I played her husband's dizzy head auntie. So at one time, I had to be cuddling and kissing her. Just now I was in Alicia Key's video. I was her grandmother. She come to my house and she was helping me in the kitchen, cutting up beans and the music was going 'Girl on Fire'. But up to now I haven't got paid for that.

Is it fun? It all right! You see, the point is, I got in this so late, it don't excite me. The only thing I'm proud about, I getting a little change from it, that I able to help my grandchildren. Because I'm always saying if, when I had those three boys on me own, if I'd hadda help, oh my God! But otherwise, no, I'm not excited about it.

I used to cook for Vanessa. Usually used to do rice and peas for her. Chicken. Fish cake. I'm good at me fishcake – Alan Yentob told me so. He would go to prison for me fish cake he said. And Richard Branson used to have a do up at his country home for all his workers and their family and they give me the job to make tausands and tausands of slices of cake. Rum cake. Ginger. Carrot. Banana. I made it ALL. At the time I'm saying to myself, 'What the hell you put yourself in? You think you could manage that?' But I did it!

Sometime I make cakes or I cook up tandoori chicken and certain people I know on the market, I give it to them. Like Cleo. She sell nice dresses and thing. Right at the corner of Oxford Gardens. I think it's last year she got married. On her wedding day, this beautiful dress she was wearing, she got that from Ebay for a pound or something. The dress was lovely! Now she would want a vegetarian meal. And Paul – he sell cashmere – I make him any little thing to eat and he love it. I could give him a spicy meal. And you know the spice shop? That's Philip's shop. Any little ting I cook and I take for Philip he's like, 'Mmm! Oh boy, this is SO good.'

I go most days. That's my daily exercise. Like my routine. I come out and I get little tings. And I always getting someting. I always looking for a bargain and GETTING it. Because every day there is a bargain somewhere, somehow. Me friend will come to the house, 'Where did you get this?' 'Portobello Road'. 'Where did you get that?' 'Portobello Road.' She say, 'EVERYTHING from Portobello Road?' I say, 'Everything from Portobello Road!' Plates. Cup. Saucer. Old Stool. Every flipping thing in the house I get it from Portobello Road.

Well I'm gonna love you now and leave you. I brought you some chicken. And a yoghurt cake. You're welcome! If you like it, any time you have a party, or you know anybody having anything, I'm your caterer! Right? Tell them anything West Indian, I can make it. So keep in touch…

'Have you seen my Facebook page?'

PAUL, LOCAL RESIDENT

These are my hobbies: cooking and essential oils. Essential oils are very potent; I rub them all over me. It's hard to know quite how they make a difference because I do a lot of healthy things so I'm not quite sure which one is the more profound … But the oils definitely help to centre you and boost your life force. I'm convinced of that.

I find the whole idea of ingesting goodness and absorbing goodness fascinating. So every day you're taking care of yourself by ingesting the right food and you're also absorbing the right oils at the same time. And often the oil is the same as the food: basil, rosemary, thyme. Marjoram as well. But I avoid marjoram because it's lousy for libido.

Have you seen my Facebook page? I try to inspire my friends in terms of everything that's coming into the market.

Chard came in last week. Wet walnuts are coming in from France. The prickly pears seem to be around. A lot of different varieties of cauliflower are coming in. The purply cauliflower. But I don't eat that to be honest – it's a bit too recherché. The damsons have just arrived, which is great. I buy kilos of them and boil them all up and then I put the juice into ice trays and use them in the winter on ice cream. Or damson base with an upside down sponge. Wicked. I don't touch asparagus now because it's all coming in from Chile. So asparagus is over for me really. There are plenty of alternatives. I ask where everything's from; most of the time they know.

Monday and Fridays are the buying days: the two days I do my Pilates. If I'm doing a day like that I eat a banana and a load of houmos. Separately. Houmos is great. It's what the Lebanese farmers go to the fields with. I get through three to four tubs a week from Mr Christian's. If I'm in a hurry I'll just use my teaspoon and scoop it. Because I'm really just using it to put energy inside me, ready for Pilates. And a banana; Potassium. What does that do? I've no idea but I'm told it's good for you. You're off to Pilates and you've got all that lovely houmos and the banana lining your stomach. Grab a detox tea from the Coffee Plant and walk to the exercise.

Come back from the exercise and eat again. Fried eggs or some other food. Then go down to the market. Roam around the stalls. Maybe Lynn's and Eddie's. Then I'll go up to the place opposite The Coffee Plant as well just to see if he's got something interesting in. He has some good juicy limes there. And then I conjure up the meat that I've bought from the Farmers Market or the Ginger Pig, and then I just piece it together thinking, 'That would be nice with that. That would be good with this.' Hmm. Hmm. Mmm. Mmm. And that's a moment of therapy. Just thinking about nothing else except how you're going to plan the food for the rest of the week or the weekend. It's really relaxing.

How long? Depends how inspired I am. Whether or not I'm hitting it quickly or whether I'm having to search it out. I walk around the stall several times in a day – on the buying days – before I make my decision. It's part of the ritual. Thirty, forty-five minutes around those stalls one way or another.

Here's Facebook. My personal page. See, that's from the market. That's endive with pastise. It's a thigh and leg of chicken – organic from Waitrose. And that is endive that has been sweated, gently, in the juice from this chicken and then, as it's started to soften, throw some pastise into it and just let it all … come together … in a big wok.

That's a sarsaparilla and vodka cocktail that I invented. I wanted to come up with a cocktail that was good for energy at the same time as depleting the vodka. So that's it. That's vodka, sarsaparilla, lime juice, a little agavi and an egg white – shaken. Oh, and passion fruit. The passion fruit's from the market. The chap opposite the coffee shop. They just looked like they'd be pretty fruity.

Those are the wet walnuts. They're quite bitter. You put them in a salad of rocket and bits and pieces and maybe you can use some orange zest, just to give it that little fragrance. They're great for ravioli. Mix them in the filling. And that's a lamb stew. There's some chard in there, I think. There's some tomato. There might even be some fennel as well. I did this vacuum packed style. I got a vacuum bag from a friend with a kitchen and then I fried off the meat very quickly – just to get some colour on it – put it into the vacuum bag, with a whole bunch of vegetables and seasoning and tomato puree and tomatoes, and then immersed it into a bain-marie and cooked it for eight hours. It makes a very delicate stew. It's great.

That's black olives with aubergines. It looks quite mysterious doesn't it? It looks like an asp could come crawling out of there. And I tried it with some white truffle oil. That's gravadlax I made. That's Lynn's dill.

What am I hoping to do with my page? Just inspire people to get inspired by food and the local community. They've got the market stalls here. It's all available. They're just little foodie tips. And it inspires people overseas. Some people come to the market because of it. There was a smoked fish stall that opened for two or three weeks. On one of the days they said 'I think most of the business we've done today is because of you.' Their smoked mackerel was fantastic – best I ever had. So it's just about inspiring people to enjoy themselves and cook.

You know the first time I came to Portobello was when 192 was open. Because I used to live in Campden Hill Square, I used to pop down to have supper at 192. It was all quite crucial over here, back in the day. And I wasn't that crucial. It was quite edgy wasn't it? Seemingly.

Then I moved to Dorset for fifteen years, while the children were growing up. A director friend had just rented a flat opposite The Electric and he said 'Paul, go and have a look at these flats. You'll be surprised. It's not noisy. It's got very good ambience coming up from the street: people enjoying themselves and chatting and village life.' So when one of the flats became available I popped up and had a look at it and thought 'Yeah. This is great.' And I bought it.

I love living right on the market. I don't have any issues with noise up there at all. It's not traffic noise. I've got double glazing on the front, in case on Saturday you want it to be a little quieter. Because there are a lot of street buskers. If you're not that keen on what they're singing, you might want to quieten it down a little.

I say hello to everybody in the market if I come home late – which doesn't happen very often. Lynn gets there at 3.30 on Saturday, 3.45. It takes that long to put the stall up. I go 'Morniiiinng!' and then I go to bed! Or I'm on the terrace in the summer and there's a few of us up there after the Electric, or whatever it happens to be, and before you know it the sun's coming up. I don't do that very often. I wouldn't like to give the wrong impression. But it's quite nice, when you've got a balmy summer night, to sit on the terraces up there and call down to the market traders as they're all arriving.

In the summer, when I'm on the terrace, I'm seeing the whole life of Notting Hill going up and down. The rituals and who says hello to who. Brilliant.

I know the stretch in front of me and a few down at the far end. I try to buy from everybody. It's great. It's a really strong sense of community that you get, I think, with that market. It's particularly reinforced for me because I walk out of my door and immediately I'm saying, 'Hello, Hello, Hello.' Within ten seconds. So even on a lonely day, when you might be feeling a little miserable, you always know that you can roam around and talk to at least fifteen people. That's really nice.

She's very fit, Lynn. You should see her in the morning. Back and forth, back and forth, back and forth. It's amazing. Eddie's always the same. Breezy. Resigned. He knows how to talk to his clients. And who's the loud one? Cheryl! Blimey. The language that comes out of her mouth if someone offends her – it's something else, isn't it? She does it with such aplomb. If somebody annoys her – just takes them apart! I buy from her on the days when Lynn's not there. She supplies the Electric with a lot of fruit and vegetables. And there's a stall on the next block that goes down to Westbourne Park Road. She caters for a slightly different audience at that end so you'll see some more exotic items in there. She's the one to get prickly pears from. She's also the one to get gooseberries from and hob nuts. What else has she got? Fresh turmeric. Really good purple garlic. It's on my route to Pilates so I always have a quick look and see if there's something coming in.

I'm probably eating a greater variety of food now. Down in Dorset, although everybody talks about Hugh Fearnley-Whittingstall and all the Dorset food, actually you have nowhere near the variety that we have on Portobello road. You aren't going to find prickly pears in Dorset, that's for sure. And those little baby aubergines, in front of Coffee Plant.

I stay off the street on Saturday. I go nuts. They're all ambling along at half a mile an hour. They all stand outside my door, stuffing themselves with hot dogs. I've got a very loud 'Excuse me!'

Supper tonight? I've got two small sirloin steaks from the Ginger Pig. I haven't decided what's going to go with it yet – I've got to go and look at the market. Almost certainly some chard. Chard can be quite nice by adding some maple syrup to it, making it quite sweet. My mouth's watering now, thinking about that.

I've got a big sausage roll that I bought from The Ginger Pig for lunch today. That's going to be great. I don't like to feel full. I hate that feeling of feeling full. I think it's the quantity of food we eat that's the biggest problem.

Big portions. Second portions. Not pacing yourself throughout the meal. Allowing yourself to get to a point when you're so hungry you end up eating like a hyena and then you think, 'Oh God, I'm feeling full' because you've catapulted yourself into eating too much food. If I feel hungry, I have to eat. I go to the fridge. Open the houmos.

'Every day is a battle'

LES, SOLDIER, SALVATION ARMY

I must be one of the most photographic person in Portobello Road. Since the film, there's more tourists now then there are British people out here. I've had pictures go round the world. I've had pictures come back from Russia, Australia …

You don't have to wear a uniform but everyone does. It's a way of showing outward that you're a group of people that will … fight is not the right word … but will … stand up for their beliefs. Do I like it? It's okay. Can be a bit confusing sometimes with traffic wardens and things like that, but most people recognise it. I had mine made; they don't quite come up my size.

I was born in Bow. My mum was working in the local sweet factory over there, Dad working in the local brewery in Whitechapel. I left school when I was fifteen and worked on a barrer down in what used to be called Club Row – a big Sunday morning market. I used to get up at half past three in the morning and pull seven stalls. Then I went and worked in a metal foundry; I worked on a building site as a labourer; I was doorman on a cinema.

I moved when I got married – thirty years ago. I worked for the council for a short time, collecting the rubbish. I done the stint down the market. It was raining and I slipped over on a wet cabbage leaf: busted me ankle. And then they sacked me for leaving the route without permission. Because the supervisor was too busy up the pub; we couldn't find him. I went into a couple of other jobs then I had a heart attack so I had to give up work.

I was bored so I come here one day. On a Friday they used to do a jumble sale – teas and all that. I got talking to one of the old ladies. I remember her saying 'There's always a place for you; all you gotta do is find it. And you can only find it if you're walking it with the Lord.' I started getting interested. I thought to myself 'Well, look around. They're all happy so there must be something in it.' I can't say 'I saw a mighty light' and all that. To be honest, I didn't. I just felt in myself. I was happy when I was here and you just know that's the way to go.

I was an adherent for three years and then I took the decision to be a soldier. It's like levels of faith in a way. An adherent – yes, they wanna become a member of the congregation, but they don't wanna get too involved. Whereas a soldier says 'I wanna become a member of this church. I wanna get involved in the growth and the moulding of it.' In a way, an adherent is more important than a soldier. With a soldier, you've already converted them, shall we say, in a way, whereas adherents are sort of fifty-fifty. It's like the battle. It's no good preaching to someone who's already a believer. You get out to the ones who's not the believers. Every day is a battle. Oh definitely. Not a battle as in punching up or fights – it's a battle against evil. There's always people who wants to put you down because you believe.

I started volunteering here when I become soldier. On a Friday we have a coffee shop. There's plenty of coffee shops in Portobello Road but not everyone can afford two, three pound for a cup of coffee. Plus you can't take buggies in and when you go in they want you out straightaways. Whereas you can come here, you can have a cup of tea or a coffee, a sausage roll, bit of toast or whatever, soup, a chat – it's more like a community meeting place.

The local vendors are always coming for their tea because they've got nowhere. Plus there's no toilet for them. The reason why we keep the toilets locked is there's a lot of drugs around. They buy their drugs; they come in our toilet; they shoot up, whatever. We know 'cause of the length of time: if they're injecting theirself, they're normally out for about an hour or so. Come in for a cup of tea, yes. But you're not allowed to smoke in here; you can't drink in here. If you're a drug user, you're a drug user. We won't criticise you but we will say 'No, you can't do it here.'

And what is the best place to hide something like that? They know that we're not going to get searched. When we shut down, we had it remodernised. When they ripped the toilets out, they found hidden drugs. It's the main reason why them toilets across the road are shut down. 'Cause they done a police raid and they come out with three bags full of syringes and that. It's one of the darker sides of the area but it's improving. It's not so much evident now than when it was in the late 1970s, '80s. We were having literally a battle then – 'NO, this is our … and you're not coming in' –

because when we were doing the homeless meals they used to try to intimidate the weak and the homeless people for money or to carry their drugs as runners and that.

Plus there's other things going on what we don't agree with. Like, a few months ago, we found a couple in the toilet making love – well, if that's what they wanna call it. I saw a woman go in. All of a sudden I thought 'I'm sure I saw a man there just now.' I thought 'Ah, he's gone into the Gents.' Then I noticed the gents toilet key was still hanging up and I'm thinking 'NO!' So as I've come out I could hear, obviously, the noise so then I just asked them to sort of vacate the premises. I was very, shall we say, diplomatic about it. They just come out and they were laughing. They looked quite respectable. It could have been they were playing a game – go and find the most unusual place or most risky place. Who knows! So obviously, we've got to sort of keep it safe for people who genuinely need to use it.

This is a church. 'Cause we've only got one little building, we've gotta use the one hall for everything. We're not a very big core at the moment because we've been shut for such a long time. Now we're starting to build it back up and we're getting out to the community more. So it's more, I think, back to the roots, getting out to meet people. Some people are not comfortable walking in because they're homeless and they may be a bit … um … personal hygiene may not be … 'cause they live on the street. So we will go out to them and we'll talk to 'em.

We got two regular homeless that'd come in, get their coffee, go out. To start with. But now they're coming in and they're staying for a bit. A little chat and that. Then they'll wander off and then they'll come back for a bit longer. And each time it's that slowly, slowly catching monkey sort of thing. If they convert, that's a bonus. But if not, it doesn't matter. As long as they know there's someone here who will be concerned about them.

Saturday's I normally stand out and collect. I sell War Cries – what helps to pay for the upkeep of the building, the lights, the coffee, tea and all that. And again it's another way of saying 'We're here to talk if you wanna talk.' And you do get people come up. Personally, I will not force my beliefs onto anybody. If they don't wanna talk about Christ or that, then that's fine. If they wanna talk about the weather, it's contact. But you hope that within time you can persuade them that you're better off with Christ in your life than not with him. If they join the Salvation Army all very well and good, but if I can persuade someone to go to church regular and praise the Lord, that is the battle won.

How much do we take? It varies. Sometimes it's not even worth collecting, to be honest. I think the littlest has been about £3, £4. But, as I say, you're not there just for the money; you're there so people can see. Sometimes you get the odd jeer like. They want to shout at me, they shout at me. I don't mind. While they're shouting at me, they're leaving other people alone. All I do, if it gets too offensive or that, I just come in shut the door. They soon go away.

You still get a lot of the old timers come down and have a little chat. There's one, bless him, always comes down and puts a 10p in the box. And that was for the cup of tea that someone gave him on Dunkirk. They had the wagons out then. He's just one of the locals. I haven't seen him for a while I must admit … so he may of … gone.

Has it changed my life? Definitely. I'm more, shall we say, contented. Before I used to get very short tempered with people. Everyone used to be able to wind me up just so easy. But now it's water off a duck's back. Now I have inner peace. I know that, with the Lord's help, I can handle anything. You may think you're on your own but you're never on your own. It's like that old 'Footsteps': You was with me then You left me … The proof is there's only one pair of feet in the sand. The answer to that is 'No, that's when you were down and I was carrying you.' It don't matter how bad you are, there's always someone you can turn to. That's the important thing.

'Everyone is treated the same'

NICK, MARKETS MANAGER

I was Security Supervisor for American Airlines. I was signing for something like 300–400 people's lives on a plane. I had to give over a document saying that all passengers were fit to fly and the flight was secure. When 9/11 happened, I watched it on TV in the baggage control room in Heathrow. From then it was a downward spiral: they shrunk the number of flights and I was made redundant.

It was a bit of light relief. In fact, when I had my debrief, one of the guys said to me, 'Nick, the whole world's been removed from your shoulders. You look quite different'. And now I look to Portobello Road where I'm semi in control of, say, something like two to three hundred traders and forty thousand visitors. Sometimes when I stop and think about that you kind of go 'Hold on, have I actually improved my life in terms of what I control?' But I have.

The council is the custodian of this world which is Portobelloville, or whatever you want to call it. Disney World. Portobello World. Many times I've joked with the traders 'If we put a barrier at the top and charged everyone a pound for coming down the hill, we'd all be rich!' Monday to Thursday it's a local market, with a number of tourists who haven't read the tourist books and go 'Where's the market?' Friday's second hand and Saturday is their attempt to become the next Lord Sugar.

How does it work? Well, to become a casual trader people come in to say 'I want to sell something.' We ask them for details. If it's an obvious thing that we have a mass of – such as ladies fashion – we'll just say there and then 'Unfortunately, we've got enough of that.' If you've got something special, we'll consider it. We ask people to email so that we have kind of a filter mechanism.

What have we said No to? We've had one guy wanting to sell puppies. We had one guy wanting to do proper tattoos on the street – and we've gone 'Gotta be joking!' In terms of the kind of bizarre products, we've had a stall selling a whole collection of leather dog collars and different things for dogs. We're talking £40-£50 upwards All top notch stuff which you kind of stop and go 'On a market stall?' But it worked for a little while. We had someone who wanted to do … um … dress up kind of stuff … the latex variety and that kind of thing … which lasted a few weeks with a few wigs and different things. We stopped them short of the toys though. That's one of the sensibilities that I do have. If I'm walking along with my eight year old and my five year old and they go 'What's that?' I don't want to have to explain to them. The basic premise in the back of my head is a grandma, a mum and a daughter. If it gets through those different ranges, then you're okay. And that's what you should have at the back of your head. Because it's important to make it a family market, as it were.

What do people get upset about? Fakes. Counterfeit goods. Watches, bags, you name it. It's mostly watches and bags. Our trading standards have picked up on a few being sold in the second hand section. Kind of been put in 'Oh yeah, it's a Louis Vuitton but it's a second hand one.' It's not; it's brand new and you're selling it as something else.

Another thing people complain about is being short changed. Cash allows that flexibility for traders to … um … be creative, shall we say … In fact recently we've had Trading Standards come through to ensure that everyone follows a clear pricing regime, that weights and measures are being respected, that scales are correct. What did they find? They found one that shouldn't ever be used. They found a number still using imperial measure which, technically, is illegal. However this wasn't a creative exercise in creating more metric martyrs. It would be nice and it was suggested, and advice and education, but it's not about coming down like a sledgehammer to say you need to throw away that and you need to buy a new one and all your pricing needs to be priced up in kilos, which a number of people choose not to understand or wouldn't understand – in terms of locals.

Those customers who have built up a relationship with certain traders know what they're getting. Those who are new to the market and are trying out different things could easily be led down the wrong way. Someone once came here and said 'By the time I got home, all the mushrooms already were rotting.' And you're like going 'Where did you get them from?' And it all came out and we had the conversation and the costermonger's reply was

'What'd she want? It's a pound a bowl.' And I'm going 'No, that's not the idea.' That's where you kind of want to say to them 'Stop and have a think.'

Do you remember the Fresh carts? That was supported by the Mayor's office and by Rosie Boycott. The whole premise was taking the bowl concept one step further by actually packaging the items in biodegradable materials and putting a clear price on it. So it's not up for anyone poking around in it. It's not up for abuses of price, of scales, or the costermongers' adding up. It's quite plain to see that's one pound, that's two fifty, that's one fifty. Now for anyone adding that up, it's straight forward.

We bought into the concept because we saw that it was offering some thing new, something fresh for costermongers to rise up to. These guys were in uniforms. They all had tabard aprons. Not whatever the trader picked up last night to put on, but all clean and presentable.

The costermongers here trashed it. They hated it. They said it didn't fit in. It wasn't a proper fruit and veg stall. It wasn't good for the image of the market. The reality is, the odd few people who bumped into us and talked to us about it said 'This is wonderful. I know what I'm getting now. I don't have to suffer the fruit and veg traders' dirty hands.' It got removed from Portobello Road though. It wasn't making money. It was difficult to compete against the pound a bowl and the other fruit and veg traders.

The antique traders are a world of their own and they're very insular and individual. There are lots of traders who are good at what they sell and know what they're selling. And there are those who come in, copy other people's ideas and start flogging them. They do have to sign a declaration stating that their goods are over 50 years old and the idea of spot checking often gets mooted. It is difficult and, again, it goes down to the issue of the council meddling. See, everyone wants the protectionism of the council. But the minute the council does something: 'Oh, you're meddling.' It's very difficult to persuade them … to say 'If you want the quality, and if you want to be known still as the World Famous Antique Market, you need to main'tain that quality as traders yourself. And be unscrupulous about your neighbours.' But they're not. They don't want to be involved with anyone.

There are some traders out there who are struggling. The whole way we shop has changed. Congestion charge took out a large chunk of shopping. You've also got the issue of parking. We stopped certain metres for four Saturdays, going back two or three years, so that parking bays came free. Who used and abused them? The retailers and the traders! Instead of … duh … letting the shoppers come and park to shop, the retailers just parked there all day!

Mugging's a problem around the area. Pickpockets are the major issue for the market as a whole. You do get a team of officers from the police who work in plain clothes to target the problem. But tourists are tourists. Cash points are cash points. That's why a lot of that trade happens very early – because you don't get many thieves who are up that early in the morning. That would be a surmise. As well, it's before most of the crowds have arrived. The antique guys do suffer. But, then again, so do the other street traders because only a human being is standing between a robber taking the takings … and that's it. And then you have the stories of a member of staff helping themselves. And because it's a cash society, it's a problem.

It's amazing the stupidity and gullibility of tourists in dealing with tricksters. Follow the lady or the matchbox tricks – those kind of gambling games. You have three matchboxes and a plant in the crowd will go 'Oh, I think it's there.' Put twenty pounds out and then, all of a sudden, all the stupid tourists go, 'Yeah, this works.' The fact they come from Spain and Italy and France where, for the most part, Eastern bloc tricksters operate anyway … you're going 'They're tricking you, conning you.' They do it on a rug or carpet and it's all very flexible so if the police turn up they can put it in their pocket and make their way. So we went through a phase of actually grabbing the carpet or the match boxes or the item. Sometimes they'd have spares but if we managed to grab all three, then they were stuffed. Some of them did decide to follow us and we'd turn round and go 'Yes? And your problem is? Would we like to talk to the police about this?' And the minute you mention the police … And then we upped the ante and the police actually arrested a number of them.

Same as DVD sellers. We went through a phase of having those out on the street. Now they're going into shops and pubs where we don't have any jurisdiction. But when they were on the street we could prosecute them for illegal street-trading because they weren't on a pitch, just standing on a street corner with a whole armful of DVDs. And you go up to them in their little English. 'Are you selling them?' 'No'. 'Are you giving them away then?' 'Oh … Yes.' And then you just shout out 'Anyone fancy a DVD?' And you start giving them out. And then they'd realise what is happening, quickly put them away and run away. And that's the kind of justice that we like. 'Cause you know they're in a tricky spot, half those people, because they're doing it under coercion or whatever. Do you go through the system? You'd like to think that the system would actually work and stop them doing it in the future, but it's very limited.

I never forget, when I first started, there used to be the guys with the wire coat hangers which they'd make into names or shapes or flowers. And we had a whole pile of them on Portobello Road. We arrested one on one of the first weekends that I actually did here when I was in plain clothes with my colleague and the police officer. So, illegal street trading. Of course he didn't speak English or have a name or address so we had to take him to the police station. In fact, we took him all the way down to Chelsea. We spent two or three hours there. Eventually an interpreter came along. The person was wanted by immigration, but not seriously enough, so wasn't going to be picked up by them. We did our interview but the reality was, getting a prosecution out of it wasn't really going to happen. Custody sergeant wrapped it all up 'Be on your way. Don't do it again.' Came outside, this guy goes to us 'Where's the nearest tube station please?' The police officer just said 'Mate, on your bike ... ' words to that effect. Thankfully, as he said at the time, he didn't have his truncheon with him or he would have walloped him one. And that took a whole afternoon. That's the problem of the system. Doing things that are going to knock it on the head or cause them a problem is often more effective than going down the full police avenue. I really don't enjoy saying that, but that's the way it operates.

I've been threatened on the odd occasion. In the summer, one of my officers was assaulted by a busker. Yeah, it happens. If ice cream vans just pull up and are waiting for trade, then it's illegal street trading. They have baseball bats, they have samurai swords, they have all sorts of things in them. No, they're not very nice people. Yes, okay, they've got to make a living but they don't go about it very nicely.

Drugs? I think there is a still a feeling that you can go into certain places where you can still pick up what you need. They aren't as visible as they used to be. Certain rundown buildings and squats and other houses have been closed down. I would say the problem has been diminished but it's still there. You get stories that some traders are involved in it. Some traders are part of it. Some traders actually stick it up their nose. It's there. It's not something that you can say doesn't happen. It's part of the society that makes up Portobello and Golborne Road, fortunate or unfortunate. If anyone gives us information we will feed it up the ladder straight away. It's not our world to get involved in because then I'm pushing the boundaries of our powers and also the Health and Safety of my team. We've got enough with ice creamies and their baseball bats, let alone going to deal with drug dealers and the other like. I think it would be quite entertaining to turn up to a drug dealer

and go 'Do you have a street trading licence for that?!' And I think they'd most probably say 'No' and there we go.

There were remnants of the old guard still here when I arrived. There was also a history in terms of … . things happening. Changes being made in terms of traders' location or someone changing their commodity into a more profitable commodity, even though really they shouldn't be allowed to. And it gets authorised without question … which suggests that certain officers weren't doing their job correctly. Market managers – going back three market managers – were all known to be, shall we say, lining their pockets and helping themselves. So goes the folklore of Portobello Road …

Back then it was distinctly them and us. There is a different understanding of the relationship between the council and the street traders now. We're a younger crowd. We're not all ex-police or ex-military. We're more willing to listen and to resolve things.

When I first arrived I was quite an officious kind of chap who'd have blazing rows with people in the middle of the street. It was that kind of test period, for market inspectors to establish where they're at. Now I think I'm respected by most traders. I'm referred to by many as 'Mr Nick'. 'Mr Nick, can you do this for me? Can you do that?' I've signed people's passports. I've helped people's inquiries into housing benefit and other things like that. And, when they're financially up against it, we can sit down and talk through the different scenarios.

In more recent times, in terms of approach, when you're telling someone off and they feel aggrieved and, straight away, the race card gets played, I remind them that, one, my name's Kasic. I'm not Brown or Smith; I'm a first generation. Born here, from immigrants. I know how difficult life is, okay? And, secondly, if I, as it were, am harassing you, well I've harassed him, him, him and him. So everyone is treated the same.

'The beat goes on'

JEROME, TIN PAN PLAYER

Excuse me, I'm smoking my spliff. You don't mind it's a spliff? My son don't smoke; my sisters don't smoke – it's just the rebels like me. Not supposed to be smoking. I suppose to be a good boy. I should have stayed in school instead of studying to go and play pan!

I was born in Trinidad 'round 1950 ... 1952 actually. I was about ten and the carnival was on. And this guy was playing this bass pan. He was playing it so smooth and so much style. And I'm standing there, saying to myself 'I have to be able to play pan better than him.'

My friends in the area they were playing with this band. I was not allowed because I was going to a well-known college in Trinidad. There's no way my parents would allow me to go in the pan yard: only the vagabonds and dregs of society will go associate themselves with that.

My friends went and I begged them so they bought me a tenor pan back. A neighbour showed me one tune. I just started playing it, over and over, annoying everybody of course. From then I just kept on playing my pan. I left college before GCS. I was not too friendly with Latin and Physics and Chemistry and I wanted to go in a pan yard. And the person who's teaching me my first tune in the panyard is the same guy who's playing the bloody bass! His name was Roxy Bellgrove: he was captain of the band! I had a good laugh.

A pan yard is just like a tent. You had to do a design and send it into the borough council to get permission or else they'll come and break it down. The roof is flat: flat corrugated iron or anything we could get to go on top there to keep out the water and the sun. More likely to keep out the sun because it was old, discarded, corrugated sheets you're getting and it used to leak when it rained. Nobody is buying proper sheets to put on no panyard. No way! You look up – it's a strainer! But it's to keep the sun off the instrument because they're heated when they're made and when the sun hits it, it tends to change the pitch of the notes.

I learned to do sign painting in the pan yard. Wire bending and decorating costumes – all in the panyard. I did any conceivable thing to make money. But I learned to make pans here.

I start with this. This is a steel drum. They make them to put chemicals and whatever in. When they're making them to take chemicals they usually come with a hole to empty it, but we order them completely flat.

My bit is the banging bit. First I get this concave. I use a steel cannonball for that, bought on Golborne Road. It's just like bouncing a ball. Once you hit it against the metal it bounces back up again and you just keep guiding it. Then you mark the notes out – so much and so much inches. When you finish, wrote all of that, you have to hammer this back. 'Cause then you shape the notes. I just try to keep it smooth. You don't want it veining up because what you get is, like if you bend wire, after time, where the point it gets, then breaks. It happens very easily sometimes. You made a hole here: you have to condemn it, throw it away.

When it's finished, the tuner cuts the drum to the right length and he will widen it a bit. You need room depending on how many notes you're making on the inside. Then he puts the notes in: he actually gets the sound to come out. And then he heats it. Because the molecules have been hammered about and messed about with, you need to heat it so it knits back itself. And when he heats it, that sound disappears. When it cools down, and he pushes it back up where he wants it to be, the sound will automatically be right round the corner.

It's nice, good; it's cool. You're just on your own. No worries. You're banging daylights out of the pan and it cannot say anything!

What do I think when I'm hitting? Various things. Sometimes I might have done something that I'm annoyed about myself with. So I hammer … I'm abusing myself verbally in my head, cursing myself. 'Why you so stupid?' … 'Silly, why you do such a silly thing? Shhhttt' … 'Why did you do that?' Various things go through your mind but I still have to concentrate on what I'm doing. You have to remember 'DON'T BURST THE DRUM! Make sure you don't put any holes in!' And then I'm thinking 'I have to go outside and have a rest. What's the time? And how soon it have to finish? It have to be done, let's finish it!'

I don't hurt people – usually meself I hurt. All the time I hurt meself! That's why it's bevexed. Sometime I go and I do silly things – probably gambling or some kind of thing. I'm annoyed with myself for that. Or I was supposed to go somewhere and I didn't do what I was supposed to do. It upsets your day. Let's pull the door a bit. You'll have to hide inside … because I don't want too much noise going out.

BAM … BAM … BAM … BOING … BOING … BOING … BAM … BAM … BAM …

Who invented the steel pan? Now that is a very, very impossible question to say that one person did it. They accredit it to one person, a guy by the name of Spree Simon, this in the '30s. Because he played the first recognisable melody, they say he is the father of pan. But people say that loads of other people, they're making steel pan at the time. It all happened because of the Carnival. They used to use bamboo. They cut the bamboo certain lengths and they'd be making music with it; they'd be playing this rhythm. The guys who started the steel pan, they didn't go and cut any bamboo. And Tuesday morning, Carnival morning, they came out and decided to go. So they took their mother's dustbin and started beating on it and, by mistake, they found that by beating on the drum it created a separation in the metal and you got different notes. That's how they started doing it.

They have over one hundred calypsonian in Trinidad and every year they do at LEAST two calypsos new. Brand new songs. Some do ten! So just imagine all this – I think they have to start to recycle now! And the costuming is the same way: every year there's a new costume. Some play military mask. They play history. Some people come with fantasy. Some even go back to Jurassic Park! Some people play American Indian mask year in, year out. There are some of those that play original and then they have fancy. The original look authentic-like, like the first Americans, exactly how they look, how they depict them in the movies – exactly like that. Some go more in depth and they copy everything. I know a guy he does the beading. Copy everything exact, exact, exact. The one who make the shoes, the moccasin, exact. Actually, he carry it a bit further. He's dressed like that whole year, call himself 'Crazy Horse'! That is his love, his thing. There those who play the fancy Indian. Now, as well, there's falling pieces decorated with rhinestone and glass and all sorts of thing, and needlework and all that sort of thing they're going through. And every year they change it!

Could you be dressed up as a Red Indian but playing calypso? Yeah! It's still calypso music – the dressing up is to go to competition. Trinidadians are mad! Lookin' at it that way, it's funny really!

Calypso actually originated in Africa. The original world is kaiso – in Trinidad we call it calypso. I think it has much more of a French influence in it then. And we have this calypso beat: it's a four-time beat. Calypso in the true sense is a commentary and basically they'll comment on anything. The humorous ones will say about two flies, about monkeys – all sort of real humorous topics. The social commentary will be what happened to a husband and wife and if there was a third party involved, what all that will go down. Then you have the political one – they will go behind politics. One guy did a song about Bin Laden. I have the record … 'Bin Laden … the dark boy … why you mash up the trouble in people place? The rude boy … the bad boy … etc.' It's a nice song 'cause they're telling Bin Laden they're looking for him because he mash up the place. Why he come in the people party and mash up the place? The 9/11 – they were commenting on that. You have to read it because there's a lot of double, lot of triple, meanings. They tell you everything there's going down. There's even one guy, he foretold that one day's going to have a black president in America. And he sang that four, five years before Obama got elected. His name is Crazy. They say that his songs are very rude because he's using expletives. He had one like 'They're looking fur King Crazy.' What he's saying? His name is Crazy … so everybody looking for him! 'They're looking for King Crazy, because he's a calypso king.'

How did I get to Portobello? I was a foundation member of the band 'Skiffle Bunch'. We came to England in '86 on tour. A friend took me down to Portobello Market – oh, it was nice and lovely there! It had loads of people milling around. Not like now: now it's packed with people! We came back here '87, '88 then '91, '92, '93, '94, '96 touring England, Scotland, Wales, Germany, France, Italy, Austria, Switzerland – all these places, just in and out, as far as Malaysia, and Singapore. In 1996 I decided to stay here to go to college and do some music. College was about two hours a week. The rest of the week I'm free. I started playing on Portobello 'cause I needed something to do.

I go when I can. Another day – it's sunny and nice. I have nothing to do today so I gonna practise in Portobello. When is the next gig coming? Who is coming to give me the next gig? Come on someone! Okay, no gig today. All right. Practise tomorrow again. Say hello to people, have a laugh. Get paid too! Because people appreciate it.

You stay there for about three hours, you will get five pounds. There's no way that you wouldn't get five pounds. Only if rain falling too hard forget it. Because everyone's studying to hold their umbrella: nobody have no time to go in no pocket. Forget that. Don't think they're going to feel sorry for you! If snow is falling, well you definitely guarantee you're getting that.

I play melodies. I only play them twice and I go onto another song. So when people are coming up, by the time they reach me from the corner they hear 'bout four, five songs. Songs from the '60s, the '20s, the '30s and Elvis Presley – it takes them back to all those years where they probably hear their parents singing, and hear it playing on the radio – the little box radio at home.

People ask me questions. They want to know where the instrument is from. What's the name of the instrument? Some want to know if I can play this song, if I can play that song. Want to hear 'Happy Birthday'. I don't really like talking to them – I rather just play.

I wear the hat just to keep out of the sun. I wear it in winter too. It's just part of the garb. Just gimmick. In Trinidad there's loads of sun. I don't like the sun: it's too hot. That's why I'm in England! Every time the sun come out, I'm looking to go Norway …

What's my dream for the future? To tune pan. To do the finish product, straight down to tuning. Right now I would really like to get together with a couple of persons and get a machine that will make the drum itself, because there's no drums in Trinidad – they have to import them from Jamaica. I would like to get equipment and make drums. In the meantime, the beat goes on!

'I refuse to be cold all the time'

GARY, BUTCHER

My family was the first family ever to have a stall licence in Portobello Road. That would have been my great-grandfather. He used to live in that house over there. Before they had licences they used to pull the stalls out early on the night before and someone used to sleep underneath them, to make sure that they didn't get moved on.

My great-nan done about ten hours a day here. There again, she had ten kids so they all helped as well. They used to sell rabbit, beetroot and celery. My family sold that for years. I've got pictures indoors of my great-great-great-grandmother with a basket and rabbits hanging over the sides of the basket. Why the beetroot? What they ate, I think, years ago. In them two end sheds down there they've got the old-fashioned beetroot boilers. It would be steaming up as they'd come out. Hot beetroots and celery. Yeah, I wouldn't fancy it. There you are.

When myxomatosis come in with the rabbits, they started on the chickens. They done mainly chickens but they done the live chickens: they wasn't allowed to kill 'em until the people actually bought them because it was against the law. So someone used to stand there and kill 'em and pull the guts out.

This stall's three foot wide by nine foot long. My granddad 'ad it made. He had it all hand-painted: there was all lovely paintings round the side. He was quite wealthy, my granddad. They do say he won the Pools three times and I know for a fact they won the Premium Bonds. He'd buy a new car every year. Plus he was a very smart man. He wouldn't go into a pub without a suit on and a tie and a trilby hat.

My granddad liked the pub life. He liked playing darts; he used to get six inch nails and he would play darts with them. I don't remember him working. He used to leave me dad 'ere and go to the pub. That's what they used to do down here: the men used to go to market early in the morning, set up and then eleven o'clock, once the pub was open, you wouldn't see them no more. That would be it for the day for them. It still happens down here now. We won't mention no names but it does happen. A lot of us, we can't afford it.

And he was a bit of a character ... I remember when we had that lock up down there. He had all his Christmas turkeys in there and he sat all night in the freezing cold with his shotgun – just in case anyone tried to rob the turkeys. And then in the morning he went home and somebody phoned him to say that his shed was unlocked. The locks had been open all night!

My dad was very quiet. He would go for a drink but not like my grand-dad used to. But he expected a Sunday roast dinner every Sunday. He'd go to the pub at twelve and expect it to be on the table at three o'clock when 'e come in. That was the way it was: it would be absolute murders if the roast dinner weren't there on a Sunday. Women nowadays, it wouldn't happen.

I came down here when I was fifteen. I used to be down here younger than fifteen, but not working. I used to come with me dad and just crawl on that shelf under there when I was tired. We used to sell just rabbits and chicken. Right round the stall we used to have rabbits in their skin – all different colours, all different feet, all hanging up by their legs. They'd pick their rabbit and you'd skin 'em 'ere. Put them on a hook and just pull 'em down. The pelts used to go under there in a box and then the skin man used to come down, take all the pelts and make the coats and that. We used to do about fifty on a Friday morning. You wouldn't get away with it now. They'd go crazy now if you put them up.

It was really busy then. And the queue: the queue went right the way down. Maybe to that next alley: it used to be massive. We used to pull out at six o'clock and they'd all be standing in the doorways waiting. Loads of them. We'd start on a Thursday morning. Do Thursday morning. Friday. Finish about eleven o'clock on Saturday morning. Do about six hundred chicken. It was real quick turnover. What do we do now? About twelve. So you have to mix it up with other stuff now. Obviously. Else you'd go out of business.

We had a large community of West Indians down here then. There used to be so many ladies and they used to argue in the queue. They were always big and always shouting. The husbands were very quiet: you rarely saw them. Sometimes they'd send them out and they were always a bit uncertain or frightened if they're buying the right thing. I think they're frightened of the wives and that. I think they are.

The ladies would come in a group: like Miss Rose, Miss Daphne, Miss Ryan. They was always called 'Miss'. They used to come on a Thursday morning and buy their stuff on credit. They'd try and confuse you. It was always about the money. They were a bit red hot with money. Whatever change it was they would stand there and check every ha'penny of it to check it's exactly right. And they'd shout 'How much you say? How much you say?' or ''Ave you made a mistake?' and they'd sort of nudge each other, joking.

And they'd say 'Give me a nice boiler.' If I took that one, they'd say 'No, not that one. That one.' And if I took that one, it'd be the opposite one. And that's just the way they were. Just to tease you I suppose. It was always chicken. Chicken pieces. Boiling chicken. They used to buy more then, see, 'cause they had bigger families. They used to have pots going and they'd eat chicken every day. We used to get a lot of Spanish here as well. They used to have rabbits, the Spanish. But I think a lot of Spanish have gone now. There's just a few of them left.

The meat came from Smithfield meat market. It still does, yeah. I must have been fourteen when I first went. The place was buzzing. Meat everywhere. Porters' barrers everywhere. And you wasn't allowed to take the meat out the cases without paying these porters: they was in a union. All that's stopped now.

I remember there used to be a lovely caff up there. Really old fashioned caff. They used to put the beef and the ham on the counter. Whole legs. And if you wanted a roll they'd cut it off the leg for yer. And salt beef was presentated in a cabinet. Really nice.

And of course the pubs was open at three in the morning so they'd be drinking in the pub like we would at two o'clock in the afternoon. It's different now. It's dried up a lot. It was good fun then.

I'm out here now from seven in the morning 'til five at night on Friday and Saturday. We have our regulars; I've known eighty per cent of these people for years and years and years – right through to their kids and grandkids. Which makes you feel very old. We can do up to forty or fifty lines now: smoked chicken; lamb chops; breast of chicken; ducks; pheasants; smoked pork; everythink really. Beef; sausages; bacon. Even eggs.

No special today, no. The special is just getting home! The cold weather's awful. Awful. I've known fresh stuff to go frozen on here. And

then, on top of that, you're touching frozen meat. Once your hands go that cold, you can't get back. There's nothing you can do. Just have plenty of hot water. Buckets and buckets of hot water. And I have the heating on all the time at home. Non-stop. I refuse to be cold all the time.

How much longer? What? Down here? Not too long now, I hope, Blanche. I've been here a long time. Forty years. I think that's long enough for everybody really, to be honest with you. Every year I think 'This is gonna be the last year' but I sort of make one more year … Perhaps that's how it might end, I don't know. Let's hope not anyway!

I wouldn't miss it. I wouldn't miss it at all … Would people miss me? Perhaps. But I've seen them all come and go. For about a month, two month, they say 'Where's so and so?' and then nobody says it anymore. Is that the harsh reality of life? I think it is, yeah. Like yesterday's news …

'The whole market knows me'

WAHID, HOUSEHOLD GOODS

So hello, how are ya? Nice to see you too! Yeah, I'm listening to music. That's my thingy. Listen to music and serve my customers at the same time. I do five, six, seven thing at the same time, y'know. Let me just stop it …

I sell everything for a house you need: toilet paper; kitchen roll; batteries; CDs; DVDs; lighters obviously … Sometimes customers start moaning about the price. They say 'I'm gonna get it from Poundland.' But, obviously, the qualities are different. For example kitchen foil, when they get it, the next day they come, they're like 'I'm sorry. From the Poundland the quality was shit'. So, I told you …

Sorry, my language is kind of slang language. Is kind of street language, you know!

– You all right sir?
– How much is a pan scrubber please?
– Ah, this one? That's 60p. Or two for a pound.
– I'll take two.
– No problem. D'you want a bag for that sir?
– No, I've got a bag here.
– Thank you sir very much.
– Thank you!

We came from Afghanistan because of the fight. In Afghanistan my dad had his own shop making car batteries. He left in 1982. That was Russian times. The war was going on. Half of my family – my aunties, my uncles –

they were living in one room. They were sitting down drinking tea. Twelve people was in one room talking. Family talk and that. And then, obviously, bomb explosion happened. And then everyone died.

My dad worked for a while to make money then he brought my mum, my two little brothers and one of my youngest sisters here. 'Cause obviously all of us couldn't come. My dad couldn't afford at that time, innit. There was seven of us.

When the war started between America and Afghanistan in 2000, because of Taliban, I came over as well. First impressions? Well obviously I was kind of shocked; there's big different between my country and here. For example, in my country people don't have licence. Cars, motorbikes, they just drive whenever they want. And there's no limit of speed. You have to be twenty-one to drive here. Nah, not seventeen. You have to be nineteen at least …

What else did I notice? The weather. Down there it's twenty-four seven sunny. Here you don't hardly see the sun. Our food is grown by the sun. Down here they mix a lot of liquid, a lot of ingredients and stuff. But ours is natural food: it tastes better. In my country no women's allowed to work. And you don't see no woman at all going outside the house. Their husbands are strict. They're all at home, doing homework.

Obviously here is kind of posh place. In my country there's a lot of sad people who lost their family. Little boys on the street polishing shoes to make money. The boys here are lucky, you know. They go to school. In my country at that time they couldn't go to school because of Taliban. I didn't go to school. Everywhere you go, there's a mine. Everywhere. You couldn't step out of your house. And there is a lot of kidnap going on. They kidnap your children and say 'Right, give me two million pound so I can let go of your son.' Even if people give their money, after that they still kill their children. Cut their head and send their head only. So, obviously, the parents wouldn't let their children go out. Our teachers used to be killed, get shot in the head, because they ain't allowed to teach. That's how bad it is, I'm telling you.

It wasn't easy to get here 'cause that time I wasn't British, innit: I had Afghan passport. So I had to wait nine months in Germany. I went to Greenford Primary school when I arrived. That was quite good: everyone was treating me nice and I had a lot of extra time spending with teachers so I can learn English properly and reading and writing. I used to go clubb-es – football club, basketball club. It was quite good.

I went to secondary school. I done my GCSE but unfortunately I failed. The thing is, with me, I'm good at doing practical work than doing education. Like for example reading and spelling – I'm not good at these stuff.

– Morning, love!
– Two packs of Rizlas.
– So that'll be five pound, love.
– There you go. Thank you, love. Have a good day.

Have I picked up market talk? Maybe! I have to say that: it's kind of respectable. If you give them respect they will come to you all the time. If you be rude to them, obviously, you're losing customers. I've got a lot of customers, you know. The whole market knows me. And obviously I'm good at talking with womens so I've got the most friendly women down here. Girlfriends? There's plenty, love, there's plenty. I've got so many girlfriends my area. Not down here. I know there's a lot of people here who wants to go out with me but there's no point me going out because I'm always working.

My dad is very strict. Most of the customers they want to stand and talk to me. If I talk more than two minute my dad is like 'Why are you talking to them? Just get them money and let them go. You don't need to talk to womans you know.' When you wasn't here, he's like 'Just answer a few question to her and let her go. Don't talk to her much.' That's what he said to me. Obviously he's kind of a holy person, innit. He wants me to be good, not be free with people. Not keep talking to them saying 'Darling', 'Hi' and stuff. Hugging them and kiss on the cheek and that. When you get free with them, more customers come to you and start hugging you and kissing you and, obviously, we Afghan, we got respect for ourself. We can't, like, hug womans in the street. Not at all.

If my dad is around, I don't talk to womans. I don't smoke in front of him. And if we have argue, I don't look at him straight; I put my head down. I don't answer him back, 'cause that's kind of rude.

Obviously, I'm a young person. I want to have my fun a bit, but I don't do everything in front of his face. I hide it.

I've been out with a lot of girls from different, different countries. I was even planning to marry an English girl. She was my first love. I had four years relationship with her. But because of my parents, I couldn't marry her. Even if she was convert into Muslim still I couldn't, because my dad's like 'The culture's different; she wouldn't understand you one day.'

'Cause, obviously, they don't like to be controlled by their husband or boyfriend and that. She will leave you one day. Then what you gonna do?

My dad is not strict with my mum. He's fine with her. As long as you trust your woman, then that's fine. 'Cause the womans, the most of them I know, they do cheat behind their husbands or their boyfriends. They do that. Most guys have girlfriend and they start chatting another girl. That's not right. You wouldn't feel right if your girlfriend would do that behind your back. You wouldn't feel right, would you? Will I be strict? Nah, not really, not really. If you be too much strict with them, they'll fall out with you. If you be friendly with them, whatever they got in their heart they will tell you.

You can't go out with Afghan girls: they don't go out. So how can you find an Afghan girl? You have to talk to their parents and you have to talk to your parents: 'Listen, I like this girl. I want to marry her.' So my family goes to her family and we start asking for her hand. And then the first thing, engagement, will happen, then marriage.

And our people, first of all we make money, we buy our own house, we get a licence, everything sorted. Then we get married. You can't just go pick up a girl with nothing. With empty hand. How you gonna feed her? What you gonna do with your life?

Until you're ready you can have a bit of fun. 'Cause when you're married then that's it, you're lock. You can't do anything.

– I don't have toilet paper love …

The other thing is, if you be too much free with the customers, then they always ask you the stuff, sometimes for free, if they don't have money. Then they're like 'Oh, I'm going to give you the money tomorrow.' I did that. Most customers didn't come back. Too friendly is not good. My dad, his point is: don't be friendly with anyone, not just womans. Even don't be too friendly with your neighbours. 'Cause then they're going to come on your land or arguing and stuff is going to happen. He's been through all this. If you be free with people, at the end of the day, they're gonna treat you like shit to be honest. They won't treat you nice.

[Customer comes and gesticulates]

I have to cooperate with these kind of people that don't understand no words. So I have to kind of sign language with them. Cause, obviously, down here most Italian, Spanish, they don't know English. So you have to do the sign language.

– Thank you love. Have a good day.

This is my dad's job, you know. I'm just working for him until I find a job. I wanted to be mechanic. I did mechanic for two years in college but then I failed on my coursework. As I said, the writing and the reading I wasn't that good so I didn't understand the questions and stuff. But the practical work I passed. In my country the difference is that young boys without education and nothing, they still know how to fix cars. They've got their own garage. Here you have to have qualification otherwise they wouldn't take you. 'Cause, obviously, they might think instead of putting the engine inside the thing, you're gonna put the engine out the back. D'you get it? It's just like, instead of putting sugar in a coffee, you're gonna put salt in a coffee. So that's why you have to have qualification here. To have a job. They wouldn't just take you like that. They wouldn't. Unless it's your own people. Then they would take you without C.V.

> *– I spoke to your dad on Saturday. He said 'As long as you pay*
>   *back today … ' He said 'People don't pay back, but you pay*
>   *back.'*
> *– Yeah, but the thing is you always do that.*
> *– By tomorrow.*
> *– I'm upset, yeah, because you always have your money for*
>   *Tescos to buy something.*
> *– My mum sends me shopping for her. I can't spend my mum's*
>   *money. If it's my own money then, yeah. You know what I'm*
>   *saying?*
> *– So why don't you ever have money on you? That's the thing …*
> *– I don't work, innit.*
> *– So that's what I'm saying. Go find a job, innit. You can't*
>   *do that all your life, keep borrowing and stuff from people,*
>   *can you?*
> *[man leaves]*

See that's what I'm saying. I mean, he's a young guy, he can fucking go work for himself … Sorry the language, but you know.

He took a lighter. He's been doing that for more than a year. Keeps taking and saying 'I'll pay you the next time.' He does pay but you can't do that always … sometime it has a limit, you know. He used to have his own stall but he's lazy. One thing I hate is lazy people. I mean you're a man, go work for yourself. He never has money himself, man. Always coming to me saying 'Oh I'll pay you next time' and that.

Do people steal often? Nah, not with me. They know me. If they cross the limit then they know what's gonna happen to them. So, obviously, I'll cross the limit as well. Most people, if they thieve down here, they're like 'Oh, just allow it.' 'Cause they're scared. They don't want to do nothing about it. But I'm not like that.

Darling, listen to this … uh … we … hold on, hold on, what was it? It's a kind of speech, yeah: 'We live by the gun. We die by the gun. That's why we call Afghan … ' So, in my country, on the street there's shooting going on. Everyone dying everywhere. No one cares no more because they're used to it. So that's what I'm saying, like. We don't get hurt because we are used to it.

Do I have support? You see them five shops: they're my cousins'. All them five shops. I've got a whole market to be honest. Everyone's with me. So I'm happy. And, obviously, I've got most black guys who's … one of them … has guns and stuff. I've got them. So they'll always back me up.

Anyway … my dad's here …

'Whatever's on 'ere is real'

RICHARD, MAKE-UP

I'm from just up the Golborne, over what they call 'The Town'– just over Golborne Road Bridge.

My mother was what they called a spotter: she used to get the marks off of clothes before they dry-cleaned them. She knew every trick in the book to get whatever out: she done it all 'er life. She worked in Hendon and she used to 'ave to get three buses. All I can remember is her carrying bags of dry cleaning with 'er, off the street, just to help get more money in.

She was a schemer. Everything was a scheme and she never ever told him nothing. It used to be 'Shh … Don't speak in front of the old man.' When I was about fifteen I used to have a bet, have a gamble, right? Anyway, we lost the rent this way. Only about three quid but it was a lot of money then. So she put two footprints in the bath – one like that and one like that – and said we'd been robbed. The toes were touching in the bath! That's just one. She done thousands of things: she never stopped.

She was older than my dad; she made out she was younger. And there's another thing: her birthday was the fifth of August but she always made out it was the fourth of August because that was the Queen Mother's birthday! It was only when she died that we realised.

Mum was from Paddington. My dad was a Welshman – a miner. He moved from Wales in 1936 for work. We used to call him 'The Quiet Man' – he just wouldn't talk about anything. He went all through the war. He joined up to do 'is bit. There's plenty of Cockneys who hid. They'd have hiding places in the sofa or under the stairs or up the chimney or anywhere. Soon as the army or the police come for them, they'd hide. He was in the front.

He never ever spoke about it but I was in the pub and Arthur, one of 'is best friends, come in on his own and he said 'Your dad,' 'e said. 'E was the one who charged up the beaches and they'd all be behind him.' And I know at the end of the war 'e was like the SAS. He was what they called A1 Plus.

The house we grew up in was in Adair Road. My room was at the top of the stairs and we 'ad a bedroom and a front room and that's all we 'ad. The cooker was just on a landing and our toilet was out in the back yard. The bottom three rooms was condemned: you couldn't live in 'em. But we used to 'ave to go down to use the toilet – down these dark stairs, through these rooms just full of rubbish and damp. My dad cleaned one room out and kept pigeons in there. They was racing pigeons but they couldn't race cause 'e never let 'em out. They used to be all on perches like that and 'e'd just sit there for two hours. They used to relax him.

It was a slum. That's what it was. It was 'orrendous. She tried 'er best for us, my mum. But the difference with being poor then, in the '40s and '50s, right, everybody was poor. The whole neighbourhood was poor. We never ever thought about it. Never. 'Olidays we used to go to Southend for a day out. They'd get up at four o clock. There used to be a bakers down Golborne Road called Holmes's. You could go there four o'clock, buy twenty-four rolls, cut 'em up, fill 'em up, and then get a train down to Southend. Have a day down there and then come 'ome. That was your 'oliday. But it was better then because there was about four different youth clubs you could go to within a two-mile radius. Play pingpong or listen to music. There's nowhere now for 'em. When you leave school, til you're eighteen, if you can't go down the pub you've 'ad it. So you've got to doss about on the corners.

In my neighbourhood there was Irish. There was black people. Though I think there was only one black family when I was little and they lived in Southam Street. The boy's name was Bluey: he used to be in my class. We just treated him like a white bloke. Then, in 1958, they all started coming. West Indians, yeah. Then the race riots.

… Thirty years ago you looked down that market half past five on a Friday morning and all you'd see was ten thousand black heads and maybe one white. Going down the market to buy their shopping. They used to buy off me and my wife: not to use, they use to buy it to send back. Used to double their money. And that stall there, Gary's stall, would be a queue for miles. That's where they used to buy their meat. Gary's dad used to live just in some flats down the bottom of Southern Row and his granddad 'ad chickens under the table. I bet he don't even know that. And he bought a brand new car – which was unheard of – and he sat on the thing all day just bibbing the 'ooter and waving at everybody that he's got this new car!

We used to go to school in what was then called Middle Row. I was never a naughty kid but I'd miss more than I'd done there. When I was eight I worked for a costermonger down 'ere called Johnny Spencer. 'E ad a bald head: they used to call 'im Cannonball. I used to work Fridays in the morning, Friday evening and then all day Saturday. And 'e give me two pound fifty which was a fortune. Millionaire I was. But as soon as you got to fifteen and you 'ad to pay tax and that, you couldn't work for 'im, cause 'e didn't want all that. But 'e was a lovely man. 'E got three years in 1962, I think, for a hundred grand's worth of tax that 'e 'adn't paid.

Then I worked for loads of different people. All my mates used to be 'ouse breakers an' all that. I just couldn't do it. I went into one and I just felt sick. I thought it was horrendous. I was never afraid of the police but I thought to myself 'If my dad knew that I was in 'ere … ' If he'd come and got me and I was doing that 'e'd 'ave kicked seven kinds of … out of me. So I just couldn't.

At that time none of our group would be working. We'd be sitting out in the sun and a bloke would say 'D'you want a couple of days work, boys?' and they'd all go 'Not this week. The sun's shining.' When I was fifteen, sixteen, we used to go to take them purple 'earts. They were like speed, weren't it? But it was worse than speed 'cause you used to take a load of them, right, and when you was on a come down you was thirsty. I remember I come back to my mum's 'ouse and she was the first woman in that street who 'ad a fridge. Anyway, I've opened the fridge and there's this great big fresh fruit trifle. I'm gasping … and it was all grapes. I ended up 'aving all the jelly … She got out of bed and screamed. It was somebody else's. She was fridging it for somebody else. Oh, she was 'ilarious!

The reason I sell make-up is my wife's nan. She used to work in Shepherds' Bush market in 1946, selling this 'alf-a-crown perfume. She 'ad a pitch in every best market – Portobello Road, East Street, Fulham – but she used to sublet 'em to everybody else.

When she died my wife used to work on a stall. I was working on the motorway. I used to work like two weeks in one, shovelling, and I used to make four hundred pounds a week. Anyway, Linda was working in Fulham. I said, ''Ow much you took today?' She said 'Four hundred quid.' Took what I earned. So I threw the shovel and went and 'elped 'er. And then we came to Portobello.

We used to go 'ere, go there, get stuff that you could only buy in the chemist. And we used to get clearance out of the biggest wholesaler. We've 'ad the best. If we're really serious, we're a threat to Boots.

We once bought a load of Superdrug stuff from a wholesaler and it all 'ad Superdrug labels on it. They bought the police out and everybody because the wholesaler was supposed to debag it. But there are like ten thousand pencils. Can you imagine? You'd be there for five years.

We used to buy testers off an Indian woman in 'ammersmith before anybody knew what a tester was, right. We used to buy them for two and three quid and sell 'em for fivers and tenners. We 'ad Trading Standards on once and he said 'It's not for sale.' I said 'Who said it ain't for sale?' He said 'Well it's got 'NOT FOR SALE on it.' I said 'I've paid for it. What d'you think I'm gonna do. Throw it down the … ?'

I've never sold anything fake. I sell smell-alikes and look-alikes and things like that. I've got a thing that I've just bought off my mate. It's called Dream Alone, right. So you know what that's a copy of? Jo Malone. In Oxford Street they sell you a Chanel Five as a Chanel Five and, when you get it home, it's got a bottle of carbolic in it. That's fake. But this is just similar. I've got D and G. It's called Dolce and Goodlife or something. The bottles are identical. The smells ain't. They can't be identical for two quid. But I tell 'em straight and if they like it, they buy it.

One bloke, he come up. He's head of a men's magazine. They had a thousand pieces of L'Oreal shampoo that were supposed to go into goody bags but they delivered it the next day. So what did 'e do with it? He sold it to me for sixty p. It was like thirteen quid each. That's how you get different stuff. Everybody can go on the wholesaler but the few people that I buy off private makes the stall different to everything else.

The other week I had a load of this REN. Have you heard of that? The face cream? Anyway, it's expensive. It's top. I bought it off this bloke and it turned out it's all stolen: the police rung me up just after Christmas. They said 'We're going to come and whatever you've got, we're gonna take.' I said 'All right'. You can't know if it's stolen. All you say to them is 'Is it stolen?' And I asked him three times 'cause it was quality stuff.

What 'ave I got on the stall now? Let me think. Revlon eye shadows. Genuinely Revlon. Revlon lipsticks. I'm selling Calvin Klein body lotion that I bought in a job lot. It's gotta be between twenty and thirty quid: I sell two of them for a fiver. I turn it over. Other people would sit on it for years: we want to be into something else. We do most stuff on there now two quid, three for a fiver. It's easy for the tourists. My son can speak a lot of different languages. He can say 'Three for a fiver' in whatever language and they understand it straight away. And 'e can understand them when they're saying it's all fake! He goes [foreign accent], 'No, no, no, no … this is not fake' and they get gutted!

The customers are all different. We've 'ad the Queen's cousin buying soaps for the Queen and we 'ave little people. We 'ave all models and all actresses and we have local women: black women; Chinese women; everything. We have people there who was in the pram and are now thirty. And they bring their kids and their grandkids. There's people come from Peru, from Brazil, from Germany for this stall only. That's all they come down that market for. It's like a cult thing. If you knew the stuff that we'd 'ad over the years, for the small money …

The Moroccans come up and you can 'ear them say 'This is where you buy the make-up. Not down there. Not over there. This is it 'ere. Whatever's on 'ere is real.' And that's what it is.

I don't buy things that I think are dangerous or dodgy. A couple of years after we started, they sent a load of these eye shadows from China but they was full of lead. They cost us sixty p each and we 'ad over a thousand. It was a lot of money. Near Christmas. But I dumped 'em all. It was awful: that six hundred quid slaughtered us.

… The worst thing about 'aving a busy stall is they 'one in on it. You know 'ow you know people are rotten? They look at you. If you come to my stall and there was all these lovely nail polishes and lipsticks you look at that. But the ones who are sudsy, they look at you. Then I don't look at their eyes: I just watch their 'ands. We call all shoplifters Veras because on Coronation Street it's Vera Duckworth got done for shoplifting. If you was over there and I thought you was a thief, I'd just say to my son 'There's a Vera over there, look.' And he knows straight away what I'm talking about. But it ain't upset 'er. 'Cause if you said 'She looks like a shoplifter,' it'd be all off, wouldn't it?

I was sitting in that restaurant there, having something to eat, and there was an old lady with a Zimmer frame. It 'ad a bag on it and she was filling 'er bag up with all my gear. So I went out and took it off 'er. I said 'Bye bye, you're barred.' That's all you do with 'em.

To little kids I'll say 'Why don't you ask? You can 'ave it.' The majority of the stuff round the front, it's a pound or two – it just ain't worth nicking. 'Cause it's a right bad stigma, innit? Anythink good we 'ave by our 'ands.

You 'ave to. 'Cause if you lose a bottle of something that's cost you fifteen quid, it's 'ard.

I get a lot of women get their purses nicked on the stall. One time there was an old woman – oh she 'ad to be eighty – 'ad 'er 'and on a lipstick on the stall and her other 'and was in the woman's bag next to her. Just like that. It 'appens all the time. Believe it or not, I give them money to get home and they can always bring it back the week after.

Most women 'ave everything in their purse dun they? My wife never. She'd 'ave money in this pocket, money in that pocket. She'd never lose it all. But she was brought up local. She was a one. She was unbelievable. This stall of mine is busy but if she could 'ave still been here, they wouldn't 'ave got round that stall. People used to come just to be with her. And they used to wait. It was like a queue here. We used to 'ave this nutter come up. He was properly mad. He used to say 'Linda, I'm gonna knock you in a wall and buy the wall and take it home.' And he used to give 'er sweets …

She caught loads of shoplifters. She caught this Irish one. She's gone up the road and Linda's chased 'er and caught her. She said 'Gis my bottle of perfume back' and she said 'Oh darrrling, it must 'ave fell in!' Ha ha ha ha ha. You know gypsies used to nick off everybody? Well they used to walk past and they'd say 'Don't stop there, she's got eyes up 'er arse.' That's true, that is!

We made more money then, because of 'er charisma. I said to 'er one day – at quarter to eight in the morning – "Ow much money 'ave we got?' She went and counted it. She had eight hundred quid. Thousands and thousands we used to make. We used to be mobbed.

There ain't no fortunes down here now. It's 'ard work now. Everybody knows the price of everything because of the internet. You could bring me up a bottle of perfume and I could scan it and it'll tell you the cheapest it is in the country. Just like that.

Is there a black market on the market? Course there is. Everythink on the market is cash. But without the black economy this country would fold. 'Alf of them people working down there are laundering money anyway. Yeah, course they are. People down there who work day in, day out, don't take fifty pound a day – there's gotta be a reason for it.

I've seen everything. Everything that could possibly 'appen on the market. I tell you something. You know when you get people coming up and they're playing music and you get a big crowd? That's when the pick pockets start to work. They all work together. So when they do that, I'll shout out 'Mind out for yer pockets.' I give 'em all a warning.

And now it's all drunks and that. All the care in the community are walking the streets 'ere. Early in the morning there's a man now. 'E's a drunk. 'E lays down. 'E pisses imself on the floor. But the police don't wanna take 'im away cause 'e's just got to go in the cell and what they gonna do with im? And I've seen plenty of stabbings. There was a stabbing up the Golborne the other week. Did you hear about it? The two fish men. They was working together. 'E sliced 'im. One of the Struttons stopped 'im … and all 'is stomach fell out. That was only a few weeks ago.

It's all right, I drink cold tea love. It's part of working on the stall. People buy it when you're setting up and then all of a sudden you go to drink it and it's freezing cold …

I'm sixty-six. I'm keeping this stall open for my granddaughters. One of them's just coming up for fourteen so I'd like to keep it going for four years. It don't earn that much now but we don't stop laughing. I say to them 'Oh, you look good today'. 'Oh do I? Thank you.' I say 'What, you been run over?' And I say 'Before I come 'ere, there was thousands of ugly women. Look at them now – they're all beautiful!' They do laugh.

I don't 'ave a bad day. Very rarely. I don't get miserable, nah. I did … The funny thing is, the day she died, I went down the market, right. But if you'd 'ave seen 'er … This Saturday she looked unbelievable. Her eyes were bright. She could 'ardly walk and she made us a cup of tea. I would never 'ave gone if she'd 'ave looked ill. My daughter rung up. She said 'Dad, I don't wanna worry yer,' she said 'but mum's collapsed. You'd better get 'ome.' We was all round 'er bed when she died. The doctor said that 'er 'ead had exploded. She had aneurisms and she was laying there and she was breathing funny. And I said to 'er 'Linda, wherever you are love,' I said, 'you wait for me, right?' And she opened 'er eyes. But they reckon she was already dead.

I still miss 'er. I'm still broken 'earted. You know what I mean? I can't get over it. Forty-five years I was with 'er. And to look after 'er and all..

That's why I've started coming back to the market. I've started to go down on a Monday. I've started one in Harrow. There's no money in it. It's just to get out of the 'ouse. Because there's too many memories in there …

'I'm very confident that it will work out'

Henry, menswear

From about the age of ten I've wanted to have a business. I was born in Leamington Spa, Warwickshire, in 1988: I'll be twenty-five on the 29th August. My dad was an entrepreneur. He started buying bone products from butchers after the War. He literally had a wheelbarrow and he'd go round, buy their scraps, get them melted down into bone marrow and sell it to people to make into soaps and ice creams. He did so many things which brought cool stories and which always inspired me I guess.

I went to school in Ampleforth, in Yorkshire. I wanted to be an entrepreneur but let's not pretend that every morning I was waking up saying 'I don't need to be here because I'm going to have a business in three years.' I wasn't some sort of Del Boy. Lots of people had young enterprises at school. Everyone sold cigarettes. I was on the committee for the school charity in my last year. I bought pint glasses and we had the school crest put on them and sold them. I bought too many. I learned from that. And I also learned that you can't sell 2008 glasses in 2009.

I did go to university. I went to Oxford Brookes and studied Real Estate. Why? I wasn't a particular academic, I had shocking predictions (a D and two Us I think) and I just thought that property was a cool course. I did a few work experiences but I never went into it. I just started trying to create a concept for a business.

I thought that men's underwear is a market which is quite untapped so I started doing some research. I wanted to create boxer shorts with really cool prints on them. Happy dogs or flying pigs or something. I'd even thought of an advert. It was going to be a guy and you can only see the desk and he's looking down and it says 'Every man should smile when he looks down.' And then underneath it would show that he's smiling at his boxer shorts not something else.

Then I realised that in order to print fabric you need to engrave big screens and the more colours that are in it, the more screens have to be engraved. I discovered that I'd be having to buy two thousand in order to get my own fabric. So the set-up costs and the quantities required were just impossible.

Whilst I was doing this I was going round to lots of people saying 'How do you make your boxer shorts? Do you have a gusset? Do you not have a gusset?' All that stuff. And a shirt maker called Emma Willis said she often used the material left over from shirt orders to make into boxer shorts. So I thought, if she's got material left over then everyone else is going to. I called them all up and they said 'We've got five metres of this, two metres of that' or 'We've got a bag of scraps' and I thought, well, if I just centralise that, contact them all and buy it, then I can start getting really, really great fabric at affordable prices and making cool boxer shorts out of it. And of course it's very sustainable. So it seemed to tick all the right boxes. My brand changed from a kind of fun, young, printed boxer short to a really cool, well-made, British, quality brand.

The thing was I needed money to do it. Given that my predictions at school weren't great my mum wasn't expecting a huge amount from university. We struck a deal. If I got a first, she'd lend me some money to start a business. I got a first and then had a bit of money to start …

Everyone's pretty friendly here. Nobody's picked on me because I sound posh or anything like that. I actually started out on Spitalfields market when I first moved to London. I was staying with my cousin in Islington and all I had was two suitcases full of boxer shorts. I didn't have a car so I used to put them in a shopping trolley I'd borrow off Sainsbury's in the morning. I'd be looking at my iPhone and I'd be like 'Which way's Spitalfields?' Everyone thought I was quite funny and they didn't begrudge me for it.

Then I moved over to West London and, obviously, Portobello's just on the doorstep. The problem with it is it's outside. When it's cold in the winter if you look behind people's stalls they'll be standing on a crushed down cardboard box. That's because your feet get very cold standing on the road and, believe it or not, that cardboard box just provides an extra layer of insulation that keeps your feet a lot warmer. Also, when the clothes that you're selling are quite valuable, and the wind comes and blows some onto the street, it's not the best to be out there with the elements. But you can make it protected and work with it.

This boxer short is a cotton poplin. Have a feel. It's soft and nice and washes well. Lasts a long time. Isn't going to shrink. On the rear of the boxer short there is a seam panel. That's the gusset. It prevents having a seam going down the middle of your two cheeks. Often they do have one. You wouldn't have thought people like having a seam down their crack, as it were, which is why I've got this gusset in. But I did a survey the other day to see if people really minded and it turns out, actually, that's what's more important to somebody is how they look. And with this gusset here it means that the panels can't be as tight fitting, which basically makes them a bit baggier. Gives them, if you like, a bit more of a diaper's shape which doesn't look as good if you're thin. So although some of the older generation had told me that the gusset was very, very important, I think I'm going to take it out. Or do both.

These are all my design. I'll print out a table and then cut two swatches: one for the waistband and one for the body of the fabric. Then I'll show my girlfriend, my housemate and my mum. Occasionally they'll be like 'That doesn't go with that at all!' but on the whole it's quite a simple process and then I'll go to the factory and get them made.

The factory's in Richmond. Yeah, London. They make boxer shorts for a lot of quite established tailors and shirt makers. For sure it's much more expensive but you're not shipping something across the world and it's good to contribute to our economy. That plus the fact that it's still just me going around. If you're a one-man band you can't, I don't think, manage quality control if it's not in the UK.

I like that it's made in Britain. It is a big part of the brand and if possible it would be nice to keep it like that. But it's also a big part of the brand to keep on going and to grow. If you ask me if I'd prefer to have a business consisting of one person making boxer shorts in England or a thriving enterprise of fifteen young people making beautiful boxer shorts in Portugal, then I would move things offshore. I don't think I'd be completely cutting my nose off if I did move things offshore. But, yes, it is part of the brand and when the demand's there I guess I'll have to review that option.

I also sell waistcoats and if people have got a special requirement, I'll make them specifically. This morning I had a customer come to my house for a wedding waistcoast fitting. He wanted a double breasted white linen waistcoat with aqua piping and mother of pearl buttons so I made that.

Were I a bit bigger and more established it would be a bit embarrassing because though it's not a student house – I try and keep it nice and tidy – it's certainly not Savile Row kind of tailoring. I share with somebody else so I can't have waistcoats in my sitting room. In fact you wouldn't really notice anything different to a normal house apart from the odd mannequin here and there and boxes with garments in. But if you were to go into my bedroom you wouldn't really be able to move. I've got an eight foot high rail with double tiers. It's six feet long and on it are about one hundred and fifty waistcoats. It's at the end of my bed. It's not a big deal. I mean, what do you do in your bedroom? You get changed and I've got a desk there but I don't need to be able to run around and dance. My house doesn't have blinds so actually it's quite good because it stops the light from getting in.

Clients come and sit in my sitting room and then I'll just bring down the ones that I think they'll want to see. I've got a mirror there and we'll decide if it wants to come in, go out. I'll wear a tape measure which makes me look very sophisticated, but in reality I'm just kind of blagging it. But I think everyone who comes round knows I'm a one-man band starting out and I think they find it a bit charming to be honest.

Do people want me to undercut? I guess. Somewhere like Favourbrooks in the Piccadilly Arcade is twice the price probably. They've got a great brand, they're well established, they're in the right place and they have a lot of rent. All of which I don't have. But I doubt Favourbrooks would send somebody to your house with a waistcoat or bike round London to get it to you on time. Or, if the postman fails, make one up in three days. I try and post it out but if somebody says 'I'm out and I need it to be left with my granny,' I'll do that.

I'm very confident that the brand will work very well and I think that the name will be instrumental in that success. It's a good name. I love puns and word games so I was just like 'What am I going to do? I'm gonna make stuff using ends of lines' and I wrote down everything that meant end of line: off cut; surplus. And then I was like 'Sir Plus'. It just sounded good. People don't get it occasionally and think it's quite poncey or for fat people. When they do find out what it's about, it works well.

With the logo I wanted to be a bit ironic because I do think that things like Jack Wills – and all of these brands which have a polo player logo – are a bit pompous. Cabbage is trade slang for factory offcuts so I thought 'I'm going to have a top hat on a cabbage.'

Who are my target customers? Um … they'd be aged twenty-five to thirty-five. Young. Creative. Individuals who read publications and set trends.

But you know, you aim at a certain person but you don't always have them buying your things. In reality it's mostly ladies who buy my boxer shorts for their boyfriends or girls who come choose a waistcoat for their husband to get married in. A sale's a sale at the end of the day.

I'm a casual trader. We have to go to the market office for seven forty-five. They put all your names in a bag. Then they pick out the names and when it's your turn you go up and choose a number pitch. I have to call up a guy called Danny to come and erect my stall 'cause my gazebo won't fit in my car. I set up and then drive back to Kensal Rise – because I save a tenner on parking – and run back down from Kensal Rise to my stall.

When you first start you've got all these expectations and so when somebody walks away you're like 'Oh no'. But now I don't really mind at all. People come and go and then they come back. And people buy and then they don't buy. It's kind of like driving. When you first start you're a bit nervous but after a while you get overtaken, you get stopped, you don't have traffic lights, you do have traffic lights, you start, you stop but you don't every time think 'Oh no, not a traffic light'. You don't bat an eyelid eventually.

On the whole I think people in markets are very self-protective. On Portobello, they've got their hands in their pockets. They've got their rucksacks in front of them sometimes. That's not a comfortable environment. So you've gotta gauge it well and let them know that you're there if they need any help but you're not going to hassle them. You're not going to rob them. I always say 'Would you like to see my underwear?' which makes some people laugh. Then they'll come and have a look at it. But other people look at you like you've harassed them.

People try and bargain all the time. The other day there was a tie. They're like, 'How much is your tie?'

I'm like 'Seventeen pounds' (which, for a tie, is reasonable – they're nice ties). She said, 'I'll give you five.' I just don't understand that mentality. I wasn't annoyed. I was just like, 'Are you joking? Go away! Do you think if you say, "Five" I'll say, "Have it for seven"?' So, yeah, people always barter but that's just the way a market is.

Someone stole my lunch box the other day; if you saw somebody eating a bacon and egg sandwich, it was mine. I think they thought it was my money-box but I always have my money on me. People's stuff's getting nicked all the time. Honestly, if you leave your phone on your tabletop it will be gone in five minutes. The other day some lady came and was very adamant that she wanted to walk behind the stall. I was saying 'No that's the back of the stall' but she walked round, had a look and then walked off. Now she wasn't there and then going to steal something 'cause she knew I was watching. She was just having a look to suss out the situation so she could send someone else in. They do all kinds of different scams so you just don't leave anything out.

Right, I think we've got maybe fifteen more minutes 'cause I'm not going to sell anything if I keep talking …

You can't really compare having a job in a boring office to doing what I'm doing. You're in charge of your own destiny. You can work really hard and make something. You're creating, innovating, meeting new people. It's the difference between sitting in a class and doing Maths and getting out and playing Hide-and-Seek in the school. It's just doing something a bit fun. Starting it from fresh. I think that's really cool.

I'm very confident that it will work out. A year and a half ago I was selling boxer shorts. Now I'm selling boxer shorts, t-shirts and people are travelling across London to come and see my waistcoats and buy them for their wedding. You've got to hang in there. And although it's a very tough retail climate I do think that if you can create the right concept and get your manufacturing and supply chain sorted then, when things start to pick up and people know you for a certain thing, it can only get better.

I want to become known for the brand that does really great quality clothing online. Better than the products in the department store but a bit less. What will I do when I make my fortune? I would definitely spend it on a few fun things. Have a party. But to buy back the house I grew up in would probably be a big goal. That would be wicked. Maybe don't print that, otherwise the guy that's selling it might charge me more …

'I don't mind who they are so long as they buy'

LAURA, HOSIERY

I'm not famous. I am a writer but I'm not famous. I was published a long time ago. It was called *The Furnished Room*. Yes, they did make a film of it. I was very lucky early; nobody really wants what I'm writing now.

The story I'm working on at the moment is called 'Where is my mask of an honest man'. There's two protagonists – a man and a woman. The woman is an old lady of my age. She gets a crush on this much younger man. He's her landlord and she's a protected tenant. Does the relationship materialise? No, absolutely not. She's interesting and so he likes her. But he's charming to everybody – he's not particular – and he actually only wants to get her flat.

What happens? He tries to throw her off the roof. But there's a sort of clown character who starts pointing at the roof and jumping up and down – putting attention on what's happening – which makes it impossible for him to push her.

What does she do? Well, she doesn't take it personally. She's in such ecstasy at being on the roof with this man, who's actually got his arm round her shoulders and is holding a glass of wine, that she's really dizzy anyway.

And the end? She gets her flat back but she doesn't see him anymore. He's no reason to come and visit.

I am a protected tenant, yes. Handsome landlord? No, I invented him: it's quite fun writing about attractive men. My landlord doesn't try anything. But obviously it would suit him if I was dead.

Sometimes I go into its world, yes. This particular little section, under the bridge, I find very atmospheric. With a lot of curved glass and moving lights you get visual distortions. Optical illusions. For instance, when a train goes past it will be reflected in the curved windscreen of a van as plunging down the windscreen.

– *Hello!*
[sotto voce] Come on, fork out. It's only six fifty!
Would you like some illustrated tights? They come as tights and
as footless. The one you were looking at is the London one …
– *Thank you!*
– *Don't thank me – buy the tights!*
– *What?*
– *I said don't thank me, buy the tights …*
[woman walks away]

Why can they think that I like it because they say 'thank you'? Some lady, she came, she hung around. She didn't want to buy anything but she said 'It's nice for you, being under the shelter when it's raining.' I mean – why should I be interested in a remark like that?

Maybe a lot of people would appreciate that. No one else is as nasty about customers, I think. But it's not customers. The customer is, by definition, somebody that buys something.

– *How much are these Mary Quant?*
– *Seven pounds.*
– *Bodystocking!! That brings me back. I had a pink one like that*
that I only threw out a few years ago because it was in bits …
Are they all one size?
– *Yeah. Everything should fit you with no problem.*
– *I'll come back to you. Thank you.*

Right … One of these 'come backs' … At least she was non-specific. The ones that say 'I'm just going to the cashpoint: I'll come back' you KNOW you'll never see again …

How has trade been going? Total shite as far as I'm concerned. Total shite. Compared to what it used to be. It's like somebody suddenly pulled a plug and all the water ran away. Suddenly. Almost overnight. About four, five years ago. Why? Well partly shops like Primark, partly the internet and partly the electronic payment card – which we can't take.

It's mostly tourists who've bought. Germans are good – they seem to like my stuff. The Americans are not. They have this awful word: awesome. I mean how can a pair of socks be awesome? It's such a misuse of language. 'Oh, isn't this just awesome! Oh, Charlotte would LOVE these!' They love everything and then they just go off leaving a mess. Some years ago the Japanese were most avant-garde and they would buy the stuff and look good in it. Recently not so much. We have Chinese girls coming now. Some of the lesser stuff here is actually made in China but they haven't seen it. Presumably they're just made for export.

I do sell to men. I don't mind who they are so long as they buy. I'd rather have a transvestite who buys something than a pillar of society who says they'll come back. Sometimes you get girls who are completely punk – they've got pink hair and studs in their noses and spiky collars – and they come with their Mums – who are obviously decked out by Marks & Spencer – and yet they're very fond and holding onto each other's arms.

I'm misanthropic by nature. There's some poem that begins 'I do not like the human race / I do not like its foolish face'. Is that how I feel? Yes. I try and restrain it …

Does my attitude affect business? Probably, yes. Well, yes, because I have this condition of not recognising people. So it could be that last week some-one's come and spent a lot of money and I've been really nice to them – 'cause I do like to be helpful – and then they come back next week and just look and I make some rude remarks. I simply can't learn faces. I always thought it was only me. Then I read some article about some writer whose name I forget and he has it. And it's got a name. It's called 'prosopagnosia'. It is a condition.

Sometimes I think of humans and I think how wonderful they are. If I think of something like the Cern particle accelerator – anything to do with maths or physics – I think how wonderful some people have got such brains. I think we're simply devalued by quantity. Anything is devalued by quantity. There's simply too many. Who should go? Well, that's the difficult point because I'm one of the too many …

This job? It's not bad. It has a certain amount of freedom, although the freedom is circumscribed. But it's got more freedom than most jobs I sup-pose. Sometimes, even if I'm doing something horrible like carrying heavy bags, I'm thinking to myself 'Freedom, freedom'.

The buying is nice. I think everyone likes buying things. Generally if you buy things you're being bad and self-indulgent. But if you're buying it for the business you're actually having the pleasure and you're being good.

No … I'm not good at buying to make money. I tend to buy the thing I like, irrespective of whether it makes a fiver each or five pence each. Like, for instance, these zip-up socks. These cost me nine pounds; I sell them for ten. But I wouldn't not stock these.

The older I get, the less weight I can carry. This stuff doesn't weigh too much. I haven't got a car so it all goes on the Tube. It doesn't cost me anything because I've got an old lady card. And my son helps.

What does the future hold? Well I don't know. It's not really in my hands. It depends if cancer occurs or doesn't. Or how long I've got my mind and my ability to read and go for walks. I'll go on here while I can, yes. I hate it when they say things on the telly like 'Why don't you visit an old person?' I don't want some bloody person coming round, calling me love, and bringing me a box of horrible supermarket biscuits! What do I want? A handsome young man pushing me off a roof? No. But someone can come round and say 'Darling' and bring a bottle of Cointreau …

'We don't have wine and sausage any longer – it's mint tea and wholefoods!'

JO, VINTAGE CLOTHING

I was born in 1947 in Weston-super-Mare. It was very conventional. My dad worked for Wills Tobacco Company and my mum was a housewife. We lived in the countryside.

I went to teachers college. I wanted to be a teacher because I was always getting crushes on teachers at school and I thought 'Oh yes, that will be nice to have all those young girls liking me!' But the reality of it was somewhat different. I started off in the East End teaching French to kids who didn't give a damn. They'd be like 'What the bleeding hell do we have to do this for?' So I thought 'Yes, why am I doing this?' And then I met my husband. He was an antiques restorer. I was going round all the markets with him and I thought 'What shall I be interested in?' It was a toss-up between china – which I really liked – and clothes. In the end I went for clothes. I became a part-time teacher and I started experimenting by going to Covent Garden market and trying to sell things.

I was getting a lot of my stock from the Brick Lane rag yards. This was in '72. There were mostly women in charge. They looked how you imagine gypsies would look – Eastern European women with their long hair swept up. They were getting on in age and they were all from the low end of society – there was no status at all attached to dealing in rags. They looked really hard and they were quite hard.

They'd bring out this huge bale and rip it open. There were 1920s swimming costumes, Edwardian tops, Victorian skirts – all mixed up. Some of it was damaged and a lot of it was sprayed against little insects so it had a particular sort of smell.

You'd go to look through it and then somebody would come along and start pushing: pulling them out and putting them under their arm, whether they wanted them or not, just to be able to go through it at their leisure. Elbowing you out of the way. I was a bit shy so I didn't push myself forward; I would just clean the rejects up afterwards. They had only been rejected because they needed work on them and I was prepared to do the work. In fact I like restoring. I like to find something in a poor state and work on it.

In '75 I started at Portobello. There were only a few dealers then who did vintage. There were two lovely ladies called Rose and Tricia. Rose had remarkable stuff. Wonderful Norfolk shawls from Victorian times in the most beautiful colours. We'd all have a lovely lunch together – a bottle of wine, some sausage and a hunk of bread – and be quite cheerful in the afternoon.

We saw people come and go quite a lot. There were people who would make a quick buck by selling a hundred t-shirts. We were terribly scathing about them! In those days what was very popular was 1940s and '30s crepe dresses. And Victorian chemises and nighties. There was more Victorian clothing around then. It wasn't my specialism. I was a specialist in woollen handknits from the '30s and '40s and silk underwear: cammy knickers; silk negligees and nighties. All that lovely sort of stuff.

But once I remember finding this sweet little child's hat. It was velvet, it had lovely detail on it and it was in perfect condition. I thought 'I'm going to ask a LOT for this.' I put it on my stall and I asked for twenty-five pounds. A man came past and he SNAPPED it up. I said 'Can you tell me a bit about this hat?' and he said 'Yes, it's from 1877.' I hadn't recognised it at all; I thought it was 1930s!

I think there have always been people who are interested in buying quality stuff and that's what we offered. Beautiful tailored suits, things like that. People could buy the quality and the cut for a fraction of the price of something new.

And we've always been a great source for designers; it's the cutting edge of fashion, actually, in Portobello. We see people coming from Top Shop and Marks & Spencers to find the look for next year. Famous designers come down for inspiration or send people to do a bit of reccy-ing: Jean Paul Gaultier; Dries van Noten; Stella MacCartney. Paul Smith was great: he was always buying from us and appreciating us. Cath Kidston has been buying from us since the '60s. They look for details – open work around the neck; little rickrack braid; anything that catches their eye and is a bit unusual. They call it 'sourcing'.

We hope they buy but we do get people photographing. They know, now, we're onto it so they say 'Can I just try that on?' They take it round the corner and photograph it. It's upsetting when it's so hard for us to make a living.

Nowadays there isn't so much around. In the past people would have on their stalls something that was remarkable and NOBODY would buy it. Whereas now, anything fantastic is snapped up within the first five minutes! It seems to me that the market has actually improved over the years. Originally we were just stallholders. Now there are people who've got shops as well. They're not doing too well in their shops so they come and do their stalls. They've got really brilliant stuff. And we are all trying to outdo one another to provide something exciting so quality is up. In fact we've raised the level so high that customers are blasé about it. I don't think they understand that this is the crème de la crème and that we all have to work so hard to find it now. We've had to go to all corners of Britain and abroad because a lot of vintage has been used up. The stuff that was around in the '60s and '70s has been on people's backs a second time, maybe a third time, and it's just fallen to pieces now.

People can charge whatever they want now for vintage. They put huge prices on '80s and '70s clothing because young people are into 'fashion' and this happens to be fashion! It's not what I call vintage. It makes me SO cross – they'll go and pay eighty pounds for some awful '80s dress and then they'll come to my stall and I'll have a Victorian negligee for sixty pounds and they'll baulk at the price.

Now I make things from old textiles. If there's a hole in a dress you can make the dress shorter and use that fabric, or the belt, or a little bit of the sleeve. Or sometimes I make a pleat over it and then I make another pleat on the other side, so it looks like it's part of the dress. And the sort of things that most people don't know what to do with, I make into cushions.

I'm in a very nice section where I am. I love the people around me. Around the corner there are some people who get upset if you've got a lot of people on your stall when they're not selling anything at all themselves. But we aren't competitive at all: we're very supportive. We are like a sort of fellowship really. There's something about people who do this sort of thing: they're not conventional – they're just outside society – and somehow I feel more comfortable with them. But it's more restrained now. It's not wine and sausage any longer – it's mint tea and wholefoods!

'It's just a lot of very good friends and beautiful things'

SU, FRENCH VINTAGE

I do French vintage: clothes and workwear; textiles; antique linens. Everything. And I love paper bags and buttons and boxes. I sort of fell into business with a colleague and she lives in France. So between us we source over there and sell over here.

> – *Hello, how are you?*
> – *I'm all right, how are you? How's the dog?*
> – *Put you down Pepper!*
> – *She rather liked being up there, didn't she?*
> – *You know what she's like. She's very spoiled. Come on, go back Pep … Oi … stop that. What are you doing?! Sorry …*
> – *How much are these trousers?*
> – *They're fifty-five. I just love the way they finished off to make it really, really strong.*
> – *Yeah. Double. It was the old French work so it had to perform.*
> – *Absolutely! And it has – because here it is, one hundred years later!*
> – *Lovely. But too small unfortunately.*
> – *Not bad at all. I'll put them away then. I quite like them myself.*

I think the French were better at putting things away and forgetting about them in attics. So you have all the greniers and brocantes with attic stuff. What does brocante mean? Don't know! French car boot? It could be in a village, all the way down a street, or it could be in muddy fields or concrete car parks.

Village brocantes are wonderful because you've got the cafés and they're already drinking absinthe, or something disgusting, at six o'clock in the morning, and you've got all these wonderful French peasantry in the middle of the countryside, selling off their grannies' whatever it is. If you're lucky you'll find something amongst the sea of Barbie dolls that proliferate over there. Oh, and the tools. Lots and lots of rusty agricultural tools. It's a real mix. But that's what makes it so exciting.

– *I can't see a price on this …*
– *Um … twenty-five that one. It's a wonderful stripe, isn't it?*
– *It's great. This time we're doing Sinbad. It's a series for Sky.*
– *Oh what fun! There are some nice wide ones as well.*
– *Definitely those two.*
– *Okay. Thank you.*
– *Can you give me a receipt?*
– *Yes of course. Ooh … Pepper!*

My speciality is buttons. People buy buttons. They make jewellery; they use them on upholstery. Sometimes they knit or sew and they're very creative. Or they want to change the buttons on their cardigan from Marks & Spencer.

They're all different: I've got corozo; I've got mother of pearl with metal shank; old Bakelite; old black glass – beautiful; celluloid you see – amazing. I hate brass buttons and those naval things. My ex-husband, we saw him the other day and he was wearing just that. We thought obviously the fat slag that he went off with is putting him in blazers with brass buttons. I mean how could he? Those are 1920s. I don't do enamel because they're very old and very expensive. But this stuff, this is all very wearable.

How can you know the date? You can sort of get to know. It's based on experience isn't it? But we're all wrong sometimes. You can say 'Oh well, that's that' but unless you have a date on it – like this which I love … it says that this garment, inside this garment bag, was checked on the 15th February 1947. This is a '*house à vêtements, hermetique*' against mites, dust and other nasty things. It's probably impregnated with something disgusting, but isn't it beautiful?

We picked that up because it was over an old suit and it had just been sitting there in the cellar, or the attic, and now I'm selling it because I think it's beautiful. I'll sell it for twenty quid. It's nothing very much but it's a piece of history. It probably would work if you sprayed it with what I use against moths – an anti-cockroach spray from the supermarket.

I like this sort of thing as well. It's a farm corn sack. Isn't it beautiful? Those are all corn sacks of various sorts. These are very easy to use because they're seamed at the side. So you just split them open and use them as table runners out in the garden, or lots of people stuff them with cushions and use them for garden benches.

This is a hemp picnic cloth. These are what the workers took when they went into the vineyard to begin the vendange. They all had initials on them so they didn't get mixed up. I do a lot of hemp. Oh, the dog stood on that this morning! Sometimes you get hemp and nettle. Nettle's incredibly strong. It's the nettle stalks I think. They sort of pound them down and then it makes this fibre and then they weave it. It's quite a bit coarser than this so they're all very practical.

These are mattress tickings. That one's fantastic because it's got the herringbone weave. They're old mattress covers but they're very good for upholstery or cushions. There are lots of companies that buy up old mattresses for the feathers. They rip them and take the feathers out – which is very annoying because then there's a big rip in it. You have to wash those for days and days and days and the remaining feathers float everywhere.

I use all of them. I wear linen shirts and men's linen trousers. I use linen sheets to hang on my windows. I just hang them up with pegs: I can't be bothered to make curtains. And I use things like this to throw over the back of the sofa and stuff. Far too many fabrics knocking around in my place!

- *[A fellow trader tries on a pair of trousers] I'll give you fifty-five for them. What do you reckon?*
- *They're great. They're better on you than on me, how annoying!*
- *[To another fellow trader!] Go tell her how beautiful she looks. I've sold to the lady!*
- *He's wearing a nice jacket. It was my ex-husband's and I thought it would suit Julian a LOT better …*

I was born in Huddersfield in Yorkshire. When? 1948. My parents were in the wool trade because that's what you do in Yorkshire. There are lots of woollen towns: it just happens to be where the sheep were, I suppose. My grandfather had a textiles mill so I was always brought up with textiles around. We made worsted, which is a very fine men's suiting: a plain wool with a beautiful drape. My uncle would bring it home from the mill and my mother would have a skirt made. She was quite smart and liked a good bit of cloth. So it's inherited, I suppose.

Then my uncle taught the Japanese how to make worsted. There was a big decline in Yorkshire tweeds and worsteds once the Japanese found out how to make them. That was my uncle. But at the time it seemed like a good idea.

I wanted to go to Art School and learn to be a fashion designer but my father said 'Over my dead body'. He didn't want me to go to London because he thought that was a den of iniquity. And he didn't want me to do something peculiar and arty because he thought that was bad too. Fathers had a lot of say in those days. So I went to be a secretary and then headed off to London as soon as I could and did fashion instead.

I went to work for someone in the rag trade in Great Titchfield street. The rag trade was the word for high street fashion – the cheaper end of fashion. Amazing person called Jackie Staples; she had a label called Jake. She used to just copy stuff out of Yves St Laurent, down-price it and we'd ship it into Fenwick and into *The Telegraph*. It was right at the beginning of mail order and *The Sunday Telegraph* used to do mail order. So that was great.

I was brought up in the '50s and all I wanted was a pair of denim jeans. When I went to Sunday school I still had to wear gloves and a hat. But that was the very early '50s. And then Mary Quant came. Then it was BIBA and everything became very affordable. Then there was Radley and there was Quorum, Celia Birtwell and Ozzie Clark. It was FUN then. SO exciting. I used to go and shop in Browns, spend a month's money and eat nothing for a month.

Is it time for lunch yet? I had a marmalade sandwich but that was a long time ago …

Why did I start selling? Oh, 'cause I'm always broke! Never have any money. I've always had to work and I'd rather work for ME because I come from a family who work for themselves. My mother was always very independent and I think it filtered through. When I was married I still worked. And actually I really never told my husband what I was earning, even if it was nothing very much. He had absolutely no idea EVER what I had. And I think that's probably a bad thing. Do not do that! Communicate about money.

I met Jill at some fair or other eight years ago. I said 'I want to buy some of your linen sheets but not at this price.' She spent three days saying 'No' to me and then she said 'Oh, okay. You'd better come out to Burgundy and look!'

So I did. Then we decided to work together. So she's there and does a lot of the buying and Romily, my daughter, goes and helps and I go out and help. We drive out overnight – Romily sleeps in the van ALL the way down there – and then we buy like fury, load up the van and come back again.

Ah look, we've got another pug down there! We're prolific in pugs today!

– How old's yours?
– Pepper, stop it! You're a nightmare!

The French had much more. Even the ordinary girl in the village had some sort of chest that was her marriage chest. Whereas I don't think we had quite the same here. So they'd have dozens of tea towels that were never used. And they'd have dozens of linen underdresses – this sort of thing which is sort of like a nightie, but it's not really a nightie, it's an underdress. They changed these rather more than their clothes because of course they didn't wash. These are peasant wear. This is all handfinished on the edge – it's beautifully made. Lots of people wear these. They put a leather belt on and wear them on holiday, or in the garden. They're beautiful linen.

These nightshirts are very smart. I don't know what the R was for: he was probably called Robert, you know, Ricard! The French were very good at monogramming everything. They had books with stencils telling them exactly how to do the monograms. Lots of different styles. But everything, everything. Who else would monogram their tea towel? They did then. That was part of their trousseau. They'd hand stitch them all and then they'd sit there.

Those are lace collars. Beautiful, beautiful. I sell them for eighteen, twenty-five. The workmanship is absolutely incredible. People quite often tacked them on and then moved them onto another dress. And they did the same with sleeves. Lace sleeves they would take off the dress. Lace cuffs they'd take off. As well as all the buttons. That's why I have millions and millions of mother of pearl old ones. And horn buttons and bone buttons.

I do love lace. I loved Kate Middleton's wedding dress: I thought that was beautiful. The inspiration for the dress was Princess Grace's wedding dress. She saw it in the V & A. It was a very simple dress but it had to have enough oomph didn't it? In fact, Princess Grace's dress had much more of a bell. It was the '60s … But I think it was that tight lace bodice and the long lace sleeves. Lace in a wedding – beautiful don't you think? Jane was saying the wedding veil was wrong. She has this wonderful shop up in Golborne Road, doing wedding things and using vintage but making new. The veil was too heavy:

it pressed down too much. It should have been much lighter. And Jane said they were using the wrong silk tuile. They should have known, shouldn't they?

– *What's that?*
– *It's a suit carrier.*
– *Ah … that's thirty …*
– *Okay, I'll leave it thanks … It's very nice … I'm tripping over the dog here!*

I didn't want to sell that. I didn't want to sell it to her. It's funny that, isn't it? Very naughty. That doesn't happen very often. And I don't know why. She comes round all the time. And there's one other customer who has a terrible reputation amongst all of us. She buys things with a very, very tiny waist. Her waist is twenty-one inches or something. And she comes with tape measures. All she wants to do is tell you how tiny her waist is. All the time! For the last eight years. No thank you very much! She'd pick up something like this – which is tiny – and she'd measure it and she'd say 'I think that's a little too big for me'. Well put it back then … bitch!

I'll give ten per cent to someone who deals with me regularly and buys a lot on a regular basis. I have dealers who come and they never ask me for a discount, EVER. So I always give them a bit of a discount. But if somebody's coming along, and I don't know them, and they look at something – like this is forty quid; it's early 1900s, it's handmade and it's very pretty – and they say, 'Can you do it for twenty?' NO, I can't! Why do you think I've written forty on it?' I mean, why? You go into Topshop and you pay fifty or sixty quid quite easily … I'm sorry about the dog.

People think because prices are low you can lower them even more. But then you're not making any money are you? They just think that they can bargain all the time because we're selling vintage, and you can't. You can maybe ask politely but not for half price! If you don't make your margins then you're not going to survive.

What would I like the future to hold? More money. We do the lottery: we put a pound a week on. We did win something. We certainly won back what we put on. So maybe we'll get the big one.

But If I won the lottery, I wouldn't stop this. It's just a lot of very good friends and beautiful things. Good combination.

'There's no escape'

HILARY, VINTAGE CLOTHING

I was born in 1952 in Whitechapel. My parents had just left Goldsmiths Art College. I think at the time my father was designing film posters and my mother was doing something strange like designing chequebooks.

I grew up in a ballroom: my parents had rented this amazing space in a massive mansion block, right on Clapham Common, and it was the communal ballroom for the entire block. I was there until I was six so I just remember running about in this massive space with pink columns and an Italian painted ceiling. It was totally open plan and we had one other room, the powder room, which was my bedroom and my brother's bedroom. It was all very grand for something like nineteen shillings and eleven pence a week.

I went to a rather rough little school round the corner from there and then we did the sensible thing and moved out to suburbia proper, where my mother was incredibly bored and I ended up going to a convent school. They thought it was in my best interest at the time but it was probably the worst thing they ever did. Except that it turned me into a complete rebel. Then, after that, I did the usual obligatory short stint at art school, which came to nothing, various odd jobs and then ended up doing this and working for myself.

Virtually everyone I know who's here seems to have gone to art school. I think, perhaps, at the time when we were there, it was the refuge of the imaginative but generally feckless! It was just an excuse to have a good time, take a lot of drugs and not do very much.

When I left I went and worked in various fashion shops and, very incongruously, did a management training course at Jaeger. Where I stuck out like a sore thumb. I got sacked when they caught me on the men's floor parading around in a pair of very, very short shorts. The Jaeger uniform was dire – a sort of skinny ribbed jumper and a tweed skirt – and I wanted to show off my day attire, so to speak, to the chaps. It was the end of late night shopping. I'd got changed and come down and I was standing on a stage, embracing one of the male models, whilst very scantily clad in a pair of electric blue hotpants and over-the-knee lime green platform boots. Not realising that the department manager was there …

I ended up in a shop called Jean Machine where I met my husband. Then I had a child and ended up getting a very sensible job to fit in. I actually worked as a school cook, believe it or not. And then my old school friend, Giga, and I set up a clothing stall at Covent Garden.

It was 1979, the start of the new Romantic Era, so they were all wearing vintage stuff. Among our customers were Steve Strange, Boy George, the transvestite Marilyn and all the Blitz kids. I was selling a lot of '40s and '50s clothes then. The girls in that group loved wearing boned taffeta ball gowns with loads of petticoats underneath and they all loved lacey things.

Boy George looked like Kate Bush then. He was very, very skinny and he had this mass of dark hair which he used to backcomb. And full make-up. He used to buy coats, cloaks, lace blouses: women's clothing. He'd wear suave pants (silky and gathered round the waist) and a girls' blouse which he would tuck in. And he used to cram his feet into women's shoes. He was probably about a size nine but he would actually try and cram his feet into a size seven. And he would suffer for it. He didn't care: he looked fabulous.

And Marilyn was SO beautiful looking with an androgynous kind of beauty. And then there was an absolutely gorgeous girl with porcelain skin, dark almond eyes, her dark hair swept up in a huge bee hive and red Cupid bow lips. Stunning. It was like looking at a collection of tropical butterflies and you'd just kind of marvel at how wonderful they looked.

Giga and I would never come to the market without being dressed up in seamed stockings and absolutely massive hats. Black felt hats. Huge things with ostrich feathers. I had a hat made by Steven Jones which was like a pagoda. And I wore a thin black evening coat, belted in, printed with copper abstract shapes. And voluminous copper-coloured pants shot with gold. Was I warm enough? No! I was absolutely bloody frozen all the time. You didn't care. It was fashion – you had to suffer!

We came to Portobello in 1982. It was fabulous then. There were very few tourists and lots and lots of Londoners. It was before all the parking restrictions came in so you'd get families coming and they'd all buy something.

You'd get to know a lot of local people who were really lovely and very loyal and would come to you every week. And I suppose the difference was that I would set up at this time in the morning and I would have a queue of people – dealers and local customers – waiting to see what I was bringing out.

There was quite an interest in classic English clothing then so I was selling Harris tweeds and Burberry coats which were being worn in a slightly ironic way. And collarless shirts were massive: both granddad shirts and regular striped City shirts. A lot of them were utility clothing from wartime. They had the utility mark in them: two very solid black symbolic Cs with little cuts out of them (kind of Pac-man shaped) and then it said '41' or something like that. That meant that you could purchase them with a voucher out of your ration book. The outerwear would usually be made from a fairly rough wool and the styles would be a little more basic, but by today's standards they look like absolutely wonderful works of tailoring. And the quality was fabulous.

Back in the '40s things were not washed that often so you changed your collar every day but you didn't change the shirt. Everyone wore quite hefty vests underneath so it mattered less. Also, because things were so much more of a uniform, no one really noticed. Things were so expensive then: most men would have had maybe two suits – a work suit with one jacket and two pairs of trousers and a suit for best, which would have been for weddings and funerals.

In the '80s people were wearing collarless shirts without a collar. Boys *and* girls – with the girls belting them in. And we had masses and masses of old '60s and '70s Levis, the more faded the better. Girls were buying those very big and belting them in so they were really high on the waist and really baggy in the legs.

It was an era where people were quite swamped in their clothes. It was big on top, big on the bottom, with a little waist. I think it took a lot of references from film noir. The kind of mac look. Think of lots of the pop videos at the time, shot at night, with women with men's trench coats on, pulled in tight and collars turned up. I have to say on the whole it didn't really work quite as well as, say, Katherine Hepburn doing it!

In the early '90s we had the last recession. The recession was FABULOUS for us. Absolutely fabulous. It was a different retail world then. We didn't have the likes of Primark. We didn't have people doing faux vintage. We didn't have cheap high street clothing. So we were still incredibly competitive: that's why we did so well.

Those were good days. It was so busy you'd actually have people queuing up to pay you. And there was a lady customer who used to come every week and regularly spend about five hundred pounds before I'd even started my day. It was an incredible buzz. I was making very good money: three times what I make now.

I also sold some vintage cashmere. I found a beautiful, beautiful little brown intarsia cardigan which was sprinkled with autumnal leaves, woven into the design. I sold that to Stella Tennant. She used to come round more or less every week to buy bits and pieces for her wardrobe. When she became the model for Christian Dior she was on the BBC, at the Dior Fashion show. She was on the catwalk and then, next minute, they were interviewing her backstage and she was wearing my cashmere! I saw her and I just screamed 'Quick everybody, come and have a look!' And I thought 'Wow. That's as good as it gets.'

In the '90s we saw lots of people from the music industry. Like Lennie Kravitz, the Gallagher boys from Oasis, Blur, Michael Stipe from REM and Kylie Minogue. I ended up selling her a beautiful little 1930s dress that my eight-year-old daughter used to wear – she was that tiny! And she was lovely and smiley and sweet and completely unpretentious. One still glimpses people now and then. Bob Geldof. Mick Jones from the Clash. He's quite cadaverous looking and he stalks Portobello in this elegantly-wasted way.

There's been quite an abrupt decline in sales over the last five years. Vintage has just become a label that's attached to a style. So when Topshop does 'Topshop Vintage' it's really just remakes of old styles. And the age group that I sell to are now buying things from Primark and Hennes and they are not going to be willing to spend a lot of money. So you have to think differently, move with the times and sell things in a different way.

I get every fashion magazine every month and I look at everything that's going on. I check out what my customers wear from top to bottom. Then I try and find something that I can buy in bulk and I price up as low as I can. To most young people now, '80s is vintage. And that's what sells. So I've got masses and masses of men's '80s shirts with abstract patterns – quite bright, quite gaudy. And check shirts and denim shirts – which are kind of a hardy perennial. I'm also selling quite short shorts, made from cut down jeans frayed in the washing machine.

When I started in '79 I was getting all my stuff from jumble sales. Then jumble sales started to dry up and I got a rag yard contact. It was like suddenly discovering a treasure trove. We were paying a lot more for things but we were getting amazing, beautiful things because there was so much rag going through the yard. Every week it was like an adventure: 'What are we going to get today? What gems are we going to find?'

Every rag yard is laid out differently. Most of them work from a conveyer belt which means that you'll have one chap who will barrow in all the sacks from the recycling bins and another chap who'll rip open the bags and throw the rag onto the belt. The belt goes up quite steeply and then goes back on itself and it basically shakes all the clothing apart. Then it comes past you and you have to grab what you can off it. You've got all the workers in the factory standing alongside you. They have cages in front of them – like the old British Rail type luggage containers. They'll throw in them the useful, resaleable clothes which are mostly sold to India and Africa: cotton shirts; cotton trousers; fleeces; anoraks – practical things. They're bought by the container load and shipped over to Nigeria, or wherever. Then tipped onto the dirt road and literally sold on the street, by the piece, for very little.

In the 1980s some yards would allow their staff to pull the vintage off and sell it to the traders. They would work for a very low basic wage from the management and that would be their money. So unskilled workers could take home between five hundred and a thousand pounds a week from what they were selling to the traders.

It is a dirty job. You're handling dirty clothes. Unwashed clothes. What I've noticed recently is that things have got filthier and filthier. People will chuck all kinds of tatty old rubbish into recycling bins whereas when they used to donate old clothing to charity shops, it was always clean. Now you can get filthy underwear and things like that. Anything can be in there! Even cat poo or the odd compressed rat.

In the '80s we were pulling off a lot of '60s stuff: cotton dresses with really good prints and full skirts; little reversible gabardine jackets with lovely details and designs – like little sailing boats with pink sails on a wavy line of sea just going across the back; men's short sleeved casual shirts with motifs on them like trains, boats and planes and wonderful scenes like the New York skyline and men with saxophones. I was so much more enthusiastic about it then, I have to say. I still love doing it but the kind of joy that you get from things has diminished considerably because of the quality. Today things are not intended to last. Now you go to the rag yards and the vast percentage of it will be Florence and Fred from Tesco, George at Asda and, of course, Primark.

Is it still worth it? Oh definitely. Yes. Yes. And now and then I still do have amazingly good days. But I have to work much, much harder at it. And

I am feeling old now! I'm sixty and I can't kid myself that I have the same strength or energy that I used to have. It is MASSIVELY tiring. If you look at the size of my pitch and you think I do all that on my own – get out all that stock, put up the tarpaulin and everything – it's physically very challenging.

I don't enjoy the process but I enjoy being here when I'm here. I love selling things. I love talking to the customers. I love the people that are around me. They're such a very colourful patchwork of characters and they become like your extended family because you end up knowing them for years and years.

I think we're here because we wouldn't survive anywhere else! But that's just very tongue-in-cheek. I think that we're great survivors, actually, and we would probably survive anything! Come recessions and economic meltdowns, we somehow still manage to struggle on.

There is a feeling that there is a freedom that comes with this job. But it's the most tremendous tie as well. You can't ever sit back and take it easy. If you decide you don't want to get up at half past five in the morning, or don't feel up to buying one week, then you just know that you're not going to make so much money come the weekend. So it's quite a tyrannical business really because once it's got you, that's it. After having done it for so long you are obviously utterly unemployable!

I very rarely go on holiday. If you do, you're losing money and it's costing you on top of it. So you really do have to make sure that in the week you treat yourself to something. At the moment I'm doing a comedy scriptwriting course. I have had so many hysterical moments here, one way or another. Most of them come from the people you meet and the things that they say to you. As a stallholder you attract people that are slightly out of kilter with the rest of the world. They'll come and engage you in conversation and this just leads to some really, really funny stories.

You get conspiracy theorists and their theories are just beyond bizarre. You get people who are completely delusional about their own intelligence and attractiveness. There was one chap who would come and talk about himself and his relationships. He just couldn't work out why he didn't have a girlfriend and he would say 'Well de reason is, like, I go out … like … and I'm lookin' at them and I'm talkin' to them … and then … they kind of walk away. But it's probably 'cos most of the time they think that I'm very deep … and I'm, like, too intelligent … and it sort of puts them off, you see … ' And he'd say 'I have to move out of my flat. The landlord's put it on the market for some ridiculous sum of money … So what I do is … when people come round to look at it … in the condensation on the windows I write 'Do not buy this flat'. I move the furniture around so it makes the place look smaller. I shake salt on the floor and I write 'Devil worshippers' in the salt.' Nobody bought it for two years! Every week it would be a story like this. But he had such a good heart and he's such a good guy. He's actually got a full-time job with someone now, in the market selling.

What does my future hold? Gosh … I see myself being here when I'm about seventy-five. There's no escape: I will die here! I will die here in vintage clothes and be carted off! They'll say 'Hilary for God's sake, it's time to go …'

'If I didn't take any money, I'd still go up there'

FRANCES, VINTAGE CLOTHING

I come from a very old Kingstonian family. My grandfather bought the yard on Fairfield and he used to hire horses and carts out by the day for rag men to go totting – collecting rags [old clothes] and that. People used to want to get rid of them. Sometimes they were paid and sometimes the rag man would just give the kids baby chicks. Yeah! Or goldfish. Then we'd buy it off of them. And people would bring stuff to the yard on prams. We used to buy a lot of rabbit skins. Use to make fur gloves, hats – all out of rabbit skin. And then, during the war, it was bits of lead, copper, brass and iron. When my grandfather died, it was front page of the *Surrey Comet*: 'The Death of Kingston's most colourful character. "There's wealth in waste", says Herbie.'... Oh have you got that on? Am I all right talking?

Rags were worth money in them days, because they were good quality: everything was pure; it was real. You could send them away as they were but you got three times as much money for them when they were stripped up. You'd have the old hooks – what the butchers used to hang the cows on. You'd put a coat on two hooks and rip the lining out. You sliced off buttons with a knife. After the war my dad used to do that. And Bill Alexander. He came home from the war and he didn't have any feet. Then they were all sorted – woollens, merino, serge, angora, flannel – and it all was then stripped up in bags. And the big lorries used to come and take them and they was remade into clothes. Have you seen the grey blanket, the old army blanket? Well they were made out of rags.

I was born in 1939. When I left school I became a nurse and I had Monday as my day off. The Monday market was the big cattle market and

I used to wheel over a totter's barrer full of bike bits and pieces: chains; old handlebars … I used to get them for nothing because they used to come in the old iron. I used to stand on a stall near the cows and take about two pound, three pound and I was a rich person then!

Then I got married. Unfortunately I had two children. Well, fortunately I had two children. Then my husband went off with someone else and that broke my heart. So we broke up. I never went back to nursing: I went to Kingston market. And then, in the late '50s, I went to Portobello.

Why Portobello? Because Jack went up there. Jack's family got killed in the war so my mum and dad took him in. And when Alan left me, and my dad died, we decided to get married. Men and women didn't live together then. It wasn't nice. But we was always brought up as brother and sister so it wasn't that sort of marriage. There wasn't any children or anything like that. He's had his life, and I've had mine.

… Jack went up there for years before me. He used to take pots and pans from the yard. Everyone wanted pots and pans in them days. And they'd be going away with kettles, frying pan, yer know. So happy. Everybody so happy.

The rag-and-bone men used to line up across the road. Where all the vans are now, you'd see all the horses and carts. When they'd been totting, they used to sort the good stuff out and call it 'usefuls'. They'd come up on a Friday at four, five o'clock in the morning, before the toll man came out, sell their bit of stuff and go. The toll man didn't use to come 'til about nine o clock so they didn't have to pay any money.

The people who wanted to buy it, they used to come out early. And all the people would be following the horse and cart and, "Ave to look what yer got, Harry! Oooh, take that fer me Harry! What 'ave you got Harry?' You know. All round the horse and cart. And the man used to stand up on the cart and say 'Look, d'you want this? Two bob! D'yer want this? Over there, a shilling. Take the ladies' money. Now we've got four nice coats here. I want two bob each for them. Now, who's gonna have 'em? The first one with their hand's up, gets 'em.' And you was lucky. You went home with a new coat. Because clothes were hard to get.

They were all local people. You didn't have any tourists. They were all ordinary people that lived in them houses. They weren't all toffee-nosed people because the houses weren't worth the money. Everybody was the same. Everybody had the same amount to live on. My mum used to get three pounds a week and that used to have to keep me, my twin brother and herself. For a week.

I used to get down there about five o'clock in the morning. Only on a Friday, 'cause you couldn't get a stall on a Saturday for love nor money. I was on the waiting list for nearly twenty years to get my stall Friday and Saturday. I would go in the yard and find old stuff – the old-fashioned hats, furs and all sorts of things – and put my stuff on the stall. There was no new stuff up Portobello Road then. Portobello Road was a second hand market and a fruit and veg market. Everythink was second hand: second hand cases; handbags; prams; old pushchairs; tin baths.

By the time you unloaded and sold yer stuff it was nearly dinner time. Somebody used to go down the fish shop, and get all the fish and chips. There was no takeaways – it was mainly fish and chips, sausage and chips, pie and mash with eels. There was a big pie and mash shop up the top of the road and people used to go and get pease pudding and faggots for breakfast or dinner.

Petro Lingo Gypsy Lee was on the corner then in a caravan. He was a very old man; he looked like an old Father Christmas. He came from Colchester but he had a farm under the Westway. He used to go to the market in the caravan on Friday and stay up there all night. He would tell fortunes in the day and sell bits and pieces. I had my fortune told loads of times. What did he tell me? Oh, all sorts of rubbish. I reckon he used to make it up. Jack sold him this great big box of black candles and he was selling 'em for five pound each to all the black people to keep the evil spirits away.

… There was a lot of people on the market then who couldn't read and write. I didn't like to say that but there was. They knew their pounds, shillings and pence and yards, feet and inches but it was … all the other. A lot of people in my age group, we never went to school much during the war. St. Andrews School in Cottage Grove is where I went and it all got bombed. All that was left was the hall where you had your dinner. So half the school was allowed to go in the morning and all you had was a little square slate and a piece of chalk. And the teacher would say 'Right. Table. T A B L E spells table.' And you'd sing it all. That's how we learned. We didn't have any books. And then when bombs were dropping very hard at the end of the war, nobody went. And you could tell. 'Cause you'd say to them, 'What do you think of this? Do you know where that address is?'

'Oh I can't be bothered. I'll have a look later.'

And you'd think, 'Oh well, I won't say anymore.' There was no shame to it. They just didn't go to school.

The '60s were good. Really swinging. In the war years, everything was black – you didn't even have a coloured car. After the war, everybody wanted colours.

Oh it was great. All colours. Prints. All nice curtains with fruit on 'em. Bananas on 'em.

The next generation weren't the same. They had to have what they wanted. In the olden days you never bought anything 'on the knock'. But then they'd come up the market and buy it so much a week. Even from the market. But you didn't get it 'til you paid for it – if it was still there when you'd paid your three pound!

There was one bloke who used to come up there. We used to call him Snatcher Fred. And he'd have a lovely fridge up for sale for a fiver. Well everybody wanted a fridge in them days. And he'd say 'I'll deliver it for yer, on the horse and cart. Will you'll be in?' 'Yes, that's right.' 'Okay.' Got the address and everything. The woman had gone – he'd sell it again! She'd come back next week: 'Where is my fridge?' 'You gave me this address.' 'No I didn't!' 'I've got a bad back, Madam. I can't bring it down the steps. I left it outside. What's happened to it's none of my business.' And that's how he used to carry on. He'd sell that fridge a dozen times. And then he'd drive off with his horse and cart. What could you do? You didn't say anything. You knew he was doing it but you just didn't open yer mouth and say anything. Market people never tell on anybody. You keep yourself to yourself. If you can't say anything nice about somebody, you don't say anything at all.

The yard was sold in 1964. Then I went round the jumble sales looking for nice quality clothes to sell. I don't buy anything anymore. Haven't done for years and years and years. I've filled one bedroom and my attic and I've got a garage full of stuff. My garage's forty feet long but it's FULL of stuff. You wanna go and have a look?

This was a bedroom originally. There's top hats up there, look! This one is all seal skin and this one is silk. They are quite small. People were very small in them days. That's a hat that they used to wear in the 1950s. You've seen Doris Day and all of them with 'em, ain't you? Look: this one is made out of velvet with a net on the front that comes over the face and two little jewels each side. And here's another one. Can't remember where I found them. You can't find them today; that's why I like to keep a few bits.

I try to keep it all covered up. Most of this stuff's in boxes and I line all the boxes out so no moths can get in. I don't even know what's in 'em now. I do get a nice surprise when I open the boxes. I think 'Oh wow. That's for the market. Get a few bob for that this week.' Oh yes, it will all come out when I get round to it. I gotta first get rid of the stuff out the garage. I wouldn't say I'm a hoarder, no. You've got to keep some stock.

Never had a car in here. Look. Goes right back. Look at it all! I don't know what's there. I just sort of load the car up and take a few bits each week. And I tell you I'm getting to the back of my garage now and some of that stuff hasn't been out for twenty-five years.

Yes, that's the Pope. He looks after me.

This I just found today and I've put it in here to take. It's a debutante dress. It's lilacy mauve satin, all lined with net. They used to have that for their party to pass out in. This is all the old dresses, look, all waiting to go up. I've got lots of the old evening suits and dresses. Years ago they all used to wear evening suits if they went out. Even to a Masons' do. But they don't now. They don't dress like they used to.

See look – all old handbags hanging up here … That's another old hat I just found on the floor. Old ribbon on it. Somebody'll like that. Got lots of these heads, look. They're what they used to have in the old hairdressers years ago to help people train. Bloke come up the market with hundreds of 'em. Fiver each. I only bought six: I didn't want too many. I put different hats on 'em and put them up at the stall.

I don't really know what sells anymore because it's a different generation. And I don't know what price to ask any more. My stall's right opposite the Westway, under the bridge. I chose it because I don't have to put a cover up. I used to arrange it a bit more but I'm too old now. I have got a cafe there. They call me Tea Wee because I drink tea and go to wee. I go 'All right. Cup of tea.' And then they bring me a cup of tea out and mind the stall while I go to the loo.'

People still bring me stuff. They work in Holland Park and the madam will say to them 'Oh, you've been so good. Look, I don't really like this handbag. Would you like it?' 'Ooh yes, I'd like it.' And they bring it to me and ask me to sell it and we have half each. The Chelsea Pensioners often come up the market and say hello. Angela Rippon came to my stall. She bought a blouse with big cuffs. She loves them.

If I didn't take any money, I'd still go up there. Well, I mean I'm seventy-two now – what would I do? I go up there; I got my car and I sit in the car door like an armchair. Everybody comes and talks to me. I earn a little bit of money sometimes, just enough to pay the stall. Sometimes I don't earn much. But I love it up there: it's a way of life.

Have I been any help to you? Have I really?

'Always a happy, jolly face'

PAUL, JEWELLERY

I wasn't an abused Barnardo's child. I had a perfectly normal family, normal up-ground, mother, father still alive – what else d'you wanna know?

I was from … what's that got to do with our past if anything? Fulham. And my family originally from South East London but they live in Fulham. So that's it in a nutshell.

What did my dad and mum do? They had me! Ha ha ha ha ha ha. Worked at a building society and worked as an engineer.

Oh darling, I didn't know it was a tape recorder. I'm thrown now. I feel really nervous. I feel all quiet. I thought it was questions about the market. You're very delving into my personal cupboard. You're going too quickly too deep, darling. I feel very, very … I don't know you're not Inland Revenue, do I?

What brought me here? Just say I got drawn the short straw! Ha ha ha ha. I trained as a chef but I just collect things. So it got out of hand. Ha ha ha. It just overwhelmed.

When did I start collecting? I've always had an eye for it. You either have an eye for it or you don't have an eye for it. It's like when did you want to be a reporter? You're always naturally very nosy! Ha ha ha ha.

What was I buying as a child? Oh I can't remember. I didn't have many friends and I had curly hair and I was the last in the sports field so I had to collect. There was nothing else to do. Obviously you don't have any money then do you? So shells and conkers. Marbles. Just a magpie, you know. But a natural interest. You read stuff. You just naturally pick up and learn as you go along. Takes ten, twenty years to learn everything. It's like one day you might work for the *Independent* and you'll know what I mean. But we've all gotta start somewhere. Ha ha ha ha ha.

Darling you caught me on the spur. I'm not prepared for this. Mentally. You've done this on purpose, 'aven't yer? It's a hot day, I've just had lunch and I'm psychologically drained by a thousand nutters. Ha ha ha ha ha. No, but some of them are hard work, you know. A hard work customer is somebody who wants everything for one pound. And I mean one pound. Ha ha ha ha ha.

Darling I can't think of what to say. You're not giving me very interesting questions anyway. Very boring … dry … questions. Everything from a year onwards is data protection. I'm not interested in history. I'm only interested in right here and now.

I'll do you a cracking interview and I'm word perfect and everything you want to know in the world – any other day after today. When I'm better in the mood. I just feel a bit off colour today. I didn't even sleep last night. And I'm not as sharp as normal, as you've probably noticed …

[Eight months later …]

Come on. Sensible head. No questions about weight or anything like that. Ha ha ha ha ha ha.

I've been doing this for twenty years. I'm always buying and always selling. It's continuous. They support each other. Obviously I collected and I liked car boots and all that palaver to start with. But you can't keep everything can you? And then you buy boxes of things and you realise that you can sell a few things. And I was good at doing what I do and I enjoyed doing it and turned it into a business so to speak.

It was mainly jewellery to start with. Jewellery seemed the most easiest thing to sell with the space you had to start off with. I didn't always have bigger stalls like this as I do now. I started with smaller stalls. And obviously jewellery is easy to carry – smaller and more compact – and it always sells. And then it escalated to vintage stuff across the board: vintage clothes, jewellery; anything old of interest.

There are different areas of my table. The middle table's the best stuff. The dear stuff. The gold and silver and rarities. One side is your pick and mix pound rubbish. Tat. And the other side's vintage clothes, vintage handbags, vintage shoes – quality bits and pieces. So you get the clothes people on this side. You'll get the council peasanty people, the pound merchants, on this side. And you'll get the quality ones in the middle, where the glass boxes are. They tend to not mingle on the inside. Ha ha ha ha ha.

I'd never sell one item 'cause one item's too risky. That's the art of dealing: never have tunnel vision. I tune in to what people want rather than what I want and that works. There's a million housewives round here come to me and they'll buy a pair of earrings for two quid but they wouldn't buy anything out of the dear stuff trays. They don't really want to spend any money; they just want a quick ring or pair of earrings to cheer themselves up. And they will come back every week like clockwork – you can set your watch by some of them. If you get forty or fifty of them in one day that's a hundred quid just for a pile of rubbish! Ha ha ha ha.

It's a bit of a social hub as well. A lot of people pour out all their emotional problems and that. I'm not really that interested but I make out I am. That's part of what brings them back!

Do I tell them my troubles? No. Always a happy, jolly face. Ha ha ha ha ha ha.

The nicest thing that ever happened to me … A regular of mine got breast cancer – this is a true story, a very sad story – and she was in the Royal Brompton. She disappeared for a while and then she came down with this carer woman. She had had all her chemotherapy: she had no hair or anything like that. She said to me 'The medication's stopped working for me at the moment. I've only got weeks to live.' She said 'The only thing that cheers me up is to come down here, talking to you.' And that was like … a bit of a … even I didn't say anything to that. This last knockings, her life's over, but the only thing that cheers her up in all this is coming down to the stall … Which I found really quite choking. That made me glad to do this job. Because it's something nice, you know?

People come to get away for five minutes from whatever's going on with them. They like a little bit of a laugh. You learn who you can make a joke with and who you can't. I'm not going to make one of my bad jokes on somebody's who's standing there with a Chanel bag and posh shoes. I'm not going to say something too low-key. But I will make a little comment that she'll find funny. If she's looking at the glasses I'll say, 'Stop making a spectacle of yourself' – something like that. Some little sort of icebreaker.

> – *Can I look at this in the light?*
> – *I'll have to tie your shoelaces together Madam. Ha ha ha ha ha ha ha ha …*

Things like that people find funny. Things like that will make a sale. 'Cause people let their guard down. They laugh. When they laugh you've hooked 'em in. They'll shop and shop and shop then and just relax.

– *I've bought something else. A hat and a collar.*
– *All right darling. Oh lovely. That's what you need with summer coming!*
– *Ha ha ha ha ha. See she liked my joke …*
– *I'm having a live interview with one of my regular customers, Rosie. Come over here. Tell her about the service you get.*
– *This is Rosie, the market cleaning supervisor. What do you think of the service on my stall?*
– *Beautiful.*
– *And what about the things you buy over the years? Quality?*
– *Quality, good quality. Nice stuff.*
– *Have you ever had counterfeit stuff?*
– *Never.*
– *All genuine?*
– *Yeah.*
– *Right, you go and pick your fiver off the lady over there! Ha ha ha ha ha ha …*

If I wasn't as chatty as I was, I wouldn't sell fifty per cent as much as I sell. It would be a lot lower. Because it wouldn't go off the table on its own … A lot of these stalls are not really that sociable, are they? I wouldn't even go shopping around a lot of them, to be honest with you. Why not? Little attitude problems. The more good you are at something, the more you're hated. The better you are at doing it, the worse you're liked. They all like to come to me and get good deals off me but behind my back they despise me! Ha ha ha ha ha. Some of them don't make a lot of money. They can't understand why I do and they don't. It's simple things – good product, fair price – isn't it, at the end of the day?

I'm just watching the gloves over on that corner. Everything's all right: I'll know when to move. You're going to get the odd thing stolen but I'm not really bothering about that side. They're welcome to it! Ha ha ha ha ha ha. Last week a pair of Christian Louboutin shoes went for a walk without the legs in them. That was my fault: I put them both together. I should have only put one out. But it's not the end of the world, is it?

There's meant to be security. There's no security here. If anything happens, nobody would help you. You do get the odd incident but I know how to handle a situation. If somebody nicked a pound ring and they was drunk, I'd just let them have the bloody ring. I wouldn't really cause a scene over a pound ring. Other people might and that's when you get trouble isn't it? It's not really worth the aggravation.

I've had hoodies trying to kick my table upside down and trying to rob money. It wasn't my fault. The car broke down because my partner put diesel in and it was meant to be petrol. Not a good move. So I was here at seven thirty at night. It's low-life around here at that time: all the things come out the pond. Dogs walk around in pairs at that time of night here, Ha ha ha ha. And they was all hanging around and I was the only one here. I got all the good stuff away but they're all come round the table. I knew they was going to try something. And then they're pinching little pound watches ... I just let them get on with it. And then a couple of them got funny and started shaking the table and all the rest of it. But luckily enough the little girl around there, Julia, helped me. She's only a little pint size but she's got a big mouth on her. She came running round the corner shouting like a Banshee ... They must have thought she was an absolute lunatic and they run off! Ha ha ha ha ha. There was six men down on that stall there: they all looked the other way.

In the morning it's all vagrants sleeping here. Because it's dry, isn't it? So it's a bit like shelter. Usually they wake up when they're rattling the tables and that and get up of their own accord. There's one who likes to sing in this chair here and piss in this chair. Nightmare. In one word: nightmare. Seventy-four he is. He knows every song ever written in the world and he will sing it to you, every word perfect, from start to finish. Does he sing it nicely? Not really, no. Just like a wailing old drunk! Ha ha ha ha ha ha. He threw a bottle of cider over one of my customers wearing a Chanel coat and then had the audacity to turn round and blame her for it and demand she buys him another bottle of cider.

Sometimes he does it all day. Depends if he's on a bender. But usually he collapses or goes to prison. One of the two. 'Cause he starts fighting everybody and it all goes out of hand and he goes to prison for three months. Which I think is where he's gone now. Ha ha ha ha. He was in sheltered housing down there for the elderly people. He got thrown out because he wasn't living there and he rented it out, the ground property, to four Polish workers for one hundred pounds each a week and he lived out on the street drinking!

Drugs? What do you want to know about that? Of course I notice things going on. You notice everything going on. There's shoplifters round here. They'll offer you stuff. Meat out of the supermarkets, God knows what. I'm not going to admit to eating any of it though. Ha ha ha ha ha ha. There was a time when you could order your leg of lamb and belly of pork and all that. They'd come and ask you 'What d'you want for your Sunday dinner?' then they'd go and get it! Ha ha ha ha ha. But that one's got obviously arrested and disappeared.

- *I'm doing an interview dear. News of the world! News of the world! I'll be in the Sunday paper!*
- *I'll take the two. Although I don't know if I need another watch. But I'll take it.*
- *Stylish. You can always put them on ebay and make a few pound for yourself. At the end of the day. If you need money. Not that you need the money ...*
- *I need money!*
- *You don't look like you do. You look like you've got loads with your outfit! You look like you just come straight from the Ivy.*
- *I'm coming from home ... and an hour ago.*
- *Well when you go out I'd like to see ... It must be amaaazing. You look fabulous now.*
- *Thank you. You're 'bout to make a killing off me!*
- *Darling, I'll sell that stuff at that price anyway. You're not dealing with Chinese rubbish here.*

How have I learned what's what? Well you just learn. I can tell the difference between fakes and not fakes and Chinese and not Chinese. I can say that's '20s, that's '30s that's '40s. I can see a gold ring over by that café and know it is gold. I sense it. You can actually smell gold rings to tell they're gold. It's not really that hard!

Never looked at a catalogue in my life. No catalogues, no books, no other people. Just buying it and selling it and buying it and selling it and learning along the way. Making mistakes along the way, of course, and trying not to do them again. I've sold Chanel bags for two quid and platinum rings for a pound ... not for a few years, ha ha ha, but loads of them. Mistaken white gold: thinking something that's silver is silver when it's white gold 'cause they look exactly the same. Very easy one to make. How do

I know? Usually when the other person tells you, who's just bought it, and laughs at the same time! Ha ha ha ha ha. Ha ha ha ha ha. People are not nice: it's a wicked world …

Obviously you get better as time goes on. You try not to buy the rubbish things anymore but just the good things. Personally I like antique old things and quirky things of course. I'm buying all the time. Five days out of seven, from the crack of dawn: auctions; boot sales; word of mouth; house clearance people; charity shops; everything. I've got fingers in lots of pies. Ha ha ha ha.

Where do I put it? My whole house is supported along the foundations by stuff. Kind of difficult to get in. Three rooms of jewellery. You open the oven to trays of broaches – all on the shelves in the oven. In the toilet a sea of broaches. Every crevice has got jewellery.

Daunting? Daunting is the word! Completely unliveable. Very dodgy area when it comes to relationships and all the rest of it. Many times he's run off for days and come back again. Ha ha ha ha ha. I do live with a minimalistic person who makes life from getting totally out of control. They hate it. I love it. So it kind of works. If they did like it as well it would be a big problem. Ha ha ha ha ha.

And I give loads of it away. All them peasants up there who plead poverty – those old women who set their little stalls up with the supermarket trolleys they pinched – come wheeling along destitute with nothing and I give them stacks of the stuff. After I can't sell it, you know. Left over bits.

– *Hello love.*
– *D'you want to take over the interview? I'm tired now – I've been grilled for forty minutes!*

Is that all right for today? The future? I don't see much of a futurbut my God I've had a past. And that's the end of the interview for today. Thank you. Ha ha ha ha ha ha ha.

Now was that GOOD?

'It's like looking at the entrails of humanity'

Andrew, haberdashery

Why do I find it interesting? Because it's life. Every aspect of life. This is the costume of thirty, forty, fifty years ago but the players were the same as they are now. People don't change. So when you see all this at the market, spilled onto the floor, you see life for what it is: this continuous play, rolling on. It's like looking at the entrails of humanity, spread out over the street for people to pick through.

And it's the first man's first trade. When he first moved out of the cave, he went to a place to sell things. And that would have been a market.

And it's also the pureness of the trade. You bring something to a market, you ask the price and someone buys it or not – there's no one in between. We're obsessed with transparency now and it's as transparent as you can get. Though sometimes that can be the saddest thing in the world. I hate seeing people come to the market and not sell anything. They've invested so much of themselves into doing it and they're there because they probably need the money. It's like the little Match Girl – it just makes me want to burst into tears.

I was born in Rotherham, South Yorkshire in 1962. My parents both worked so I lived with my grandparents, three miles down the road. Then my grandfather died and I had to move back in with my parents.

We moved to Bournemouth in '74. I was profoundly dyslexic so they put me in a remedial class with all the gypsies from the New Forest. Our school had these pre-fabricated classrooms on the other side of the playground and that way they could keep the gypsies and the remedials away from the normal children and we would not really cross apart from playtime.

I remember my first day. The first years had to come in a day before the older kids and I remember this little kid being really cheeky and I remember hitting him. This boy I'd met said, 'I wouldn't have done that if I was you.' There were two big families – the Sheens and the Coopers – and I'd hit one of the Sheen kids. I didn't know that the next day the rest of the family were going to turn up. That did make my life hell for the first year or so.

I played truant all the time. Up the road was Bulstrodes auction house. There were sofas at the back and you could just sit there and while the day away. By the time I left school I knew all the prices of English furniture. I'd know a Georgian corner cupboard would cost two hundred and forty quid and a gate leg table was eighty. But I didn't have any money. So I was armed with this knowledge but I couldn't do anything with it.

I left before the exams. (We weren't allowed to take real exams anyway: instead of taking Maths we did this thing called 'Money Management'; instead of taking Science we did 'Combined Science'.) I started a motor mechanic apprenticeship but they found out I had no qualifications so I didn't last long.

My friend's mother had a market stall and his father was a props buyer for the BBC. I loved their house: it was full of things to look at. In our house we had new shag pile carpet and G plan sofa. They had rugs and pictures on the walls. It was a very different kind of thing.

I also had an Auntie Nora who lived in Sheffield and was really into collecting. Her house was great: there was just stuff, stuff, stuff. I now know a lot of it was mass produced Victoriana; it wasn't great antiques. But I loved going there. Lots of grownups don't have time for you, do they? But she had a lot of time to play, get things out and show them to you.

People like that are a catalyst. By the time I left school I'd been accumulating things for years. Not buying them, finding them. Pulling them out of skips. I'd filled my, bedroom up with bits and pieces. My friend's mother was always saying to me 'Andrew, you've got a real eye. Clear out your bedroom and take it down the market.' So I started. My very first stall was in Wimborne. I took fifty-six pounds that day – I can remember exactly. My apprenticeship had paid sixteen fifty a week. So I thought 'This is the way forward.'

The gypsy children's dads had the tenders for council dumps. And in those days, especially round the New Forest and Bournemouth, there were so many retired Colonels and other military types that what turned up was extraordinary. You could open a suitcase and it would be just full of brilliant, brilliant items. I could buy a carful for twenty pounds. If I could get the roof full and the car full it might cost me forty.

... I'd also buy from auction. I bought stuffed animals because no one wanted them: a fake mermaid, a Siamese sheep – all kinds of mad things   all for a pound. And tea chests of pots and pans: all, again, for a pound. And the two brothers who ran the auction, because they'd seen me sat there for years, would always let me take the goods and pay them the following week. Which is unheard of in auctions, or anything, nowadays.

There was no shortage of stock I could find. I didn't specialise. Sometimes I'd buy things because they were a certain colour; because I wanted to have a stall full of red that week. Or I'd put shapes together, irrelevant of their value or what they were. And then sometimes I'd just pick out wonderful items because I thought they were interesting. There was no conception that this was going to be the way I was going to make my living. It was just something I was doing. It was like I left school because the summer holiday started and I feel like I've been on summer holiday ever since!

By then I'd left home and I was completely left to my own resources. But it was really good fun. My friends had gone to college and they never had money. I had a car and I had some money in my pocket. I mean not a lot: I never had a lot. It was very, very difficult to have a vehicle that worked, some money to buy some stock with AND somewhere to sell things. To have the combination of the three seemed virtually impossible. You've got everything going and your car breaks down and you haven't got any money to fix your car because you've spent it on stock and you don't know where to go to get money. I had tons of traumas. Usually vehicle traumas. Always something going wrong. Why? Well my capital for buying a car was usually about two hundred pounds and I was driving them hundreds of miles a week, completely overloaded with stock. I remember sometimes, coming back from market, the oil light would come on and I couldn't afford to get any oil. So I'd cross my fingers, hope I'd get back ... and blow the engine up. Then I'd be back to square one again.

I'd just have to work it out. I'd have to do something in order to get by. I used to collect batteries because you could get the lead out of them. I'd find caravans and strip them for aluminium. I'd collect anything that you could find lying around which you could make some money out of.

What brought me to London was working for a guy called Peter Freight. He dealt in antiques but he'd lost his driving license so I used to drive to London for him. It was fantastic. I was seventeen, eighteen by then and I'd be driving this big van into town, full of antiques, going to all the antique shops that he used.

His wife used to do lace and clothing. One day she prepared about five or six boxes and gave me a map of how to get to Portobello and who to go and see. And when I got here, that's when I knew I'd got home. Because I was wearing old suits and anything I could find on the tip and all of a sudden everyone else around me was dressed in old clothes. It was a proper homecoming: I just suddenly fitted in. I really felt 'This is it. This is where I belong.' And that was a brilliant thing.

It's the fitter-outers that fit in here. The oddballs. Everyone is welcome at a market. That's why markets are so magical and important and wonderful. They act as a sponge for society to soak up people who don't have a place to fit. People who everyone has turned their back on. It gives structure to their week. Something to do and to focus on. A reason for getting in and out of bed.

You do become aware of other people's mental health issues. There are some people who come to the stall who've got Tourettes'. There are some compulsive obsessives. But you don't judge them for it. Sometimes it's what makes them interesting.

You used to see lots of fly pitchers. And for a lot of those people, coming out of home and putting down three or four pairs of shoes on the floor was their way of being part of society, rather than being sat at home. It's a tragedy they've gone. The council thought they should clear that up because it was unsightly and it didn't look great for your Kensington rate payers. But it was a very, very valuable thing.

And the personal interaction that you have with people – you can't put a value on that. Multinationals can't touch the reality of a market. Because they can't say to someone, 'That's fine, pay me next week' or 'You can have that for half the price.' And that's very, very important. And markets also give shoppers a chance to meet people they wouldn't normally meet: all nationalities; the very poor and very rich. The market is a place where they can come together and strike up a conversation. That's why I'm amazed the market isn't full. I'm absolutely amazed. Because for thirty-five quid you can stand in the middle of Kensington and Chelsea and you've got the opportunity to sell to the full spectrum of life.

Only this last two years I've been on a council pitch. That's because of the way they used to treat people. They really looked at us like we were Dickensian scum. When you used to go to the office, they would shout at you and marshall you around and treat you like thieves and vagabonds. I just thought, I don't want to be talked to like this'. But then the market died. On Friday you'd look up and down the road and there'd be no one on the street.

So I thought 'Great, I can spread out.' I've got three pitches now and they've really begun to be a bit more human – a number of the girls are really nice.

… I've had gaps: it hasn't been continuous trading. And I've usually had a shop as well. So Portobello Road has just been a tiny part of what I've done but it's been a regular tiny part. Portobello has actually been a saviour for me because a lot of the time I've gone off on very crazy schemes and ended up losing money. And then I've always come back to Portobello Road in order to work my way back out of trouble again.

… In fact, I was working myself back out of a hole again when I started this haberdashery. I had gone into a property partnership. My grandfather had always warned me about partnership; he used to say 'a partner-ship is the worst ship that sailed'. Well it soured and I was virtually wiped out. I somehow managed to beg, borrow or steal ten grand and I used it to buy a whole job lot of vintage ribbon. Striped vintage ribbon. I spent every penny I had on it. Just like Jack and the Beanstalk.

Why? Because I thought it looked beautiful. And even I could count that if I got a pound a roll there were more than ten thousand rolls of it. I think I bought three and a half tonnes in weight. It was nearly two Sprinter vans – full, full, full, as high as you can get. And I was probably overloaded as well.

I got my old stall back – outside a shop where I'd rented before. The stall looked AMAZING – covered in all this striped ribbon. The first customer wanted to buy two metres. I didn't have a pair of scissors or a ruler because I thought people were going to buy it by the roll. So I borrowed them, came back, cut it and they said 'How much is that'. And I said, 'Oh I dunno: two quid a metre?' Then I looked in the back of my van and I thought, 'Wow. If I get two quid for every metre that's in the back of that van, that would be really good.'

I didn't think about becoming a haberdasher: I just thought about sur-viving. So I'd come every week and sell this ribbon. Then I realised that it was going to take years to sell so I started buying other vintage haberdashery and fabrics and trims. I just applied the same rules as I did to anything else: if it was nice, buy it.

I really enjoy it. I really enjoy it because I don't pre-judge my customers thinking whether or not they're going to spend. I stopped enjoying antiques when my expenses were too high. Because I would look at a customer and I would pre-judge them and then try and sell them something because I'd got my rent coming up. So when they came in, sometimes I was just thinking, 'Get yer chequebook out. I've got my effing bills to pay!' And that is not a very nice way to be. But now, on the market here, I've got as much time for someone buying something for ten p as spending a hundred quid. I really don't mind which because, through the day, it will even itself out.

I love the bit where I am. I really love it. There's no animosity or anything between us: we really would help each other and do anything for each other. And it's a stretch with such a history. Michael Moorcock used to work in 307 in the '60s printing *New Worlds* magazine. It was a very famous recording studio: you'd see people like Fortune and the Clash filing in and out to record. And that shop 297 used to be called 'Lord Kitchener's Valet'. It was the very, very first shop to import those Afghan coats and they sold all that military clothing that Jimi Hendrix wore.

I can't say that the mood was that much different when I started at Portobello. If anything, that's why I still love it now: because the essence of what I loved then is still here. A lot of the people are the same and a lot of them have come, have gone. There are people who were there and then, all of a sudden, they disappear. Then someone tells you that so and so has died and you think 'Oh I wondered where that funny bloke who sold the shoes was'.

When is it time to stop trading? There's no time, is there? Why should you stop? You work on the market so no one tells you what to do, so who's going to tell you when to stop! It's all down to personal circumstances, isn't it? One might stop because he gets cancer. The other one might stop because he wins the lottery. My lower back hurts and my knees are a bit shot but apart from that I'm really fit and well. If I suddenly sold a painting for two million quid, I don't think I'd bother coming down the market for a while, but I wouldn't rule out not ever coming back because I enjoy it. It's good.

That's really what I would like to say. About me, I want you to be very concise. What I want to put across is how brilliant the market is. How wonderful and how valuable it is. And how it should be celebrated.

'It informs everything I do'

PIP, MILLINER

I was born in Basildon. I was a bit of a freak there really. At fourteen I was the only punk in my school and I was chucked out for wearing a hacking jacket. There was a very small punk movement in Basildon. It's funny, we all did something in our own weird way. I've recently been in touch with Alison Moyet on Facebook. She had looked at my website and she was like 'Ooh, that's lovely. I had no idea you were doing that! Isn't it interesting that we all got away!' And there was also Vince from Depeche Mode. There was such a small gang of us. We used to meet at our Woodlands youth centre and see our first band, the Vandals, and then go up to South End for punk gigs.

I was really into music, fashion and clothes. And fashion as a statement. Nothing normal. I was a New Romantic as well. So I went from punk, making my own clothes, to New Romantic dressing and getting all sorts of clothes from jumble sales. Vintage was the best way of dressing because you could get amazing dresses and they didn't cost anything.

I couldn't wait to get to London. I was always bunking the fares, coming up to London all the time. I'd go to Kensington market and I'd buy 1940s jackets for six quid, seven quid. I've still got my first one which still fits. Amazing.

I really wanted to go to art school but my parents were very against paying for me to go to college. They thought it would be better for me to work behind the counter at a bank or a building society. So I had to save the money myself. I worked for the Institute of Chartered Accountants from sixteen – in this little funny uniform. I had bright red, henna'd, hair. There'd be me, in this little blue skirt, hobbling around with mad red hair. I always thought I managed to tame myself down for these conferences with proper accountants and doctors and lawyers but when I left my boss said, 'You never fitted in. You were much too bright for this place!'

I think I got to where I am today purely because my parents weren't going to go and write the cheque. It made me very determined. I made sure I was top of the class and when I got to the Royal College I won every competition that was there. I just worked so, so, so hard. I was there for seven days a week 'til ten o'clock at night. It was the most amazing experience and it taught me the discipline that you need to run your own business. And now I'm lucky enough to take Friday mornings off to go to Portobello. That's my only treat.

I don't quite know how it crept up on me, the every Friday thing. The first time I met Virginia we were both looking at a dress or something and she'd got one end and I'd got the other. It was a bit like in *The Lady and the Tramp* when they picked up the bit of spaghetti! The dealers introduced us and we just became best friends. Now we meet every Friday religiously. We'll have a cup of coffee on Golborne Road and we'll go round the bric-a-brac and go and do market.

Our dress styles have changed. When I first started getting to know her we were both into '50s clothing. It used to be really strange: we'd never talk to each other about what we were wearing but we would both turn up in a '50s dress in matching colours. I used to find it really funny because I've never met anyone that dressed like me, ever, and I thought it was so unusual that we were so in tune with each other. It was like being a doppelganger. I'm still into '50s, but I vary quite a lot now. I'm not into '60s: it's a bit short and it's nylon. I don't like nylon. I do '30s and I've gone quite into '20s recently. But I tend to wear '50s for work because it's really practical. It's cotton and I can wear it on a bike. The '20s and '30s fabrics are a lot more delicate so you have to be careful.

Why do I love '50s? It's the prints. The colour. I'm mad for colour. Every morning I'll be like 'What shall I put on today? Today I'm into red.' And then it's blue or lilac or whatever. It just really cheers me up. Makes me really happy.

Do I ever feel shy? No. I think that that comes from when I was a punk: I'd be wearing leopard skin trousers and a turquoise mohair jumper and I'd have orange spiky hair. And my mum would literally be dropping me off at the train station, driving away with my legs still in the car because she was really embarrassed of what I looked like. But I live in my own world. I dress for myself – I don't really let things affect me.

It can't be like a uniform though. I do wear designer clothes. I'll wear Piers Fionda … Westwood … I bought a McQueen jacket just before he died. And one of my girlfriends insisted that she buy me a pair of jeans when I went to LA. But I generally only wear jeans when I'm depressed or I'm moving studio.

I've always worn hats. Again, it's another colour on your head. It's self-expression. I started off wearing turbans made of tartans and velvets and raw silks. Give me a bit of fabric and I'd make something out of it. The first hats I made to sell were like berets with beadwork sewn on them. I was at college and a friend and I didn't have money to buy presents so we thought we'd make hats for people. We made these hats and they were really cool so we were like, 'Let's sell them on Portobello market!' I must have been about twenty-two then, so it was a long time ago!

My first degree was in film and photography. I started working as a photographer but I still carried on making hats. Then I worked for the film industry, doing styling and costume. But still making hats. Then a friend of mine said 'Your hats are great. You should do an exhibition one day.' So I did an exhibition of hats and costume and photographs and jewellery and all the hats sold and the press picked up on it. It was during the recession in the '80s when there were lots of empty shops and galleries. I was able to take a shop in St Christopher's Place for eight or nine months and I opened a hat shop. Vogue came down and they picked up on it. And then I thought, 'Oh God, I think I'm quite good at this. I'd better go and learn a bit more.' So I found out what the best courses were and went to learn couture at the Royal College.

I think I've just always wanted to create and make. And my inspiration's always come from things that are unusual, that have got some history. I love to get an old piece of 1940s veiling and then turn it into something contemporary. Or I'll find a vintage frock and think 'What hat would I make to go with that frock?' and then I'll create something.

I would say I've been shopping seriously at Portobello since I set up the business fifteen years ago. To start with, I'd look for vintage feathers or flowers or ribbons for the hats. But then I started looking for the dresses and the handbags and the shoes.

The lure of Portobello kind of creeps up on you. I think it started when I started getting to know the traders and it became a really social thing. Because, with millinery, I'm here on my own. I found a lovely rapport popped up with people knowing … 'Ah Pip, I've got this beautiful mink flower for you; you'll love it' or 'Pip, have a look at the Victorian beadwork on this'. Then, because I'm noticeable, people would always go 'Oh hello, hello. Ooh I like your outfit today!' So you got chatting to people. And when Virginia and I met there were two of us and it became 'Oh, it's the '50s girls!' Now I know practically everyone that's on there – if they've got good stuff. You have to go every Friday because sometimes you'll get an amazing thing and other times there won't be anything for ages. But for me it is research. It informs everything I do. And it's who I am, really.

Most of the things I make come from me. I'll tend to make something for myself and then put it in a range. You can pick up a dress and you just look at it and go 'That's stunning and really unusual colourwise' and then those colourways will influence something.

These are 1930s gowns. I just love these. Literally every time I wear that it goes under the arms. You put it on, you darn it. You put it on, you darn it. But they just look so lovely. Just the colours of them.

This dress is a classic 1950s. Classic, frothy tulle. They used to wear these in mid-town America. They look brilliant on – like a real fairy princess – but they are … mad. So this started influencing these little hair combs which are from a little '50s range that I do. This piece is actually called Sherbert Pip. It's a collection of contemporary flowers mixed in with vintage. These pansies are vintage. You just can't get really beautiful printed velvets anymore.

I've become obsessed with felt. These felt flowers are 1940s. That's when they used to do the classic beautiful felt cut-out flowers. Again, now you can't get nice felt flowers at all. It's impossible. So I have to hunt and hunt and hunt for these.

These leather flowers I got on the market. I was just really, really lucky to find those. Hand pressed leather. That's pressed velvet. That's a paper rose. That's a peach bloom felt.

This is my latest thing – mink pompoms. I've been putting them into hats. I saw Linda with some mink flower shapes recently. And sometimes you can find old Victorian feathers and Victorian boas. You can get contemporary ostrich feathers now but they're not a patch on the beautiful old Victorian curled ones. The quality's just gone. Whereas the old ones … they're just lovely.

I made a film of my hats recently. My production manager was saying 'It's got to be all about the hats.' But I'd styled it all with vintage clothing and I said 'No, I want the whole look.' For me it's about the entire head to toe. I see hats as accessorising: they're the perfect accompaniment to a well-turned-out woman. I wanted the film to have a real old school elegance to it so it was inspired by Cecil Beaton. The models just loved the dresses and the hats. They felt so elegant. They were like 'Where do you get these?' They were all my dresses: the dresses that had inspired the hats!

This was my mum's favourite dancing dress. A classic grosgrain. Black and white rose print. I remember her going out in that. I used to wear it to clubs. This was hers as well. Classic early '60s, isn't it? A bit lamé-ish. A bit green. I remember wearing that clubbing as well. See I can't let go of them: I'm still hoarding things! To be honest, the wonderful thing about vintage is it's so green. You're recycling all the time.

A lot of people I know who collect vintage will wear it once and then they'll pass it back out. I find that quite difficult. If they're kind of boring day wear, sure enough, but when you find beauties … It's like these prom dresses. I must have about eight of them. Look how big they are! And so it's insane at home 'cause you can't fit everything in.

I'm not a great businesswoman honestly – I just want to make beautiful things. And if someone gives me a sob story then I'll sell it really cheaply. That's what all those traders do. They want their things to go to beautiful homes. So if it's going to be appreciated, then they're happy to take less money. I really love that community. I'm so in there with those women. That's why I took myself away from doing the runway shows. Fashion is cut-throat. I'm actually not tough enough. And I'd rather just be doing my own thing. I'm really happy having my own little niche and pottering along. I don't think I've ever had high aspirations. But I've had amazing achievements. Really good stuff happens to me. At the moment, my hats have just come back from a Mario Testino shoot. They're coming out in Italian Vogue in July. Then there are others coming out in British Vogue in August. I've worked with some really cool photographers this year: Ellen von Unwerth, amazing, gorgeous photographer; Zena Holliday, who's an underwater photographer so I saw the hats go underwater for this amazing shoot.

How were they afterwards? Totally ruined. Did they buy them? NO! It's fashion, darling! All they do is they take your stuff and they wreck it! I remember my bird hat – the one I won't sell. That went out to Hilary Alexander – I think it was for *The Daily Telegraph* – and she sent it back with its wing broken. I was like 'Oh My God, my favourite hat!' I fixed it – put it in splints – as best I could. Accidents happen, unfortunately. They have to do whatever they have to do to get a shot. If the hat's not working and they've got to cut off a bit, then they'll do that. But if you get a great shot out of it, it'll be worth it.

The Testino's ones are now fixed. I just got my needle out and spent a few hours. If there's a lovely picture, I'll be well happy. And if not, I'll have forgotten about it. The key is: fix the hat as soon as you get it back. There's a moment when you open it up and go 'sharp intake of breath'. And then you go 'Breathe deeply … paper bag … fix it and then it'll all be done and you won't think about it.' You have to be philosophical …

'After all these years
I still get a good kick out of it'

Brendan, bric-a-brac

I was born in the West of Ireland, County Mayo, in about the 1960s. There were four of us: four brothers. I'm the youngest. Two of them went to college but of course I was a bit of an old useless article – I just wanted to get away. Ramble around. Then myself and an older brother were selling this stuff down in Frankfurt. Mostly antiques – furniture, mirrors, clocks, pictures … every sort of tack. They loved it: especially if it came from Ireland.

This tack here now, at the moment, came from a house clearance. The estate agents get in touch when they sell a house. You've got to clear every damn thing. That one was a rough old dump. That one was a fairly nasty one. There wasn't one item touched, I'd say, except they had the jewellery taken: I could see the empty little boxes.

You don't know whether they've died or whether they're moving or where they are. You don't really ask. You don't really think, I'll be honest about it. It's like an undertaker I suppose: you have to just go in. I've got another one now on Monday. That one's fairly tidy, as far as I can remember. She's a Belgian girl.

Honest to God, after all these years I still get a good kick out of it. It's like – you could say – gold, what's in the drawer. Like being a burglar? Oh no, no it's not. In fact the thing is, you might find something but the minute you find it – ah, you don't give a damn. It's just the kick of finding it. It's good fun.

You do get the odd bit of jewellery and the odd good painting. Sometimes I put the odd piece into the auction. I found a violin recently; I got one thousand three hundred quid for that

You wouldn't BELIEVE it, the mixture of money in that fellow's house. I've got all this off the same bloody house. That's Turkish is it? That's an old

Irish punt. Look at these old things, look. That's … five hundred thousand drachma. They could do with that now! What the hell is this? Lira. 1939. Nice one. They might change these still, would they? Yeah, we'll get the whiskey money, champagne money on that.

This was an achievement award. That must have been what he got, the poor old bugger. 'This is certify that T. H. Colt has completed the requirements for the Kuwaiti System Design course.' This must have fallen out of a chest of drawers or something. What do we do with this stuff? We just dump it.

– Good morning. Hello! Top of the morning!
  I'm just setting up at the moment. Nah, you're all right.

Do you get an insight into people when you clear a house? No, you wouldn't. You get more here selling it, you would. You get to know them. You see, I can see that fellow there now. About two pound would be maximum you'd get out of that fellow there.

– Top of the Morning! You buying today or just … .
– Yeah, yeah.
– He's Polish I'd say. Are you Polish, man? Chinese?
– Not Polish.
– Where are you from?
– Romania.
– Buying for yourself or to sell?

You get the same dealers. People are hooked on it. They're hooked on this business. Especially English people I think – more so than any other nationality. By Jesus, it's got to be an old drug. I think it's the kick of finding something, that's what it is. I mean – let's be honest about it – that stuff there is not too exciting is it? No it's not. Really. But you look at their faces. It was quite funny here yesterday. I had so much rubbish. They were into it – pulling and dragging. It was quite funny to watch them.

Am I addicted? Well d'you know what, I think I am sometimes. At the weekends I get up at about five o'clock and hop out to the old boot sales buying stuff and hunting. There used to be loads of money in this old business but not now. There's no money in it lately at all. The prices are about the same as they were, I'd say, twenty years ago. But it's better than working! It's kind of a carefree old business. I mean, I don't need to do this stall if

I don't want to, but I just do it. Can you imagine getting up at five o clock in the morning? Sore neck. Sore shoulder. Hangover. Honest to God, it gets you up. There's nothing else that will get you up.

> – *Morning …*
> – *How much are these chairs?*
> – *The chairs?*
> – *D'you sell 'em separately?*
> – *I'll sell them any way at all! How many did ye want?*
> – *One.*
> – *Oh damn. Well listen. D'you see that one over there, at the*
> *back? That one is stiffer than the others. You can have that one*
> *for a fiver if it's any use to you. The other ones are a tenner each.*
> – *What about this one?*
> – *Ah, the old Captain's chair. You're too sharp this morning!*
> *That one is sixty quid … Or here you've got the old kitchen*
> *one. A tenner.*
> – *Nah.*
> – *What d'you want it for?*
> – *I've got a little desk in my studio.*
> – *Right, you want a nice chair. Go on. Buy this captain's*
> *chair off me.*
> – *It's the wrong colour. I'd have to stain it.*
> – *Fifty quid? I'm on a roll this morning …*
> – *It's the wrong colour. I've got too many different colours.*
> – *Have a think anyhow … We'll stick it in the back of the van*
> *for yer.*
> – *All right …*

I've got the beer money for the night! That photograph? That photograph there came out of a house. It was actually in the top of a wardrobe; they must have been hiding it away from the wife! It's a girl's butt. She's leaning over a penny farthing bicycle with her arse sticking out and her left hand behind the back of her head and she's only wearing a pair of socks and a pair of high heeled boots. Oh yes, her breast is on the handlebar. That's right it is! I didn't notice that one yet!

I was just taking a wardrobe apart to dump it and it was on the top. It came flying down. Full of dust. I'm trying to sell the bicycle so I thought I'd just put it up there to wind them up. Oh I can't reveal where the house was! I don't know what his profession was but his son was a solicitor. What he was I don't know. But no more information!

– *How much is?*
– *Fiver. It's some sort of a lamp isn't it?*
– *Bouillear. Samovar.*
– *Oh is it now?*
– *Yes, yes it is. In French bouillear … .*
– *That there? What's that? Oh some slides is it? Fiver!*
– *Dave! How are things? Dave, this girl is writing a book*
– *Oooh … I'm collecting. I buy tree plate. Four books. All kind of fun ting.*
– *You're kind of hooked on it Dave, are you?*
– *Yeah, I kinda hooked – you could say that.*
– *You see honest to God, Blanche, this exists …*
– *The thing is about it, is not money. Antique thing is not plenty money. A little five pound and I can come away with ten book, sometimes, six book.. very interesting book.*

   I live on me own. When you live on your own you're okay about tings. You get things, put them away and pack them up. The only thing you don't do is to cover your bath and your toilet. And your bed where you're sleeping. But any little space you get, you shove things and keep them.

   I like them old time medical book. My grandmother was a herbalist so I kind of have that in me. Everything before was common sense. Not this high-tech ting they have now.

   I like old, old celebrity thing. Them people in the old days who make their story and gone. I like to collect Churchill book. He's just ordinary; you can see that. People man. I like his soul. I have a lot of the Queen book. I like the Queen. The Queen don't do much of nothing. The Queen never get up going and shoot anybody. She do what she have to do.

   Do I read a lot? Well not really. Some of them I read and some of them I just keep them. I still work. I work with the Metropolitan Police: clean up the office and them kind of things. But when I retire I could sell them. I have tings that I buy here for almost nothing and if I go to sell it back, that's money. Brendan know the kind of ting I like. He's a very nice man you know. Even say if you don't have any money he still tell you go on and then next week bring me money. Yeah, he's a very nice fellow. I will leave you with Brendan now. All the best. Nice to meet you.

He gave me a cure there for little aches. It's something he made up. I don't know what's in it but I'd say there's a drop of alcohol anyhow. He gave me that one day and, d'you know, when I rubbed it in my neck – you get plenty of cricks in the neck in this old business – it did cure it I think. And I tell you what, I done the old cartilage in my knee and I rubbed it in and now it seems to be in fairly good shape again.

It's raining a little. Ah it'll be all right. Yesterday it was fine until one o'clock. We had a good morning selling. I was winding them up yesterday. Where's the recession? No recession! Look how busy I am! The weather has a lot to do with the market … whether they're in the mood. You can see some days they're never in the mood at all. Then, if it's too hot, no mood at all for buying. Today'd be fine now if it doesn't rain. A day like today, they've nothing else to do. You see it's only some place for them to go. That's it! And then 'Oh God … look at that table and chairs. We'll buy it!' They no more need it then …

Do people come down for company? Oh yeah. Joe here, he must have about five dossers about him full time. There's only one now but he'll have a few more. It's probably too early.

> *– Good morning.*
> *– Good morning.*
> *– That lamp? Seventy-five quid. 'Tis a nice one, isn't it?*
> *– Very nice.*
> *– It's worth more than that in scrap!*
> *– Minim minim?*
> *– Damn it, that's the best I can do. You know that dealer under-neath the bridge? He was going to give me seventy-five quid for it if he had space for it. Seventy quid if you want it! I was going to two hundred quid for that but it's gonna rain …*
> *– Let me speak with the boss.*
> *– Yeah, you speak with the boss then.*

– Does she like it? She likes it! She loves it! Buy it for her!
You can pick up a new lampshade. Anyhow listen. If you want
to spy on the wife you can look through the lampshade!
– Greeting Gareth! Did you see I'm only here half an hour
and I've a woman picked up already!

Am I married? Not now. I used to be once upon a time, you know, when I was a young fellow. Now it's just … unlucky girls. Women don't trust me after a few weeks, that's all. This girl would know. She sells clothes up there on the corner.

– You're in the mood to buy something today. I can tell that eye
… Where's that nice white chest of drawers?
– I'll have a look at it later.
– I've got a helper here today. She's a policewoman! Inland
Revenue? Nah …

Did you hear what she said? 'We're not making enough money to pay the Inland Revenue!' Ha ha ha ha hah! She's all right. She's all right … They're gypsy girls. They doubt everyone.

The thing is about Portobello: it isn't that exciting for the prices but it's exciting for the people – the people who are selling. Here's nice people, good fun, as you can see … And you get all different nationalities here. You can sell to twenty different nationalities in a day. You could even find an English person down Portobeller!

– Isn't that right Gareth? I'm telling Blanche here you could even
find an English person in Portobello Road the odd day!
– Occasionally!

The future? Ah, I never think about the future. Nah. Next week is another week. That's how it goes. It's always been like that.

So Blanche, you're all right now? You can pop by any time you like and have a yap around. You'll be all right. Get that book published, you'll make a couple of million for yourself!

'Now it's very, very nice'

ROLANDAS, REFUSE COLLECTOR

I from Lithuania. First I come in, exactly, maybe I think for couple of years, but I live now twelve years in UK. I move my family. Everything's here. I got house, pay mortgage, everything …

I come in in builder job! Exactly. 'Cause you know all people, when coming from any countries, it's builder jobs.

What can I tell? We collecting rubbish. Rubbish is rubbish you know. How many peoples? Is four. No bins anymore because too much it's danger.

Before was lifting system. In busy market time, it's not safetly. If lifting up … sometimes crazy people is going around … No see when lifting. Sometime is jumping underneath when I lifting up bin.

Only couple years, you know, one guy … trying from back pass lorry … I was driver … What happen … it's pulling legs underneath wheels. So it's crush legs. He's broken leg.

Lorry not going anymore in market. It's too much big risk. Just morning now and later, after six o'clock. We go and clean. Everything cleaning around. Taking this … electric car. It's call 'puv'. P.O.V. Before was mess everywhere. Peoples sometimes, stall keepers, not cleaning around; they are spilling everything everywhere … Now it's very, very nice. Now it's fantastic.

Is big truck. It's twin part – rubbish and recycling. Before was everything in one but that's losing money. It's big money, you know, for recycling.

It's not clean lorry. Before was only market lorry. She not only market lorry. Sometimes taken night shift, evening shift, if need. Before was cleaning every morning in washer. Now not doing because saving money. And, oh my

goodness, … very, very stink. Because it's maybe one time or couple of times per month just washing inside, around, when going in MOT or service.

I like it, this market. It's nice market. It's good because it's very old market … It's one hundred; one hundred-years market. I know old families whole life is working. Was grandfather, father, I remember. This is very history.

I know traders. We go around sweeping – around stalls, underneath stalls, everywhere! If I come and picking up rubbish: 'How are you? Are you all right?'

Not all stalls it's keep clean. But it's all right. It's no problem because it's my job. We must clean everything. It's not very nice if I come and talk to him about 'What you doing. Why you messed in floor?' Because sometimes people's not happy … 'Why are you talking to me?' Because it's not his business. All right. It's not my business. I only clean. If need … okay … it's market … it's manager, it's contract to market stalls …

Do I shop here? Sometimes. This really expensive market. Its price a little bit jumping for tourism. If you want for full family, for couple weeks, seventeen pounds only for fruits … But if just little bit, it's all right. It's not big problem.

About future? What can I tell you? It's job. Exactly.

'My photo goes all over the world'

Ron, local resident

There's a photo you can 'ave. I get plenty of them…so you can 'ave that one. That's the book. The woman met me down Portabella like you did and she asked if she could come up here, have an interview and all that. She wanted to make a poem of me. They're supposed to be poems. Dirty big pages, look! And just that little bit there: 'Ronald Downs had a harsh start in life …'. No, I never even looked at it.

I was born in Hastings in 1937. We was a big family – two sisters and four brothers. I was nine years old and I'd come in at twelve, one o'clock in the morning. Me dad took me to court in Hastings and 'e said 'We can't 'andle 'im.' 'E 'ad me put in an approved school. 'E 'ad to pay ten shillings a week for me to be there. I stayed for five years. I never 'ad one visit in that time and I was the only one out of ninety-five boys that never went home on any 'olidays.

I suppose I made friends. I was adopted at fourteen. They put me in a car with one of the teachers and, next thing you know, I was took to a big 'ouse in Golders Green. I think they were Jossies. Jews. Four by twos. That's what they were, yeah. No, they never came to the school to see me first. Well, they was elderly. Right elderly. They're dead and gone. Well buried by now.

They 'ad a string of wet fish shops. They 'ad one at Muswell Hill where I went to learn the trade. But I found out where the money was and I took it. It was under wet fish! Yeah! In plastic so it couldn't get wet. Bosh – I 'ad it. 'Ad it all. Eighty, ninety pound, which was a LOT of money in them days.

I was a pure bastard: there's no point in saying I wasn't. I was. But life was good, lady. Life was good. I was rich. I went in cabs all day and fucked about. Anyway, it didn't take long before I got nicked. Next thing you know I'm in the senior approved school. That was a bastard that. You got the cane more there and there was fights all the time.

But soon as I was eighteen – bosh, I was in the army. National Service, yeah. I fucked off same day I joined. I had army uniform on so I smashed the winder of a tailor's shop and took the dummy out. I got caught in the West End by the Military Police and I went to court for nicking the suit. 'You won't run away from the next place,' the judge said. I was flown to Cyprus two days later. In the mail plane. I went from there to Germany. In the end, I liked the army so much I tried to sign on. But they wouldn't 'ave me because I'd fucked off in the beginning. Twenty-two years I was going to sign on for.

They give you a ticket to your nearest home station and that's it. I had no parents. (I've no memory of my mother, nah. She must 'ave died.) Nowhere to go. I slept in motors. Then I stole motors and got myself into prison. For that? Well mostly …

There used to be a cinema in Shepherd's Bush called the Oseldo. How do you spell that? Fucked if I know. Don't ask me. Me and the bird had a thing and I got the sack. She was on the desk. I was tearing the tickets on the inside. They 'ad to be torn in 'alf. But I never used to tear them: I used to give them a bit that somebody 'ad left on the floor and give the ticket back to the bird so she could sell it again. We went 'alf each. It were a nice little fiddle. Because a pound in them days was a pound. I mean you worked all the week for seven quid. So it was a lot of money when you nicked a few quid, believe you me. I got the sack and went back and robbed the gaff. I got eighteen months for that. I also done a smash and grab but I got away with that. I'm not going to tell you about that. That was a naughty one …

In 1958 I got into the birds. There was plenty of them on the game: from Shepherds Bush roundabout, right the way up to Marble Arch, on every corner there was a bird. There used to be a few cafés about. Dog stalls. Open all night. And I met a bird. Veronica 'er name was. Veronica White. Never forget 'er. I worked in a little hut. It was a taxi rank really but so many birds and ponces started going in there that the taxi drivers moved out. I used to serve there at night. Mess about, wash up and all that game. Anything to get a few quid.

One night I was on the floor, 'aving a kip, and there was a knock at the winder. I'll never forget. She 'ad black 'air. Dyed. It was pissing down with rain and all the dye was dripping down 'er face. Anyway I got talking to 'er. I give 'er something to eat, gave 'er a couple of bob and she fucked off.

Obviously she was going out grafting. Next thing you know the geezers were saying to me 'Ron, what's up with yer? You've got an earner there. She wants to know, I'm telling ya. Fucking get in. If you don't cop 'er, someone else will.'

So anyway, she says to me 'Where do you sleep Ron? Where d'you go home at night?' I said 'Go 'ome?' I said, 'There.' 'Well,' she said, 'I just got a flat in St Steven's Gardens.' Which, round 'ere, was notorious for brasses. She 'ad a basement flat off of Peter Rachman, who I worked for later. So I moved in with 'er. I was with her seven years. Oh, there was no love there. She knew that.

I dunno why it ended. I think I never give her nuffin for Christmas. Yeah, that was it. She give me a watch or sum'thing. I 'ad several of them anyway. Next thing you know, she flew off. I had a few quid so I didn't care. I had a nice car. Plenty of clothes. Rings. Watches. How much did I make? I'm not telling you! Who are you anyway? I'm telling you too much here, en' I? Hey? I'm letting out a bit too much here …

Did I work? Shut up, will yer? I'm beginning to dislike you immensely when you start talking about work. Especially honest work. Nah, I never thieved. Not thieved, thieved. I never broke into 'ouses or nothing like that. I don't know why I didn't. Because sometimes I was starving.

I did work for Rachman, yeah. He owned a lot of property, Peter. And he owned two 'ouses up on the Scrubs. I got to run the two houses, collect the rents and everything. I lived there for nothing. There was a bit of a garden and we had four or five Alsatians down there. I had to feed them and let them out on the Scrubs. 'E 'ad them for his mob. If you 'ad a flat in a house he owned and he wanted you out. By law you couldn't do that in them days. But if you made enough fucking nuisance of yerself, with dogs running up and down and shitting all over the fucking place, then they fucking went on their own.

Anyway, I was gambling at the time. I collected the rents and fucked off with all the dough. I lost it all. Spanish Jo and a couple of hard men come two days later for his rent. Well I didn't 'ave it. We had a fight on the Scrubs and I got cut from 'ere to 'ere. I've got a big scar. But I didn't lose me job. He said 'He won't do it again, will you Ron?' I said 'No, I won't be doing that no more!' Huh huh.

When Veronica left, I got selling rubbers to the pros on the corners. That was a lovely job. Suited and booted. Long way to walk. Every night. But they knew me. They knew what time I come. They'd come up. 'How many you want tonight, Jessica?' She'd say 'Well I ain't gonna be out long tonight, but I want a few to start me off tomorrow night. Twelve? Fifteen?' They were three for a shilling so that was a nice little earner.

Veronica got murdered down the West End. We only knew by other birds on the game. They might have had a client, a policeman or something like that. The coppers were the filthiest lot of bastards you come across in them days. They had a beautiful fucking life taking money off us. Especially detectives. The copper on the street had fuck all. But the detectives, plain clothes, they fucking earned hundreds. And the police, if they wanted to do you up, they done you up. I was waiting at a bus stop at Notting Hill Gate to go down to Shepherds' Bush. A mate of mine come past in a car. Pulled up and said 'Where you going Ron?' I said 'I'm only going to the Bush.' 'Jump in.' He got pulled up halfway down Holland Park Road. Bent car. I got six months. They wouldn't believe me. 'Yeah, you two know … The both of you are in it'. Bosh. I got half a stretch. Wrong place. Wrong time.

Then I started on the dust. A lot of prisoners come out and get on the dust. Actually, it was advertised in the prison. It's a job they never wanted no papers. And it was terrific around 'ere, years ago. You 'ad your certain roads to do and once you finished, home. You started at seven and you was 'ome by eleven o clock. So then I used to go out totting. Not with a horse and cart, nah. They was expensive. I'd just drive around the streets with a van. People put gear out. When someone dies or somethink like that, bosh – sling it out on the street. You'd see old washing machines on the street corners in the old days and you would bung it straight in the scrap. Money in yer 'and.

And there were empty 'ouses and the gear that people leave in there. Like fireplaces. Used to go in and rip them out. Anythink that'd earn money. You see money. See it, with your eyes. You'd see an old bronze statue in someone's garden. 'Oh, get in there!' Knock on the door: 'Love, d'you want all that cleared away?' Act a bit soppy. 'Would yer? I'll give yer some money.' Used to give yer money and all, to take away somethink that you want!

I used to take the dog with me. Me last thirty years I've had a dog on my shoulders. Sammy snuffed it. Body's in the garden out there. This one's six-teen now. Mitzi, she's called. Nah, it's a funny thing. I've never trained none of them. Mitzi takes a fag from yer mouth. I've never trained her. Doubt she'll do it now, she ain't had a drink. She eats them, that's the only thing. But that's all right. Goes through the system doesn't it.

It's vodka she likes. If I get the bottle of Vodka from there and put it on the table with this Coke, she's there at three hundred miles per hour. She's a funny old dog, I tell yer. She'll drink the lot.

Oh she loves me. She kisses me. She licks me 'ead now and again. And me face. I close my mouth, mind you. She's always done it. Won't leave me alone. I don't mind. Someone loves me, dun they! But you watch her when she don't like it. (Starts biting the side of her face) Grrr … Grrr … Rrrrrr … Rrrrrr … (Bares her teeth). But she's never bit me …

She sings when I sing. Waw … waw … waww … (Dog joins in) Rrr … rrrrr … URrr … RRrrrrr … Waow … All right, my lovely. Huh Huh Huh! Terrific, ain't she? Oh I love 'er. Love 'er to death. I love my dogs better than a woman. I don't think there's a woman who I've ever thought anything of.

I was married, yeah. Only two years, love. I couldn't wait to get out of it. I made a mistake. Was a good mistake in one way, because I got my daughter. And that was terrific. And I was given to her. I didn't 'ave to go to court and fight. Because she was rubbish …

I met 'er in the Carnarvon. Right there on the corner – where the Golborne goes into the Portabella. We both got drunk. Then she come home. Stayed for two weeks. Were in the Carnarvon one night and I got down on me 'ands and knees. I said 'I think I'll marry you.' Why? I dunno. Don't know what come over me. I was forty-one then. She was seventeen.

Anyway, I tried everything to get rid of her. Threw dinners at her and all that. But she see through me. She'd say 'I know your fucking game. You're trying to get rid of me, ain't you? You don't want to go to the registration.' Before you know it, we went up the altar. Well not up the altar. Kensington Town 'all. Reception at home. It was pissing down with rain. We were all drunk. Couldn't be a worse day! The market was full of people and I had a white suit on and I was lying in the gutter outside. Drunk as a skunk. Paralytic. Wey … Wey … Weyyyy.

I never see her for three days after that. Nao! Not that night or nothing. She said 'You was always fucking drunk, Ron. When I come home, you was always drunk.' I said 'Ah, don't worry about it. Come on, you're back now.' Huh huh huh. It was funny. Anyway, she fucked off from me in the end and I ended up with the baby. I got through it. I changed nappies and all that game. I 'ad to. Either that or she'd be dumped like me. All around the fucking world. And I thought 'That ain't 'appening to 'er.'

I couldn't work because I had her to look after. Used to take her to the nursery and go out totting. You could always earn a living out there on the street. I got enough gear that I 'ad a stall in the Golborne Road for years. I made some lovely money down that Golborne Road. It was good down there one time.

There used to be a lovely bread shop. There was a pie and mash shop and a butcher a couple of doors down. They had pigs' trotters. Oh it was nice to dig out the meat between the pig's trotter. I'd buy a sausage roll in the old days. I'd buy baked potatoes. A knob of butter. Bit of cheese. Cause we used to 'ave fires down there in the road. Used to bung wood on them and sit out there like that. In the winter. When I was trading.

It stinks down there now. I like the smell of bacon and eggs and stuff like that but I don't like the stink that comes out of there now. Yeah, I do go in the Lisboa. They're polite, nice people. Sometimes I go in and 'ave two or three cakes. But I wouldn't 'ave a sausage roll or nothing …

I am race prejudiced. Very race prejudiced. They've swamped this area. I'm glad I'm the age I am now because I wanna die. I wanna snuff it. Can't be quicker than next week … Really can't be. Because I can see what's this gonna be in ten, twenty years' time. I hate to think. There won't be a white man about here …

I go down Portobella every Saturday. For definite. I'd crawl down there. I love the Portobella on a Saturday. Bands and people playing in the street. I love all that: it cheers me up for the week. And I get a lot of notice, I suppose. I'm getting recognised. And I think I'm helping keep Portabella on the map. Keeping it going. 'Oh you must see the bloke what goes through the Portabella with a dog.' … My photo goes all over the world. No one's photographed so much.

The Japanese are good photographers. They put plenty about, they do, the old Chinese and Japanese. I like it when they ask. That means they're not ignorant. When they just snap and don't fucking ask I do get the 'ump. I put the dog on the floor then. Cause they don't want me. Obviously they want the dog. Sometimes I tell them to fuck off. Or I stick me tongue out.

I've been on adverts. I dunno what for. Someone told me I was on during the week. Four o'clock. See people come and take your photer, don't say nothing – next thing, I'm on the telly. I won't have no BBC. They won't give yer nothing, the BBC, if they can get away with it. And they've got snakey little photographers. I've got no time for these with these big lenses and things like that. They're definitely after summin. In fact I broke a camera one day there. He kept taking, taking. I put the dog down and he kept hanging about. Hiding and coming back. You don't do that if you're a tourist. If you know you're not fucking wanted, go away. Simple as that. I got hold of my walking stick and hit it. It fell out his hand and went on the floor. He dived down to pick up the camera and flew. Nah he didn't get cross. He was only a little geezer. I think if he'd 'ave flew at me he'd have got 'urt. Not only that, you touch me, this dog'll bite your fucking fingers off. Oh yeah. I couldn't kiss you on the cheek to say goodbye. She'd fly at yer. Even my daughter has to kiss me this side. She gets very jealous. GRRRRRR she goes. Oh yeah. She looks stupid but she ain't. Oh no, my baby. You know I'm talking about you …

She loves the Portabella, yeah. When it's Saturday she knows. She sees me getting ready. I make an extra effort. Have a bath: cause a lot of women want their photo taken near yer. A bit of aftershave makes a lot of difference. Things like that.

I 'ave a sandwich 'ere before I go out. You must put something in your stomach before you go out. Especially if you're an old geezer like me. Then I don't eat until I come up 'ere and get fish and chips from George's. Always get fish and chips on a Saturday.

No, I don't buy a thing. Not down that market. I don't like the food that's down there. You don't know what's in it. That's why I wait. I get all my fruit and veg from Sainsburys. I get my clothes at charity shops. Why buy off of them? That's all they're doing.

I'm not out long. I get tired. When I come in here – ooh, I'm like a bag of shit. I close the fucking door and get underneath this blanket. And she gets in up next to me here. 'Cause she's tired and all.

How much longer? As long as I last. Until I die. Simple as that. And that can't be quick enough. That's how much I hate around here now. How this 'as become. If I won a million I wouldn't stay 'ere two minutes. Pss – I'd be gone. I'd leave this just as it is. Leave the fucking lot. Leave the television. Leave everything. I'd be out in no time.

I'd still walk down Portabella. Oh yeah. Well I'd 'ave enough money to buy myself a nice car. Get a chauffeur. Which I would do if I 'ad the money. Drive in the Roller. The 'borghini … or whatever I got.

I don't take a penny off any photos down that Portabella on a Saturday. Not a fucking penny. Only what people's offered. And I wouldn't steal a thing now. In fact I give. I don't know why: it's not in me no more. You could get money off the market, yeah. There's fiddles going on down there you've never 'eard of. Through the market. Any market. Not only Portabella. Money changes 'ands for something or the other. Oh yeah.

All that going down, is it? You listen to all this? Uh – gotta watch you: I might put myself in it. Might be telling you summin' that the Old Bill … Yeah, I'd like a different name. That would be very tasty. Photograph? Well that could be anyone. Don't worry about that. Yeah. That ain't me …

Postscript

Compiling this book has made me acutely aware of the value of Portobello Market.

Before working on this book I hadn't realised how many wonderful things you can buy, if you know when and where to go. I hadn't appreciated the hard graft and expertise of the traders or how much fun it is to get to know them. And I had no idea what a difference Portobello makes to people's lives.

Portobello Market gives anyone and everyone the opportunity to make a living. Some people (like Peter Simon, the founder of Monsoon) start major businesses from there. Others are able to pay their rent. Either way, the market makes all the difference. And Portobello gives everyone the chance to have a face-to-face chat. And that, in this age of text messages, email and self-service supermarkets, is a rare treat indeed.

The market may be at risk but it isn't a charity case. I don't feel the need to go there out of duty or pity but because I benefit from it. Every time I walk through the market my mood improves. Whatever I've needed – be it a wedding present or a smile – Portobello has come up trumps. Now I sleep in vintage linen, know (thanks to Josie) how to pick both a good melon and a good man, and gaze contentedly at the calves of a seventeenth-century knight. Getting to know the market has been a wonderful experience and one I cannot recommend highly enough.

Some people have commented on the fact that I have chosen to represent the way in which people speak in this book. This was a very conscious decision. My aim is to bring to life the people who frequent the market, so that you can meet and get to know them as I did. I wanted to portray the reality of the market, not a dumbed down, standardised version. I hope that it is this wonderful reality that comes across in this book. That, certainly, was my intention.

Blanche Girouard
July 2013